WESTERN POLITICAL THOUGHT

WESTERN POLITICAL THOUGHT

Dr. Y.S. Mathur
Mukesh Kumar Singh

ANMOL PUBLICATIONS PVT. LTD.
NEW DELHI-110 002 (INDIA)

ANMOL PUBLICATIONS PVT. LTD.

Regd. Office: 4360/4, Ansari Road, Daryaganj,
New Delhi-110002 (India)
Tel.: 23278000, 23261597, 23286875, 23255577
Fax: 91-11-23280289
Email: anmolpub@gmail.com
Visit us at: www.anmolpublications.com

Branch Office: No. 1015, Ist Main Road, BSK IIIrd Stage
IIIrd Phase, IIIrd Block, Bangalore-560 085 (India)
Tel.: 080-41723429 • Fax: 080-26723604
Email: anmolpublicationsbangalore@gmail.com

Western Political Thought

First Edition, 2010

ISBN 978-81-261-4560-7

PRINTED IN INDIA

Printed at Mehra Offset Press, Delhi.

Contents

Preface

Western political system has derived stability and legitimacy through underlying basic principles and ideals evolved through the works of many renowned political thinkers and experience of centuries. All western democracies thrive on rule of law, freedom of press, freedom of conscience, free elections, universal adult suffrage, etc., reflecting the political thought of the government and the governed. This book brings together a genealogy of thoughts on peace, war and ethics in Western political philosophy highlighting their legacies for contemporary theories on International Relations. Throughout this exciting history, the reader discovers important arguments against some of the mainstream narratives of International Relations, such as the contextualization of neo-realism in Hegelian philosophy rather than in an ostensibly realist tradition of international political thought.

Political thought is a wider term, which includes all aspects, which have been covered in the history of political ideas. It covers all sorts of statements, theories and evaluations on politics. By political thought we understand the reflections on, or the exposition of political ideas.

This book is an introduction to western political thoughts, spanning from the ancient to the modern times. It aims to give students the opportunity to study a range of thinkers who are considered to be key in the 'canon' of western political thought. Written simply and directly, it presents the basic ideas and dilemmas of western political thought through an in-depth analysis of a limited number of major thinkers--from Plato to Karl Marx. It views the thinkers in historical context and examines them in terms of the changing relationships of ethics and politics in western political thought.

—Author

1

Plato

Plato (428/427 BC – 348/347 BC), was a Classical Greek philosopher, who, together with his mentor, Socrates, and his student, Aristotle, helped to lay the foundations of Western philosophy. Plato was also a mathematician, writer of philosophical dialogues, and founder of the Academy in Athens, the first institution of higher learning in the western world. Plato was originally a student of Socrates, and was as much influenced by his thinking as by what he saw as his teacher's unjust death. Plato's sophistication as a writer can be witnessed by reading his Socratic dialogues. Some of the dialogues, letters, and other works that are ascribed to him are considered spurious. Interestingly, although there is little question that Plato lectured at the Academy that he founded, the pedagogical function of his dialogues, if any, is not known with certainty. The dialogues have since Plato's time been used to teach a range of subjects, mostly including philosophy, logic, rhetoric, mathematics, and other subjects about which he wrote.

Early Life

Birth and Family: The exact birthdate of Plato is unknown. Based on ancient sources, most modern scholars estimate that he was born in Athens or Aegina between 429 and 423 BC. His father was Ariston. According to a disputed tradition, reported by Diogenes Laertius, Ariston traced his descent from the king of Athens, Codrus, and the king of Messenia, Melanthus. Plato's mother was Perictione, whose family boasted of a relationship with the famous Athenian lawmaker and lyric poet Solon. Perictione was sister of Charmides and niece of Critias, both prominent figures of the Thirty Tyrants, the brief oligarchic regime, which followed on the collapse of Athens at the end of the Peloponnesian war (404-403 BC). Besides Plato himself, Ariston and Perictione had three other children; these were two sons, Adeimantus and Glaucon, and a daughter Potone, the mother of Speusippus (the nephew and successor of Plato as head of his philosophical Academy). According to the *Republic*, Adeimantus and Glaucon were older than Plato. Nevertheless, in his Memorabilia, Xenophon presents Glaucon as younger than Plato.

Ariston tried to force his attentions on Perictione, but failed of his purpose; then the ancient Greek god Apollo appeared to him in a vision, and, as a result of it, Ariston left Perictione unmolested. Another legend related that, while he was sleeping as an infant, bees had settled on the lips of Plato; an augury of the sweetness of style in which he would discourse philosophy. Ariston appears to have died in Plato's childhood, although the precise dating of his death is difficult. Perictione then married Pyrilampes, her mother's brother, who had served many times as an ambassador to the Persian court and was a friend of Pericles, the leader of the democratic faction in Athens. Pyrilampes had a son from a previous marriage, Demus, who was famous for his beauty. Perictione gave birth to Pyrilampes' second son, Antiphon, the half-brother of Plato, who appears in *Parmenides*.

In contrast to his reticence about himself, Plato used to introduce his distinguished relatives into his dialogues, or to mention them with some precision: Charmides has one named after him; Critias speaks in both *Charmides* and *Protagoras;* Adeimantus and Glaucon take prominent parts in the *Republic.* From these and other references one can reconstruct his family tree, and this suggests a considerable amount of family pride. According to Burnet, "the opening scene of the *Charmides* is a glorification of the whole [family connection ... Plato's dialogues are not only a memorial to Socrates, but also the happier days of his own family".

Name: According to Diogenes Laertius, the philosopher was named *Aristocles* after his grandfather, but his wrestling coach, Ariston of Argos, dubbed him "Platon", meaning "broad," on account of his robust figure. According to the sources mentioned by Diogenes (all dating from the Alexandrian period), Plato derived his name from the breadth (*platytes*) of his eloquence, or else because he was very wide (*platýs*) across the forehead. In the 21st century some scholars disputed Diogenes, and argued that the legend about his name being *Aristocles* originated in the Hellenistic age.

Education: Apuleius informs us that Speusippus praised Plato's quickness of mind and modesty as a boy, and the "first fruits of his youth infused with hard work and love of study". Plato must have been instructed in grammar, music, and gymnastics by the most distinguished teachers of his time. Dicaearchus went so far as to say that Plato wrestled at the Isthmian games. Plato had also attended courses of philosophy; before meeting Socrates, he first became acquainted with Cratylus (a disciple of Heraclitus, a prominent pre-Socratic Greek philosopher) and the Heraclitean doctrines.

Works

Thirty-five dialogues and thirteen letters have traditionally been ascribed to Plato, though modern scholarship doubts the authenticity of at least some of these. Plato's writings have been published in several fashions; this has led to several conventions regarding the naming and referencing of Plato's texts. The usual system for making unique references to sections of the text by Plato derives from a 16th century edition of Plato's works by Henricus Stephanus. An overview of Plato's writings according to this system can be found in the Stephanus pagination article.

One tradition regarding the arrangement of Plato's texts is according to tetralogies. This scheme is ascribed by Diogenes Laertius to an ancient scholar and court astrologer to Tiberius named Thrasyllus. In the list below, works by Plato are marked (1) if there is no consensus among scholars as to whether Plato is the author, and (2) if scholars generally agree that Plato is *not* the author of the work. Unmarked works are assumed to have been written by Plato.

I. *Euthyphro, (The) Apology (of Socrates), Crito, Phaedo*

II. *Cratylus, Theaetetus, Sophist, Statesman*

III. *Parmenides, Philebus, (The) Symposium, Phaedrus*

IV. *First Alcibiades* (1), *Second Alcibiades* (2), *Hipparchus* (2), *(The) (Rival) Lovers* (2)

V. *Theages* (2), *Charmides, Laches, Lysis*

VI. *Euthydemus, Protagoras, Gorgias, Meno*

VII. *(Greater) Hippias (major)* (1), *(Lesser) Hippias (minor), Ion, Menexenus*

VIII. *Clitophon* (1), *(The) Republic, Timaeus, Critias*

IX. *Minos* (2), *(The) Laws, Epinomis* (2), *Epistles* (1).

The remaining works were transmitted under Plato's name, most of them already considered spurious in antiquity, and so were not included by Thrasyllus in his tetralogical arrangement. These works are labelled as *Notheuomenoi* ("spurious") or *Apocrypha.*

- *Axiochus* (2), *Definitions* (2), *Demodocus* (2), *Epigrams, Eryxias* (2), *Halcyon* (2), *On Justice* (2), *On Virtue* (2), *Sisyphus* (2).

Plato's Dialogues

The exact order in which Plato's dialogues were written is not known, nor is the extent to which some might have been later revised and rewritten. Lewis Campbell was the first to make exhaustive use of stylometry to prove objectively that the *Critias, Timaeus, Laws, Philebus, Sophist,* and *Statesman* were all clustered together as a group, while the *Parmenides, Phaedrus, Republic,* and *Theaetetus* belong to a separate group, which must be earlier (given Aristotle's statement in his *Politics* that the *Laws* was written after the *Republic;* cf. Diogenes Laertius *Lives* 3.37). What is remarkable about Campbell's conclusions is that, in spite of all the stylometric studies that have been conducted since his time, perhaps the only chronological fact about Plato's works that can now be said to be *proven* by stylometry is the fact that *Critias, Timaeus, Laws, Philebus, Sophist,* and *Statesman* are the latest of Plato's dialogues, the others earlier.

Increasingly in the most recent Plato scholarship, writers are skeptical of the notion that the order of Plato's writings can be established with any precision, though Plato's works are still often characterized as falling at least roughly into three groups. The following represents one such devision which is relatively common. It should, however, be kept in mind that many of the positions in the ordering are still highly disputed, and also that the very notion that Plato's dialogues can or should be "ordered" is by no means universally accepted.

Early dialogues

Socrates figures in all of these, and they are considered the most faithful representations of the historical Socrates; hence they are also called the Socratic dialogues. Most of them consist of Socrates discussing a subject, often an ethical one (friendship, piety) with a friend or with someone presumed to be an expert on it. Through a series of questions he will show that apparently they do not understand it at all. It is left to the reader to figure out if "he" really understands "it". This makes these dialogues "indirect" teachings.

- *Apology*
- *Charmides*
- *Crito*
- *Euthyphro*
- *Ion*
- *Laches*
- *Lesser Hippias*
- *Lysis*
- *Menexenus*
- *Protagoras* is often considered one of the last of these "earlier" dialogues.

The following are often considered "transitional" or "pre-middle" dialogues:

- *Gorgias*
- *Meno*
- *Euthydemus*

Middle Dialogues

Late in the early dialogues Plato's Socrates actually begins supplying answers to some of the questions he asks, or putting forth positive doctrines. This is generally seen as the first appearance of Plato's own views. The first of these, that goodness is wisdom and that no one does evil willingly, was perhaps Socrates' own view. What becomes most prominent in the middle dialogues is the idea that knowledge comes of grasping unchanging forms or essences, paired with the attempts to investigate such essences. The immortality of the soul, and specific doctrines about justice, truth, and beauty, begin appearing here. The Symposium and the Republic are considered the centrepieces of Plato's middle period. The Parmenides and Theaetetus are often considered to come late in this period and transitional to the next, as they seem to treat the Theory of Forms critically (*Parmenides*) or not at all (*Theaetetus*).

- *Cratylus*
- *Phaedo*
- *Phaedrus*
- *Symposium*
- *Republic*
- *Theaetetus*
- *Parmenides*.

Late Dialogues

The *Parmenides* presents a series of criticisms of the theory of Forms which are widely taken to indicate Plato's abandonment of the doctrine. Some recent publications (*e.g.*, Meinwald (1991)) have challenged this characterisation. In most of the remaining dialogues the theory is either absent or at least appears under a different guise in discussions about kinds or classes of things (the *Timaeus* may be an important, and hence controversially placed, exception). Socrates is either absent or a minor figure in the discussion. An apparently new method for doing dialectic known as "collection and division" is also featured, most notably in the *Sophist* and *Statesman*, explicitly for the first time in the *Phaedrus*, and possibly in the *Philebus*. A basic description of collection and division would go as follows: interlocutors attempt to discern the similarities and differences among things in order to get clear idea about what they in fact are. One understanding, suggested in some passages of the *Sophist*, is that this is what philosophy is always in the business of doing, and is doing even in the early dialogues.

The late dialogues are also an important place to look for Plato's mature thought on most of the issues dealt with in the earlier dialogues. There is much work still to be done by scholars on the working out of what these views are. The later works are agreed to be difficult and challenging pieces of philosophy. On the whole they are more sober and logical than earlier works, but may hold out the promise of steps towards a solution to problems which were systematically laid out in prior works.

- *Sophist*
- *Statesman*
- *Philebus*
- *Timaeus*
- *Critias*
- *Laws*.

Narration of the Dialogues

Plato never presents himself as a participant in any of the dialogues, and with the exception of the *Apology*, there is no suggestion that he heard any of the dialogues firsthand. Some dialogues have no narrator but have a pure "dramatic" form (examples: *Meno, Gorgias, Phaedrus, Crito, Euthyphro*), some dialogues are narrated by Socrates, wherein he speaks in first person (examples: *Lysis, Charmides, Republic*). One dialogue, *Protagoras*, begins in dramatic form but quickly proceeds to Socrates' narration of a conversation he had previously with the sophist for whom the dialogue is named; this narration continues uninterrupted till the dialogue's end.

The three dialogues, *Phaedo, Symposium*, and *Theaetetus*, also begin in dramatic form but then proceed to virtually uninterrupted narration by followers of Socrates, and all, apparently, based on their distant memory or secondhand reports. *Phaedo*, an account of Socrates' final conversation and hemlock drinking, is narrated by Phaedo to Echecrates in a foreign city many years after the execution took place.

The *Symposium* is narrated by Apollodorus, a Socratic disciple, apparently to Glaucon. Apollodorus assures his listener that he is recounting the story, which took place when he himself was an infant, not from his own memory, but as remembered by Aristodemus, who told him the story years ago. In the beginning of the *Theaetetus* (142c-143b), Euclides says that he compiled the conversation from notes he took based on what Socrates told him of his conversation with the title character.

The rest of the *Theaetetus* is presented as a "book" written in dramatic form and read by one of Euclides' slaves (143c). Some scholars take this as an indication that Plato had by this date wearied of the narrated form. With the exception of the *Theaetetus*, Plato gives no explicit indication as to how these orally transmitted conversations came to be written down. Other dialogues, such as the *Phaedo*, *Symposium*, and *Parmenides*, do suggest that such conversations were faithfully recalled and transmitted by Socrates' followers.

Trial of Socrates

The trial of Socrates is the central, unifying event of the great Platonic dialogues. Because of this, Plato's *Apology* is perhaps the most often read of the dialogues. In the *Apology*, Socrates tries to dismiss rumours that he is a sophist and defends himself against charges of disbelief in the gods and corruption of the young. Socrates insists that long-standing slander will be the real cause of his demise, and says the legal charges are essentially false. Socrates famously denies being wise, and explains how his life as a philosopher was launched by the oracle at Delphi. He says that his quest to resolve the riddle of the oracle put him at odds with his fellow man, and that this is the reason he has been mistaken for a menace to the city-state of Athens.

Unity and Diversity of the Dialogues

If Plato's important dialogues do not refer to Socrates' execution explicitly, they allude to it, or use characters or themes that play *a part in it. Five dialogues foreshadow the trial: In the Theaetetus* (210d) and the *Euthyphro* (2a–b) Socrates tells people that he is about to face corruption charges. In the *Meno* (94e–95a), one of the men who brings legal charges against Socrates, Anytus, warns him about the trouble he may get into if he does not stop criticizing important people. In the *Gorgias*, Socrates says that his trial will be like a doctor prosecuted by a cook who asks a jury of children to choose between the doctor's bitter medicine and the cook's tasty treats (521e–522a).

In the *Republic* (7.517e), Socrates explains why an enlightened man (presumably himself) will stumble in a courtroom situation. *The Apology* is Socrates' defense speech, and the *Crito* and *Phaedo* take place in prison after the conviction. In the *Protagoras,* Socrates is a guest at the home of Callias, son of Hipponicus, a man whom Socrates disparages in the *Apology* as having wasted a great amount of money on sophists' fees.

Two other important dialogues, the *Symposium* and the *Phaedrus,* are linked to the main storyline by characters. In the *Apology* (19b, c), Socrates says Aristophanes slandered him in a comic play, and blames him for causing his bad reputation, and ultimately, his death. In the *Symposium,* the two of them are drinking together with other friends.

The character Phaedrus is linked to the main story line by character (Phaedrus is also a participant in the *Symposium* and the *Protagoras*) and by theme (the philosopher as divine emissary, etc.) The *Protagoras* is also strongly linked to the *Symposium* by characters: all of the formal speakers at the *Symposium* (with the exception of Aristophanes) are present at the home of Callias in that dialogue. Charmides and his guardian Critias are present for the discussion in the *Protagoras*. Examples of characters crossing between dialogues can be further multiplied. The *Protagoras* contains the largest gathering of Socratic associates.

In the dialogues for which Plato is most celebrated and admired, Socrates is concerned with human and political virtue, has a distinctive personality, and friends and enemies who "travel" with him from dialogue to dialogue. This is not to say that Socrates is consistent: a man who is his friend in one dialogue may be an adversary or subject of his mockery in another. For example, Socrates praises the wisdom of Euthyphro many times in the *Cratylus,* but makes him look like a fool in the *Euthyphro*. He disparages sophists generally, and Prodicus specifically in the *Apology,* yet tells Theaetetus in his namesake dialogue that he admires Prodicus and has directed many pupils to him. In Cratylus (384b-c), Socrates says that he studied with Cratylus, and took his one-drachma course because he could not afford the full fifty-drachma course. Socrates' ideas are also not consistent within or between or among dialogues.

The Quest for Justice in *The Republic*

One of the most fundamental ethical and political concepts is justice. It is a complex and ambiguous concept. It may refer to individual virtue, the order of society, as well as individual rights in contrast to the claims of the general social order. In Book *The Republic,* Socrates and his interlocutors discuss the meaning of justice. Four definitions that report how the word "justice" (dikaiosune) is actually used, are offered. The old man of means Cephalus suggests the first definition. Justice is "speaking the truth and repaying what one has borrowed." Yet this definition, which is based on traditional moral custom and relates justice to honesty and goodness; i.e. paying one's debts, speaking the truth, loving one's country, having good manners, showing proper respect for the gods, and so on, is found to be inadequate. It cannot withstand the challenge of new times and the power of critical thinking.

Socrates refutes it by presenting a counterexample. If we tacitly agree that justice is related to goodness, to return a weapon that was borrowed from someone who, although once sane, has turned into a madman does not seem to be just but involves a danger of harm to both sides. Cephalus' son Polemarchus, who continues the discussion after his father leaves to offer a sacrifice, gives his opinion that the poet Simonides was correct in saying that it was just "to render to each his due." He explains this statement by defining justice as "treating friends well and enemies badly." Under the pressure of Socrates' objections that one may be mistaken in judging others and thus harm good people, Polemarchus modifies his definition to say that justice is "to treat well a friend who is good and to harm an enemy who is bad."

However, when Socrates finally objects that it cannot be just to harm anyone, because justice cannot produce injustice, Polemarchus is completely confused. He agrees with Socrates that justice, which both sides tacitly agree relates to goodness, cannot produce any harm, which can only be caused by injustice. Like his father, he withdraws from the dialogue. The careful reader will note that Socrates does not reject the definition of justice implied in the saying of Simonides, who is called a wise man, namely, that "justice is rendering to each what befits him," but only its explication given by Polemarchus. This definition is, nevertheless, found unclear. The first part of Book I of the Republic ends in a negative way, with parties agreeing that none of the definitions provided stands up to examination and that the original question "What is justice?" is more difficult to answer than it seemed to be at the outset. This negative outcome can be seen as a linguistic and philosophical therapy. Firstly, although Socrates' objections to given definitions can be challenged, it is shown, as it stands, that popular opinions about justice involve inconsistencies. They are inconsistent with other opinions held to be true. The reportive definitions based on everyday usage of the word "justice" help us perhaps to understand partially what justice means, but fail to provide a complete account of what is justice.

These definitions have to be supplied by a definition that will assist clarity and establish the meaning of justice. However, to propose such an adequate definition one has to know what justice really is. The way people define a given word is largely determined by the beliefs which they hold about the thing referred to by this word. A definition that is merely arbitrary or either too narrow or too broad, based on a false belief about justice, does not give the possibility of communication. Platonic dialogues are expressions of the ultimate communication that can take place between humans; and true communication is likely to take place only if individuals can share meanings of the words they use.

Communication based on false beliefs, such as statements of ideology, is still possible, but seems limited, dividing people into factions, and, as history teaches us, can finally lead only to confusion. The definition of justice as "treating friends well and enemies badly" is for Plato not only inadequate because it is too narrow, but also wrong because it is based on a mistaken belief of what justice is, namely, on the belief grounded in factionalism, which Socrates does not associate with the wise ones but with tyrants. Therefore, in *The Republic*, as well as in other Platonic dialogues, there is a relationship between conceptual analysis and critical evaluation of beliefs. The goals of these conversations are not merely linguistic, to arrive at an adequate verbal definition, but also substantial, to arrive at a right belief. The question "what is justice" is not only about linguistic usage of the word "justice," but primarily about the thing to which the word refers. The focus of the second part of Book I is no longer clarification of concepts, but evaluation of beliefs.

In Platonic dialogues, rather than telling them what they have to think, Socrates is often getting his interlocutors to tell him what they think. The next stage of the discussion of the meaning of justice is taken over by Thrasymachus, a sophist, who violently and impatiently bursts into the dialogue. In the fifth and fourth century B.C.E., the sophists were paid teachers of rhetoric and other practical skills, mostly non-Athenians, offering courses of instruction and claiming to be best qualified to prepare young men for success in public life. Plato describes the sophists as itinerant individuals, known for their rhetorical abilities, who reject religious beliefs and traditional morality, and he contrasts them with Socrates, who as a teacher would refuse to accept payment and instead of teaching skills would commit himself to a disinterested inquiry into what is true and just. In a contemptuous manner, Thrasymachus asks Socrates to stop talking nonsense and look into the facts.

As a clever man of affairs, he gives an answer to the question of "what is justice" by deriving justice from the city's configuration of power and making it relative to the interests of the dominant social or political group. "Justice is nothing else than the interest of the stronger." Now, by contrast to what some commentators say, the statement that Thrasymachus offers as an answer to Socrates' question about justice is not a definition. The careful reader will notice that Thrasymachus identifies justice with either maintenance or observance of law. His statement is an expression of his belief that, in the world imperfect as it is, the ruling element in the city, or as we would say today the dominant political or social group, institutes laws and governs for its own benefit. The democrats make laws in support of democracy; the aristocrats make laws that support the government of the well-born; the propertied make laws that protect their status and keep their businesses going; and so on.

This belief implies, firstly, that justice is not a universal moral value but a notion relative to expediency of the dominant status quo group; secondly, that justice is in the exclusive interest of the dominant group; thirdly, that justice is used as a means of oppression and thus is harmful to the powerless; fourthly, that there is neither any common good nor harmony of interests between those who are in a position of power and those who are not. All there is, is a domination by the powerful and privileged over the powerless. The moral language of justice is used merely instrumentally to conceal the interests of the dominant group and to make these interests appear universal. The powerful "declare what they have made-what is to their own advantage-to be just." The arrogance with which Thrasymachus makes his statements suggests that he strongly believes that to hold a different view from his own would be to mislead oneself about the world as it is. After presenting his statement, Thrasymachus intends to leave as if he believed that what he said was so compelling that no further debate about justice was ever possible. In *The Republic* he exemplifies the power of a dogma. Indeed he presents Socrates with a powerful challenge. Yet, whether or not what he said sounds attractive to anyone, Socrates is not convinced by the statement of his beliefs. Beliefs shape our lives as individuals, nations, ages, and civilizations. Should we really believe that "justice [obeying laws] is really the good of another, the advantage of the stronger and the ruler, harmful to the one who obeys, while injustice [disobeying laws] is in one's own advantage." The discussion between Socrates and his interlocutors is no longer about the meaning of "justice." It is about fundamental beliefs and "concerns no ordinary topic but the way we ought to live."

Although in Book I Socrates finally succeeds in showing Thrasymachus that his position is self-contradictory and Thrasymachus withdraws from the dialogue, perhaps not fully convinced, yet red-faced, in Book II Thrasymachus' argument is taken over by two young intellectuals, Plato's brothers, Glaucon and Adeimantus, who for the sake of curiosity and a playful intellectual exercise push it to the limit. Thrasymachus withdraws, but his statement: moral skepticism and relativism, predominance of power in human relations, and non-existence of the harmony of interests, hovers over the Western mind. It takes whole generations of thinkers to struggle with Thrasymachus' beliefs, and the debate still continues. It takes the whole remainder of the Republic to present an argument in defense of justice as a universal value and the foundation of the best political order.

The Government of Philosopher Rulers

It is generally believed today that democracy, "government of the people by the people and for the people," is the best and only fully justifiable political system. The distinct features of democracy are freedom and equality. Democracy can be described as the rule of the free people who govern themselves, either directly or though their representatives, in their own interest. Why does Plato not consider democracy the best form of government? In the Republic he criticizes the direct and unchecked democracy of his time precisely because of its leading features. Firstly, although freedom is for Plato a true value, democracy involves the danger of excessive freedom, of doing as one likes, which leads to anarchy. Secondly, equality, related to the belief that everyone has the right and equal capacity to rule, brings to politics all kinds of power-seeking individuals, motivated by personal gain rather than public good. Democracy is thus highly corruptible.

It opens gates to demagogues, potential dictators, and can thus lead to tyranny. Hence, although it may not be applicable to modern liberal democracies, Plato's main charge against the democracy he knows from the ancient Greek political practice is that it is unstable, leading from anarchy to tyranny, and that it lacks leaders with proper skill and morals. Democracy depends on chance and must be mixed with competent leadership. Without able and virtuous leaders, such as Solon or Pericles, who come and go by chance, it is not a good form of government. But even Pericles, who as Socrates says made people "wilder" rather than more virtuous, is considered not to be the best leader. If ruling a state is a craft, indeed statecraft, Plato argues, then politics needs expert rulers, and they cannot come to it merely by accident, but must be carefully selected and prepared in the course of extensive training. Making political decisions requires good judgment. Politics needs competence, at least in the form of today's civil servants. Who then should the experts be and why? Why does Plato in the Republic decide to hand the steering wheel of the state to philosophers?

In spite of the idealism with which he is usually associated, Plato is not politically naive. He does not idealize, but is deeply pessimistic about human beings. Most people, corrupted as they are for him fundamentally irrational, driven by their appetites, egoistic passions, and informed by false beliefs. If they choose to be just and obey laws, it is only because they lack the power to act criminally and are afraid of punishment. Nevertheless, human beings are not vicious by nature. They are social animals, incapable of living alone. Living in communities and exchanging products of their labour is natural for them, so that they have capacities for rationality and goodness. Plato, as later Rousseau, believes that once political society is properly ordered, it can contribute to the restoration of morals. A good political order, good education and upbringing can produce "good natures; and [these] useful natures, who are in turn well educated, grow up even better than their predecessors."

Hence, there are in Plato such elements of the idealistic or liberal world view as the belief in education and progress, and a hope for a better future. The quality of human life can be improved if people learn to be rational and understand that their real interests lie in harmonious cooperation with one another, and not in war or partisan strife. However, unlike Rousseau, Plato does not see the best social and political order in a democratic republic. Opinions overcome truth in everyday life. Peoples' lives and the lives of communities are shaped by the prevailing beliefs. If philosophers are those who can distinguish between true and false beliefs, who love knowledge and are motivated by the common good, and finally if they are not only master-theoreticians, but also the master-practitioners who can heal the ills of their society, then they, and not democratically elected representatives, must be chosen as leaders and educators of the political community and guide it to proper ends.

They are required to counteract the destabilizing effects of false beliefs on society. Are philosophers incorruptible? In the ideal city there are provisions to minimize possible corruption, even among the good-loving philosophers. They can neither enjoy private property nor family life. Although they are the rulers, they receive only a modest remuneration from the state, dine in common dining halls, and have wives and children in common. These provisions are necessary, Plato believes, because if the philosopher-rulers were to acquire private land, luxurious homes, and money themselves, they would soon become hostile masters of other citizens rather than their leaders and allies. The ideal city becomes a bad one, described as timocracy, precisely when the philosophers neglect music and physical exercise, and begin to gather wealth. To be sure, Plato's philosophers, among whom he includes both men and women, are not those who can usually be found today in departments of philosophy and who are described as the "prisoners who take refuge in a temple." Initially chosen from among the brightest, most stable, and most courageous children, they go through a sophisticated and prolonged educational training which begins with gymnastics, music and mathematics, and ends with dialectic, military service and practical city management. They have superior theoretical knowledge, including the knowledge of the just, noble, good and advantageous, but are not inferior to others in practical matters as well. Being in the final stage of their education illuminated by the idea of the good, they are those who can see beyond changing empirical phenomena and reflect on such timeless values as justice, beauty, truth, and moderation.

Goodness is not merely a theoretical idea for them, but the ultimate state of their mind. If the life of the philosopher-rulers is not of private property, family or wealth, nor even of honour, and if the intellectual life itself seems so attractive, why should they then agree to rule? Plato's answer is in a sense a negative one. Philosophical life, based on contemplative leisure and the pleasure of learning, is indeed better and happier than that of ruling the state. However, the underlying idea is not to make any social class in the city the victorious one and make it thus happy, but "to spread happiness throughout the city by bringing the citizens into harmony with each other... and by making them share with each other the benefits that each class can confer on the community." Plato assumes that a city in which the rulers do not govern out of desire for private gain, but are least motivated by personal ambition, is governed in the way which is the finest and freest from civil strife. Philosophers will rule not only because they will be best prepared for this, but also because if they do not, the city will no longer be well governed and may fall prey to economic decline, factionalism, and civil war. They will approach ruling not as something really enjoyable, but as something necessary.

Objections against the government of philosopher-rulers can be made. Firstly, because of the restrictions concerning family and private property, Plato is often accused of totalitarianism. However, Plato's political vision differs from a totalitarian state in a number of important aspects. Especially in the Laws he makes clear that freedom is one of the main values of society. Other values for which Plato stands include justice, friendship, wisdom, courage, and moderation, and not factionalism or terror that can be associated with a totalitarian state. The restrictions which he proposes are placed on the governors, rather than on the governed. Secondly, one can argue that there may obviously be a danger in the self-professed claim to rule of the philosophers. Individuals may imagine themselves to be best qualified to govern a country, but in fact they may lose contact with political realities and not be good leaders at all. If philosopher-rulers did not have real knowledge of their city, they would be deprived of the essential credential that is required to make their rule legitimate, namely, that they alone know how best to govern. Indeed, at the end of Book VII of the Republic where philosophers' education is discussed, Socrates says: "I forgot that we were only playing, and so I spoke too vehemently," as if to imply that objections can be made to philosophical rule. As in a few other places in the dialogue, Plato throws his political innovation open to doubt. However, in Plato's view, philosopher-rulers do not derive their authority solely from their expert knowledge, but also from their love of the city as a whole and their impartiality and fairness. Their political authority is not only rational but also substantially moral, based on the consent of the governed. They regard justice as the most important and most essential thing. Even if particular political solutions presented in the Republic may be open to questioning, what seems to stand firm is the basic idea that underlies philosophers' governance and that can be traced back to Solon: the idea of fairness based on difference as the basis of the righteous political order. A political order based on fairness leads to friendship and cooperation among different parts of the city.

For Plato, as for Solon, government exists for the benefit of all citizens and all social classes, and must mediate between potentially conflicting interests. Such a mediating force is exercised in the ideal city of the Republic by the philosopher-rulers. They are the guarantors of the political order that is encapsulated in the norm that regulates just relations of persons and classes within the city and is expressed by the phrase: "doing one's own work and not meddling with what isn't one's own." If justice is related to equality, the notion of equality is indeed preserved in Plato's view of justice expressed by this norm as the impartial, equal treatment of all citizens and social groups. It is not the case that Plato knew that justice meant equality but made it inequality, as Karl Popper believed. In the ideal city all persons and social groups are given equal opportunities to be happy, i.e. pursue happiness, but not at the expense of others. Their particular individual, group or class happiness is limited by the need of the happiness for all.

The happiness of the whole city is not for Plato the happiness of an abstract unity called the polis, or the happiness of the greatest number, but rather the happiness of all citizens derived from a peaceful, harmonious, and cooperative union of different social classes. According to the traditional definition of justice by Simonides from Book I, which is reinterpreted in Book IV, as "doing one's own work," each social class receives its proper due in the distribution of benefits and burdens. The philosopher-rulers enjoy respect and contemplative leisure, but not wealth or honours; the guardian class, the second class in the city, military honours, but not leisure or wealth; and the producer class, family life, wealth, and freedom of enterprise, but not honours or rule. Then, the producers supply the city with goods; the guardians, defend it; and the philosophers, attuned to virtue and illuminated by goodness, rule it impartially for the common benefit of all citizens. The three different social classes engage in mutually beneficial enterprise, by which the interests of all are best served. Social and economic differences, i.e. departures from equality, bring about benefits to people in all social positions, and therefore, are justified. In the Platonic vision of the Republic, all social classes get to perform what they are best fit to do and are unified into a single community by mutual interests. In this sense, although each are different, they are all friends.

Politics and the Soul

It can be contended that the whole argument of the Republic is made in response to the denial of justice as a universal moral value expressed in Thrasymachus' statement: "Justice is nothing else than the interest of the stronger." Moral relativism, the denial of the harmony of interests, and other problems posed by this statement are a real challenge for Plato for whom justice is not merely a notion relative to the existing laws instituted by the victorious factions in power. In the Laws a similar statement is made again, and it is interpreted as the right of the strong, the winner in a political battle. By such interpretation, morality is denied and the right to govern, like in the "Melian Dialogue" of Thucydides, is equated simply with might. The decisions about morals and justice which we make are for Plato "no trifle, but the foremost thing."

The answer to the question of what is right and what is wrong can entirely determine our way of life, as individuals and communities. If Plato's argument about justice presented in both the Republic and the Laws can be summarized in just one sentence, the sentence will say: "Justice is neither the right of the strong nor the advantage of the stronger, but the right of the best and the advantage of the whole community." The best, as explained in the Republic, are the expert philosophical rulers. They, the wise and virtuous, free from faction and guided by the idea of the common good, should rule for the common benefit of the whole community, so that the city will not be internally divided by strife, but one in friendship. Then, in the Laws, the reign of the best individuals is replaced by the reign of the finest laws instituted by a judicious legislator.

Throughout this dialogue Plato's guiding principle is that the good society is a harmonious union of different social elements that represent two key values: wisdom and freedom. The best laws assure that all the city's parts: the democratic, the oligarchic, and the aristocratic, are represented in political institutions: the popular Assembly, the elected Council, and the Higher Council, and thus each social class receives its due expression.

Still, a democratic skeptic can feel dissatisfied with Plato's proposal to grant the right to rule to the best, either individuals or laws, even on the basis of tacit consent of the governed. The skeptic may believe that every adult is capable of exercising the power of self-direction, and should be given the opportunity to do so. He will be prepared to pay the costs of eventual mistakes and to endure an occasional civil unrest or even a limited war rather than be directed by anyone who may claim superior wisdom. Why then should Plato's best constitution be preferable to democracy? In order to fully explain the Platonic political vision, the meaning of "the best" should be further clarified.

In the short dialogue Alcibiades I, little studied today and thought by some scholars as not genuine, though held in great esteem by the Platonists of antiquity, Socrates speaks with Alcibiades. The subject of their conversation is politics. Frequently referred to by Thucydides in the History of the Peloponnesian War, Alcibiades, the future leader of Athens, highly intelligent and ambitious, largely responsible for the Athenian invasion of Sicily, is at the time of conversation barely twenty years old. The young, handsome, and well-born Alcibiades of the dialogue is about to begin his political career and to address the Assembly for the first time. He plans to advise the Athenians on the subject of peace and war, or some other important affair. His ambitions are indeed extraordinary. He does not want just to display his worth before the people of Athens and become their leader, but to rule over Europe and Asia as well. His dreams resemble that of the future Alexander the Great.

His claim to rule is that he is the best. However, upon Socrates' scrutiny, it becomes apparent that young Alcibiades knows neither what is just, nor what is advantageous, nor what is good, nor what is noble, beyond what he has learned from the crowd. His world-view is based on unexamined opinions. He appears to be the worst type of ignorant person who pretends that he knows something but does not. Such ignorance in politics is the cause of mistakes and evils. What is implied in the dialogue is that noble birth, beautiful looks, and even intelligence and power, without knowledge, do not give the title to rule. Ignorance, the condition of Alcibiades, is also the condition of the great majority of the people. Nevertheless, Socrates promises to guide Alcibiades, so that he becomes excellent and renowned among the Greeks. In the course of further conversation, it turns out that one who is truly the best does not only have knowledge of political things, rather than an opinion about them, but also knows one's own self and is a beautiful soul. He or she is perfect in virtue. The riches of the world can be entrusted only to those who "take trouble over" themselves, who look "toward what is divine and bright," and who following the supreme soul, God, the finest mirror of their own image, strive to be as beautiful and wealthy in their souls as possible. The best government can be founded only on beautiful and well-ordered souls.

In a few dialogues, such as Phaedo, the Republic, Phaedrus, Timaeus, and the Laws, Plato introduces his doctrine of the immortality of the soul. His ultimate answer to the question "Who am I?" is not an "egoistic animal" or an "independent variable," as the twentieth century behavioural researcher blatantly might say, but an "immortal soul, corrupted by vice and purified by virtue, of whom the body is only an instrument." Expert political knowledge for him should include not only knowledge of things out there, but also knowledge of oneself. This is because whoever is ignorant of himself will also be ignorant of others and of political things, and, therefore, will never be an expert politician. Those who are ignorant will go wrong, moving from one misery to another. For them history will be a tough teacher, but as long they do not recognize themselves and practice virtue, they will learn nothing. Plato's good society is impossible without transcendence, without a link to the perfect being who is God, the true measure of all things. It is also impossible without an ongoing philosophical reflection on whom we truly are. Therefore, democracy would not be a good form of government for him unless, as it is proposed in the Laws, the element of freedom is mixed with the element of wisdom, which includes ultimate knowledge of the self.

Unmixed and unchecked democracy, marked by the general permissiveness that spurs vices, makes people impious, and lets them forget about their true self, is only be the second worst in the rank of flawed regimes after tyranny headed by a vicious individual. This does not mean that Plato would support a theocratic government based on shallow religiosity and religious hypocrisy. There is no evidence for this. Freedom of speech, forming opinions and expressing them, which may be denied in theocracy, is a true value for Plato, along with wisdom. It is the basic requirement for philosophy. In shallow religiosity, like in atheism, there is ignorance and no knowledge of the self either. In Book II of *The Republic,* Plato criticizes the popular religious beliefs of the Athenians, who under the influence of Homer and Hesiod attribute vices to the gods and heroes. He tries to show that God is the perfect being, the purest and brightest, always the same, immortal and true, to whom we should look in order to know ourselves and become pure and virtuous. God, and not human beings, is the measure of political order.

Plato's Achievement

Plato's greatest achievement may be seen firstly in that he, in opposing the sophists, offered to decadent Athens, which had lost faith in her old religion, traditions, and customs, a means by which civilization and the city's health could be restored: the recovery of order in both the body and the soul. The best, rational and righteous political order leads to the harmonious unity of a society and allows all the city's parts to pursue happiness but not at the expense of others. The characteristics of a good political society, of which most people can say "it is mine" are described in the Republic by four virtues: justice, wisdom, moderation, and courage. Justice is the equity or fairness that grants each social group its due and ensures that each "does one's own work." The three other virtues describe qualities of different social groups. Wisdom, which can be understood as the knowledge of the whole, including both knowledge of the self and political prudence, is the quality of the leadership. Courage is not merely military courage but primarily civic courage: the ability to preserve the right, law-inspired belief, and stand in defense of such values as friendship and freedom on which a good society is founded. It is the primary quality of the guardians. Finally, moderation, a sense of the limits that bring peace and happiness to all, is the quality of all social classes. It expresses the mutual consent of both the governed and the rulers as to who should rule.

The four virtues of the good society describe also the soul of a well-ordered individual. Its rational part, whose quality is wisdom, nurtured by fine words and learning, should together with the emotional or spirited part, cultivated by music and rhythm, rule over the volitional or appetitive part. Under the leadership of the intellect, the soul must free itself from greed, lust, and other degrading vices, and direct itself to the divine. The liberation of the soul from vice is for Plato the ultimate task of humans on earth. Nobody can be wicked and happy. Only a spiritually liberated individual, whose soul is beautiful and well ordered, can experience true happiness. Only a country ordered according to the principles of virtue can claim to have the best system of government.

Plato's critique of democracy may be considered by modern readers as not applicable to liberal democracy today. Liberal democracies are not only founded on considerations of freedom and equality, but also include other elements, such as the rule of law, multiparty systems, periodic elections, and a professional civil service. Organized along the principle of separation of powers, today's Western democracy resembles more a revised version of mixed government, with a degree of moderation and competence, rather than the highly unstable and unchecked Athenian democracy of the fourth and fifth century B.C.E., in which all governmental policies were directly determined by the often changing moods of the people. However, what still seems to be relevant in Plato's political philosophy is that he reminds us of the moral and spiritual dimension of political life. He believes that virtue is the lifeblood of any good society. Moved by extreme ambitions, the Athenians, like the mythological Atlantians described in the dialogue Critias, became infected by "wicked coveting and the pride of power." Like the drunken Alcibiades from the Symposium, who would swap "bronze for gold" and thus prove that he did not understand the Socratic teaching, they chose the "semblance of beauty," the shining appearance of power and material wealth, rather than the "thing itself," the being of perfection. "To the seen eye they now began to seem foul, for they were losing the fairest bloom from their precious treasure, but to such who could not see the truly happy life, they would appear fair and blessed." They were losing their virtuous souls, their virtue by which they could prove themselves to be worthy of preservation as a great nation. Racked by the selfish passions of greed and envy, they forfeited their conception of the right order. Their benevolence, the desire to do good, ceased. "Man and city are alike," Plato claims. Humans without souls are hollow. Cities without virtue are rotten. To those who cannot see clearly they may look glorious but what appears bright is only exterior. To see clearly what is visible, the political world out there, Plato argues, one has first to perceive what is invisible but intelligible, the soul. One has to know oneself. Humans are immortal souls, he claims, and not just independent variables.

They are often egoistic, but the divine element in them makes them more than mere animals. Friendship, freedom, justice, wisdom, courage, and moderation are the key values that define a good society based on virtue, which must be guarded against vice, war, and factionalism. To enjoy true happiness, humans must remain virtuous and remember God, the perfect being. Plato's achievement as a political philosopher may be seen in that he believed that there could be a body of knowledge whose attainment would make it possible to heal political problems, such as factionalism and the corruption of morals, which can bring a city to a decline. The doctrine of the harmony of interests, fairness as the basis of the best political order, the mixed constitution, the rule of law, the distinction between good and deviated forms of government, practical wisdom as the quality of good leadership, and the importance of virtue and transcendence for politics are the political ideas that can rightly be associated with Plato. They have profoundly influenced subsequent political thinkers.

2

Aristotle

Aristotle (384 BC – 322 BC) was a Greek philosopher, a student of Plato and teacher of Alexander the Great. He wrote on many subjects, including physics, metaphysics, poetry, theatre, music, logic, rhetoric, politics, government, ethics, biology and zoology. Together with Plato, and Socrates (Plato's teacher), Aristotle is one of the most important founding figures in Western philosophy. He was the first to create a comprehensive system of Western philosophy, encompassing morality and aesthetics, logic and science, politics and metaphysics. Aristotle's views on the physical sciences profoundly shaped medieval scholarship, and their influence extended well into the Renaissance, although they were ultimately replaced by modern physics. In the biological sciences, some of his observations were only confirmed to be accurate in the nineteenth century.

His works contain the earliest known formal study of logic, which were incorporated in the late nineteenth century into modern formal logic. In metaphysics, Aristotelianism had a profound influence on philosophical and theological thinking in the Islamic and Jewish traditions in the Middle Ages, and it continues to influence Christian theology, especially Eastern Orthodox theology, and the scholastic tradition of the Roman Catholic Church. All aspects of Aristotle's philosophy continue to be the object of active academic study today. Though Aristotle wrote many elegant treatises and dialogues (Cicero described his literary style as "a river of gold"), it is thought that the majority of his writings are now lost and only about one third of the original works have survived.

Life

Aristotle was born in Stageira, Chalcidice in 384 BC. His father, Nicomachus was the personal physician to King Amyntas of Macedon. Aristotle was trained and educated as a member of the aristocracy. At about the age of eighteen, he went to Athens to continue his education at Plato's Academy. Aristotle remained at the academy for nearly twenty years, not leaving until after Plato's death in 347 BC. He then travelled with Xenocrates to the court of his friend Hermias of Atarneus in Asia Minor. While in Asia, Aristotle travelled with Theophrastus to the island of Lesbos, where together they researched the botany and zoology of the island. Aristotle married Hermias's adoptive daughter (or niece) Pythias. She bore him a daughter, whom they named Pythias. Soon after Hermias' death, Aristotle was invited by Philip of Macedon to become tutor to Alexander the Great.

After spending several years tutoring the young Alexander, Aristotle returned to Athens. By 335 BC, he established his own school there, known as the Lyceum. Aristotle conducted courses at the school for the next twelve years. While in Athens, his wife Pythias died, and Aristotle became involved with Herpyllis of Stageira, who bore him a son whom he named after his father, Nicomachus. According to the Suda, he also had an eromenos, Palaephatus of Abydus.

It is during this period in Athens when Aristotle is believed to have composed many of his works. Aristotle wrote many dialogues, only fragments of which survived. The works that have survived are in treatise form and were not, for the most part, intended for widespread publication, as they are generally thought to be lecture aids for his students. His most important treatises *include Physics, Metaphysics, Nicomachean Ethics, Politics, De Anima* (On the Soul) and *Poetics*. These works, although connected in many fundamental ways, vary significantly in both style and substance.

Aristotle not only studied almost every subject possible at the time, but made significant contributions to most of them. In physical science, Aristotle studied anatomy, astronomy, economics, embryology, geography, geology, meteorology, physics and zoology. In philosophy, he wrote on aesthetics, ethics, government, metaphysics, politics, psychology, rhetoric and theology. He also studied education, foreign customs, literature and poetry. His combined works constitute a virtual encyclopedia of Greek knowledge. It has been suggested that Aristotle was probably the last person to know everything there was to be known in his own time.

Upon Alexander's death, anti-Macedonian sentiment in Athens once again flared. Eurymedon the hierophant denounced Aristotle for not holding the gods in honour. Aristotle fled the city to his mother's family estate in Chalcis, explaining, "I will not allow the Athenians to sin twice against philosophy," a reference to Athens's prior trial and execution of Socrates. However, he died in Euboea of natural causes within the year (in 322 BC). Aristotle left a will and named chief executor his student Antipater, in which he asked to be buried next to his wife. It has also been proposed that Aristotle's banishment and death resulted from the possibility that he was involved with the death of Alexander.

Logic

Aristotle's conception of logic was the dominant form of logic until 19th century advances in mathematical logic. Kant stated in the *Critique of Pure Reason* that Aristotle's theory of logic completely accounted for the core of deductive inference.

History

Aristotle "says that 'on the subject of reasoning' he 'had nothing else on an earlier date to speak of'". However, Plato reports that syntax was devised before him, by Prodikos of Keos, who was concerned by the correct use of words. Logic seems to have emerged from dialectics; the earlier philosophers made frequent use of concepts like *reductio ad absurdum* in their discussions, but never truly understood the logical implications. Even Plato had difficulties with logic; although he had a reasonable conception of a deduction system, he could never actually construct one and relied instead on his dialectic. Plato believed that deduction would simply follow from premises, hence he focused on maintaining solid premises so that the conclusion would logically follow. Consequently, Plato realized that a method for obtaining conclusions would be most beneficial. He never succeeded in devising such a method, but his best attempt was published in his book *Sophist,* where he introduced his division method.

Analytics and the Organon

What we today call *Aristotelian logic,* Aristotle himself would have labelled "analytics". The term "logic" he reserved to mean *dialectics.* Most of Aristotle's work is probably not in its original form, since it was most likely edited by students and later lecturers. The logical works of Aristotle were compiled into six books in about the early 1st century AD:

1. *Categories*
2. *On Interpretation*
3. *Prior Analytics*
4. *Posterior Analytics*
5. *Topics*
6. *On Sophistical Refutations.*

The order of the books (or the teachings from which they are composed) is not certain, but this list was derived from analysis of Aristotle's writings. It goes from the basics, the analysis of simple terms in the Categories, to the study of more complex forms, namely, syllogisms (in the Analytics) and dialectics (in the Topics and Sophistical Refutations). There is one volume of Aristotle's concerning logic not found in the *Organon,* namely the fourth book of *Metaphysics..*

Aristotle's Scientific Method

Like his teacher Plato, Aristotle's philosophy aims at the universal. Aristotle, however, found the universal in particular things, which he called the essence of things, while Plato finds that the universal exists apart from particular things, and is related to them as their prototype or exemplar. For Aristotle, therefore, philosophic method implies the ascent from the study of particular phenomena to the knowledge of essences, while for Plato philosophic method means the descent from a knowledge of universal Forms (or ideas) to a contemplation of particular imitations of these. For Aristotle, "form" still refers to the unconditional basis of phenomena but is "instantiated" in a particular substance (see *Universals and particulars*, below). In a certain sense, Aristotle's method is both inductive and deductive, while Plato's is essentially deductive from *a priori* principles.

In Aristotle's terminology, "natural philosophy" is a branch of philosophy examining the phenomena of the natural world, and included fields that would be regarded today as physics, biology and other natural sciences. In modern times, the scope of *philosophy* has become limited to more generic or abstract inquiries, such as ethics and metaphysics, in which logic plays a major role. Today's philosophy tends to exclude empirical study of the natural world by means of the scientific method. In contrast, Aristotle's philosophical endeavors encompassed virtually all facets of intellectual inquiry.

In the larger sense of the word, Aristotle makes philosophy coextensive with reasoning, which he also would describe as "science". Note, however, that his use of the term *science* carries a different meaning than that covered by the term "scientific method". For Aristotle, "all science (*dianoia*) is either practical, poetical or theoretical" (*Metaphysics* 1025b25). By practical science, he means ethics and politics; by poetical science, he means the study of poetry and the other fine arts; by theoretical science, he means physics, mathematics and metaphysics. If logic (or "analytics") is regarded as a study preliminary to philosophy, the divisions of Aristotelian philosophy would consist of: (1) Logic; (2) Theoretical Philosophy, including Metaphysics, Physics, Mathematics, (3) Practical Philosophy and (4) Poetical Philosophy.

In the period between his two stays in Athens, between his times at the Academy and the Lyceum, Aristotle conducted most of the scientific thinking and research for which he is renowned today. In fact, most of Aristotle's life was devoted to the study of the objects of natural science. Aristotle's metaphysics contains observations on the nature of numbers but he made no original contributions to mathematics. He did, however, perform original research in the natural sciences, *e.g.*, botany, zoology, physics, astronomy, chemistry, meteorology, and several other sciences.

Aristotle's writings on science are largely qualitative, as opposed to quantitative. Beginning in the sixteenth century, scientists began applying mathematics to the physical sciences, and Aristotle's work in this area was deemed hopelessly inadequate. His failings were largely due to the absence of concepts like mass, velocity, force and temperature. He had a conception of speed and temperature, but no quantitative understanding of them, which was partly due to the absence of basic experimental devices, like clocks and thermometers.

His writings provide an account of many scientific observations, a mixture of precocious accuracy and curious errors. For example, in his *History of Animals* he claimed that human males have more teeth than females. In a similar vein, John Philoponus, and later Galileo, showed by simple experiments that Aristotle's theory that the more massive object falls faster than a less massive object is incorrect. On the other hand, Aristotle refuted Democritus's claim that the Milky Way was made up of "those stars which are shaded by the earth from the sun's rays," pointing out (correctly, even if such reasoning was bound to be dismissed for a long time) that, given "current astronomical demonstrations" that "the size of the sun is greater than that of the earth and the distance of the stars from the earth many times greater than that of the sun, then...the sun shines on all the stars and the earth screens none of them."

In places, Aristotle goes too far in deriving 'laws of the universe' from simple observation and over-stretched reason. Today's scientific method assumes that such thinking without sufficient facts is ineffective, and that discerning the validity of one's hypothesis requires far more rigorous experimentation than that which Aristotle used to support his laws.

Aristotle also had some scientific blind spots. He posited a geocentric cosmology that we may discern in selections of the *Metaphysics*, which was widely accepted up until the 1500s. From the 3rd century to the 1500s, the dominant view held that the Earth was the centre of the universe (geocentrism).

Since he was perhaps the philosopher most respected by European thinkers during and after the Renaissance, these thinkers often took Aristotle's erroneous positions as given, which held back science in this epoch. However, Aristotle's scientific shortcomings should not mislead one into forgetting his great advances in the many scientific fields. For instance, he founded logic as a formal science and created foundations to biology that were not superseded for two millennia. Moreover, he introduced the fundamental notion that nature is composed of things that change and that studying such changes can provide useful knowledge of underlying constants.

Physics

The Five Elements:

- Fire, which is hot and dry.
- Earth, which is cold and dry.
- Air, which is hot and wet.
- Water, which is cold and wet.
- Aether, which is the divine substance that makes up the heavenly spheres and heavenly bodies (stars and planets).

Each of the four earthly elements has its natural place; the earth at the centre of the universe, then water, then air, then fire. When they are out of their natural place they have natural motion, requiring no external cause, which is towards that place; so bodies sink in water, air bubbles up, rain falls, flame rises in air. The heavenly element has perpetual circular motion.

Chance and Spontaneity

Spontaneity and chance are causes of effects. Chance as an incidental cause lies in the realm of accidental things. It is "from what is spontaneous" (but note that what is spontaneous does not come from chance). For a better understanding of Aristotle's conception of "chance" it might be better to think of "coincidence": Something takes place by chance if a person sets out with the intent of having one thing take place, but with the result of another thing (not intended) taking place.

For example: A person seeks donations. That person may find another person willing to donate a substantial sum. However, if the person seeking the donations met the person donating, not for the purpose of collecting donations, but for some other purpose, Aristotle would call the collecting of the donation by that particular donator a result of chance. It must be unusual that something happens by chance. In other words, if something happens all or most of the time, we cannot say that it is by chance.

There is also more specific kind of chance, which Aristotle names "luck", that can only apply to human beings, since it is in the sphere of moral actions. According to Aristotle, luck must involve choice (and thus deliberation), and only humans are capable of deliberation and choice. "What is not capable of action cannot do anything by chance".

Political Theory

Aristotle was a Greek philosopher, logician, and scientist. Along with his teacher Plato, Aristotle is generally regarded as one of the most influential ancient thinkers in a number of philosophical fields, including political theory. Aristotle was born in Stagira in northern Greece, and his father was a court physician to the king of Macedon.

As a young man he studied in Plato's Academy in Athens. After Plato's death he left Athens to conduct philosophical and biological research in Asia Minor and Lesbos, and he was then invited by King Philip II of Macedon to tutor his young son, Alexander the Great. Soon after Alexander succeeded his father, consolidated the conquest of the Greek city-states, and launched the invasion of the Persian Empire. Aristotle returned as a resident alien to Athens, and was close friend of Antipater the Macedonian viceroy.

At this time (335-323 BC) he wrote or at least completed some of his major treatises, including the Politics. When Alexander died suddenly, Aristotle had to flee from Athens because of his Macedonian connections, and he died soon after. Aristotle's life seems to have influenced his political thought in various ways: his interest in biology seems to be expressed in the naturalism of his politics; his interest in comparative politics and his sympathies for democracy as well as monarchy may have been encouraged by his travels and experience of diverse political systems; he criticizes harshly, while borrowing extensively, from Plato's *Republic, Statesman*, and *Laws*; and his own *Politics* is intended to guide rulers and statesmen, reflecting the high political circles in which he moved.

Political Science in General

The modern word 'political' derives from the Greek politikos, 'of, or pertaining to, the polis'. (The Greek term polis will be translated here as 'city-state'. It is also translated as 'city' or 'polis', or simply anglicized as 'polis'. City-states like Athens and Sparta were relatively small and cohesive units, in which political, religious, and cultural concerns were intertwined. The extent of their similarity to modern nation-states is controversial.) Aristotle's word for 'politics' is politike, which is short for politike episteme or 'political science'. It belongs to one of the three main branches of science, which Aristotle distinguishes by their ends or objects. Contemplative science (including physics and metaphysics) is concerned with truth or knowledge for its own sake; practical science with good action; and productive science with making useful or beautiful objects. Politics is a practical science, since it is concerned with the noble action or happiness of the citizens (although it resembles a productive science in that it seeks to create, preserve, and reform political systems.) Aristotle thus understands politics as a normative or prescriptive discipline rather than as a purely empirical or descriptive inquiry.

In *Nicomachean Ethics* I.2 Aristotle characterizes politics as the most authoritative science. It prescribes which sciences are to be studied in the city-state, and the other capacities--such as military science, household management, and rhetoric--fall under its authority. Since it governs the other practical sciences, their ends serve as means to its end, which is nothing less than the human good. "Even if the end is the same for an individual and for a city-state, that of the city-state seems at any rate greater and more complete to attain and preserve. For although it is worthy to attain it for only an individual, it is nobler and more divine to do so for a nation or city-state." Aristotle's political science encompasses the two fields which modern philosophers distinguish as ethics and political philosophy. Political philosophy in the narrow sense is roughly speaking the subject of his treatise called the Politics.

Characteristics and Problems of Aristotle Politics

The work which has come down to us under this name appears to be less an integrated treatise than a collection of essays on various topics in political philosophy, which may have been compiled by a later editor rather than by Aristotle. The following topics are discussed in the eight books:

I. Naturalness of the city-state and of the household

II. Critique of ostensibly best constitutions

III. General theory of constitutions

IV. Inferior constitutions

V. Preservation and destruction of constitutions

VI. Further discussion of democracy and oligarchy

VII-VIII. Blueprint of the best constitution.

This ordering of the books reflects, very roughly, the program for the study of constitutions which concludes the Nicomachean Ethics:

First, then, if any particular point has been treated well by those who have gone before us, we must try to review it; then from the constitutions that have been collected we must try to see what it is that preserves and destroys each of the constitutions, and for what reasons some city-states are well governed and others the reverse. For when these things have been examined, we will perhaps better understand what sort of constitution is best, and how each is structured, and which laws and customs it uses. Let us then begin our discussion.

However, scholars have raised problems with the Politics as we have it. The first concerns the intended order of its eight books. Some have questioned the traditional ordering, arguing that the discussion of the best constitution should follow directly after book III. Indeed, book III concludes with a transition to a discussion of the best constitution (although this may be due to a later editor). However, cross-references between various passages of the *Politics* indicate that books IV-V-VI form a connected series, as do books VII-VIII, but these series do not refer to each other. However, both series refer back to book III which in turn refers to book I. With some oversimplification, the *Politics* is comparable to a tree trunk supporting two separate branches: the root system is I, the trunk is II-III, and the branches are IV-V-VI and VII-VIII.

The second problem concerns the order in which the books were actually written. If they were composed at very different dates, they might represent discordant stages in the development of Aristotle's political philosophy. For example, Werner Jaeger argued that books VII-VIII contain a youthful utopianism, motivating Aristotle to emulate his teacher Plato in erecting "an ideal state by logical construction." In contrast, books IV-VI are based on "sober empirical study." Other scholars have seen a more pragmatic, even Machiavellian approach to politics in books IV-VI. A difficulty for this interpretation is that in book IV Aristotle regards the business of constructing ideal constitutions as perfectly compatible with that of addressing actual political problems. Although much ink has been spilled since Jaeger attempted to discern different chronological strata in the Politics, it has not resulted in a clear scholarly consensus. Because there is no explicit evidence of the dates at which the various books of the Politics were written, argument has turned on alleged inconsistencies between different passages.

This leads to the third problem, whether there are major inconsistencies of doctrine or method in the Politics. For example, Aristotle's account of the best constitution assumes his theory of justice, a moral standard which cannot be met by the actual political systems (democracies and oligarchies) of his own day. He does discuss practical political reforms in books IV-VI but more in terms of stability than justice. This raises the question of whether books IV-VI mark a radical departure from the political philosophy of the other books. Resolution of this problem requires careful study of the *Politics* as a whole

Aristotle's View of Politics

Political science studies the tasks of the politician or statesman (politikos), in much the way that medical science concerns the work of the physician. It is, in fact, the body of knowledge that such practitioners, if truly expert, will also wield in pursuing their tasks. The most important task for the politician is, in the role of lawgiver (nomothetes), to frame the appropriate constitution for the city-state. This involves enduring laws, customs, and institutions (including a system of moral education) for the citizens. Once the constitution is in place, the politician needs to take the appropriate measures to maintain it, to introduce reforms when he finds them necessary, and to prevent developments which might subvert the political system. This is the province of legislative science, which Aristotle regards as more important than politics as exercised in everyday political activity such as the passing of decrees. Aristotle frequently compares the politician to a craftsman. The analogy is imprecise because politics, in the strict sense of legislative science, is a form of practical wisdom or prudence, but valid to the extent that the politician produces, operates, and maintains a legal system according to universal principles. In order to appreciate this analogy it is helpful to observe that Aristotle explains production of an artifact in terms of four causes: the material, formal, efficient, and final causes. For example, clay (material cause) is molded into a vase shape (formal cause) by a potter (efficient or moving cause) so that it can contain liquid (final cause).

One can also explain the existence of the city-state in terms of the four causes. It is a kind of community (koinonia), that is, a collection of parts having some functions and interests in common. Hence, it is made up of parts, which Aristotle describes in various ways in different contexts: as households, or economic classes (e.g., the rich and the poor), or demes (i.e., local political units). But, ultimately, the city-state is composed of individual citizens, who, along with natural resources, are the "material" or "equipment" out of which the city-state is fashioned.

The formal cause of the city-state is its constitution (politeia). Aristotle defines the constitution as "a certain ordering of the inhabitants of the city-state." He also speaks of the constitution of a community as "the form of the compound" and argues that whether the community is the same over time depends on whether it has the same constitution. The constitution is not a written document, but an immanent organizing principle, analogous to the soul of an organism. Hence, the constitution is also "the way of life" of the citizens. Here the citizens are that minority of the resident population who are adults with full political rights.

The existence of the city-state also requires an efficient cause, namely, its ruler. On Aristotle's view, a community of any sort can possess order only if it has a ruling element or authority. This ruling principle is defined by the constitution, which sets criteria for political offices, particularly the sovereign office. However, on a deeper level, there must be an efficient cause to explain why a city-state acquires its constitution in the first place. Aristotle states that "the person who first established [the city-state] is the cause of very great benefits." This person was evidently the lawgiver (nomothetes), someone like Solon of Athens or Lycurgus of Sparta, who founded the constitution. Aristotle compares the lawgiver, or the politician more generally, to a craftsman (demiourgos) like a weaver or shipbuilder, who fashions material into a finished product. The notion of final cause dominates Aristotle's *Politics* from the opening lines:

Since we see that every city-state is a sort of community and that every community is established for the sake of some good (for everyone does everything for the sake of what they believe to be good), it is clear that every community aims at some good, and the community which has the most authority of all and includes all the others aims highest, that is, at the good with the most authority. This is what is called the city-state or political community. Soon after, he states that the city-state comes into being for the sake of life but exists for the sake of the good life. The theme that the good life or happiness is the proper end of the city-state recurs throughout the Politics.

To sum up, the city-state is a hylomorphic (i.e., matter-form) compound of a particular population (i.e., citizen-body) in a given territory (material cause) and a constitution (formal cause). The constitution itself is fashioned by the lawgiver and is governed by politicians, who are like craftsmen (efficient cause), and the constitution defines the aim of the city-state.

Presuppositions of Aristotle's Politics

Aristotle's political philosophy is distinguished by its underlying philosophical doctrines. Of these the following four principles are especially noteworthy:

The principle of teleology Aristotle begins the Politics by invoking the concept of nature. In the Physics Aristotle identifies the nature of a thing above all with its end or final cause. The end of a thing is also its function, which is its defining principle. On Aristotle's view plants and animals are cardinal examples of natural existents, because they have a nature in the sense of an internal causal principle which explains how it comes into being and behaves. For example, an acorn has an inherent tendency to grow into an oak tree, so that the tree exists by nature rather than by craft or by chance. The thesis that human beings have a natural function has a fundamental place in the Eudemian Ethics II.1, Nicomachean Ethics I.7, and Politics I.2. *The Politics* further argues that it is part of the nature of human beings that they are political or adapted for life in the city-state. Thus teleology is crucial for the political naturalism which is at the foundation of Aristotle's political philosophy.

The principle of perfection Aristotle understands good and evil in terms of his teleology. The natural end of the organism (and the means to this end) is good for it, and what defeats or impedes this end is bad. For example, he argues that animals sleep in order to preserve themselves, because "nature operates for the sake of an end, and this is a good," and sleeping is necessary and beneficial for entities which cannot move continuously. For human beings the ultimate good or happiness (eudaimonia) consists in perfection, the full attainment of their natural function, which Aristotle analyzes as the activity of the soul according to reason (or not without reason), i.e., activity in accordance with the most perfect virtue or excellence.

This also provides a norm for the politician: "What is most choiceworthy for each individual is always the highest it is possible for him to attain." This ideal is to be realized in both the individual and the city-state: "that way of life is best, both separately for each individual and in common for city-states, which is equipped with virtue." However, Aristotle recognizes that it is generally impossible to fully realize this ideal, in which case he invokes a fall-back principle: it is best to attain perfection, but, failing that, a thing is better in proportion as it is nearer to the end.

Aristotle's perfectionism was opposed to the subjective relativism of Protagoras, according to which good and evil is defined by whatever human beings happened to desire. Like Plato, Aristotle maintained that the good was objective and independent of human wishes. However, he rejected Plato's own theory that the good was defined in terms of a transcendent form of the good, holding instead that good and evil are in a way relative to the organism, that is, to its natural end.

The principle of community Aristotle maintains that the city-state is the most complete community, because it attains the limit of self-sufficiency, so that it can exist for the sake of the good life. Individuals outside of the city-state are not self-sufficient, because they depend on the community not only for material necessities but also for education and moral habituation. "Just as, when perfected, a human is the best of animals, so also when separated from law and justice, he is the worst of all." On Aristotle's view, then, human beings must be subject to the authority of the city-state in order to attain the good life. The following principle concerns how authority should be exercised within a community.

Principle of rulership: Aristotle believes that the existence and well-being of any system requires the presence of a ruling element: "Whenever a thing is established out of a number of things and becomes a single common thing, there always appears in it a ruler and ruled.... This [relation] is present in living things, but it derives from all of nature."

Just as an animal or plant can survive and flourish only if its soul rules over its body, a human community can possess the necessary order only if it has a ruling element which is in a position of authority, just as an army can possess order only if it has a commander in control. Although Aristotle followed Plato on this principle, he rejected Plato's further claim that one form of rule is appropriate for all. For Aristotle different forms of rule are necessary for different systems: e.g., political rule for citizens and despotic rule for slaves. The imposition of an inappropriate type of rule results in disorder and injustice.

The aforementioned principles account for much of the distinctive flavour of Aristotle's political philosophy, and they also indicate where many modern theorists have turned away from him. Modern philosophers such as Thomas Hobbes have challenged the principles of teleology and perfectionism, arguing against the former that human beings are mechanistic rather than teleological systems, and against the latter that good and bad depend upon subjective preferences of valuing agents rather than on objective states of affairs. Liberal theorists have criticized the principle of community on the grounds that it cedes too much authority to the state. Even the principle of rulership which Aristotle, Plato, and many other theorists thought self-evident has come under fire by modern theorists like Adam Smith and F. A. Hayek who argued that social and economic order may arise spontaneously as if by an "invisible hand." Modern neo-Aristotelian political theorists are committed to defending one or more of these doctrines against such criticisms.

It is in these terms that Aristotle understands the fundamental normative problem of politics: What constitutional form should the lawgiver and politician establish and preserve in what material for the sake of what end?

Political Naturalism

Aristotle lays the foundations for his political theory in Politics book I by arguing that the city-state and political rule are "natural." The argument begins with a schematic, quasi-historical account of the development of the city-state out of simpler communities. First, individual human beings combined in pairs because they could not exist apart. The male and female joined in order to reproduce, and the master and slave came together for self-preservation. The natural master uses his intellect to rule, and the natural slave uses his body to labour. Second, the household arose naturally from these primitive communities in order to serve everyday needs. Third, when several households combined for other needs a village emerged also according to nature. Finally, "the complete community, formed from several villages, is a city-state, which at once attains the limit of self-sufficiency, roughly speaking. It comes to be for the sake of life, and exists for the sake of the good life."

Aristotle defends three claims about nature and the city-state: First, the city-state exists by nature, because it comes to be out of the more primitive natural associations and it serves as their end, because only it attains self-sufficiency. Second, human beings are by nature political animals, because nature, which does nothing in vain, has equipped them with speech, which enables them to communicate moral concepts such as justice which are formative of the household and city-state. Third, the city-state is naturally prior to the individuals, because individuals cannot perform their natural functions apart from the city-state, since they are not self-sufficient. However, these three claims are immediately followed by a fourth: the city-state is a creation of human intelligence. "Therefore, everyone naturally has the impulse for such a [political] community, but the person who first established [it] is the cause of very great benefits." This great benefactor is evidently the lawgiver, for the legal system of the city-state makes human beings just and virtuous and lifts them from the savagery in which they would otherwise languish.

Aristotle's political naturalism presents the difficulty that he does not explain how he is using the term "nature" (phusis). In the Physics nature is understood as an internal principle of motion or rest. If the city-state were natural in this sense, it would resemble a plant or an animal which grows naturally to maturity out of a seed. However, this cannot be reconciled with the important role which Aristotle also assigns to the lawgiver as the one who established the city-state. For on Aristotle's theory a thing either exists by nature or by craft; it cannot do both. Aristotle can seemingly escape this dilemma only if it is supposed that he speaks of the city-state as "natural" in another sense of the term. For example, he might mean that it is "natural" in the extended sense that it arises from human natural inclinations (to live in communities) for the sake of human natural ends, but that it remains unfinished until a lawgiver provides it with a constitution.

He then adds that "the common advantage also brings them together insofar as they each attain the noble life. This is above all the end for all both in common and separately." Second, what are the different forms of rule by which one individual or group can rule over another? Aristotle distinguishes several types. He first considers despotic rule, which is exemplified in the master-slave relationship.

Aristotle thinks that this form of rule is justified in the case of natural slaves who (he asserts without evidence) lack a deliberative faculty and thus need a natural master to direct them. Although a natural slave allegedly benefits from having a master, despotic rule is still primarily for the sake of the master and only incidentally for the slave. (Aristotle provides no argument for this: if some persons are congenitally incapable of self-governance, why should they not be ruled primarily for their own sakes?) He next considers paternal and marital rule, which he also views as defensible: "the male is by nature more capable of leadership than the female, unless he is constituted in some way contrary to nature, and the elder and perfect [is by nature more capable of leadership] than the younger and imperfect."

Aristotle is persuasive when he argues that children need adult supervision because their rationality is "imperfect" (ateles) or immature. But he also alleges (without substantiation) that, although women have a deliberative faculty, it is "without authority" (akuron), so that females require male leadership. (Aristotle's arguments about slaves and women appear so weak that some commentators take them to be ironic. However, what is obvious to a modern reader need not have been so to an ancient Greek, so that it is not necessary to suppose that Aristotle's discussion is ironic.) It is noteworthy, however, that paternal and marital rule are properly practiced for the sake of the ruled (for the sake of the child and of the wife respectively), just as arts like medicine or gymnastics are practiced for the sake of the patient. In this respect they resemble political rule, which involves equal and similar citizens taking turns in ruling for one another's advantage. This sets the stage for the fundamental claim of Aristotle's constitutional theory: "constitutions which aim at the common advantage are correct and just without qualification, whereas those which aim only at the advantage of the rulers are deviant and unjust, because they involve despotic rule which is inappropriate for a community of free persons."

The distinction between correct and deviant constitutions is combined with the observation that the government may consist of one person, a few, or a multitude. Hence, there are six possible constitutional forms (Politics I.7):

	Correct	**Deviant**
One Ruler	Kingship	Tyranny
Few Rulers	Aristocracy	Oligarchy
Many Rulers	Polity	Democracy

This six-fold classification (which is adapted from Plato's Statesman) sets the stage for Aristotle's inquiry into the best constitution, although it is modified in various ways throughout the Politics. For example, he observes that the dominant class in oligarchy (literally rule of the oligoi, i.e., few) is typically the wealthy, whereas in democracy (literally rule of the demos, i.e., people) it is the poor, so that these economic classes should be included in the definition of these forms. Also, polity is later characterized as a kind of "mixed" constitution typified by rule of the "middle" group of citizens, a moderately wealthy class between the rich and poor.

Aristotle turns to arguments for and against the different constitutions, which he views as different applications of the principle of distributive justice. Everyone agrees, he says, that justice involves treating equal persons equally, and treating unequal persons unequally, but they do not agree on the standard by which individuals are deemed to be equally (or unequally) meritorious or deserving. He assumes his own analysis of distributive justice set forth in Nicomachean Ethics V.3: Justice requires that benefits be distributed to individuals in proportion to their merit or desert. The oligarchs mistakenly think that those who are superior in wealth should also have superior political rights, whereas the democrats hold that those who are equal in free birth should also have equal political rights.

Both of these conceptions of political justice are mistaken in Aristotle's view, because they assume a false conception of the ultimate end of the city-state. The city-state is neither a business association to maximize wealth (as the oligarchs suppose) nor an agency to promote liberty and equality (as the democrats maintain). Instead, Aristotle argues, "the good life is the end of the city-state," that is, a life consisting of noble actions. Hence, the correct conception of justice is aristocratic, assigning political rights to those who make a full contribution to the political community, that is, to those with virtue as well as property and freedom. This is what Aristotle understands by an "aristocratic" constitution: literally, the rule of the aristoi, i.e., best persons. Aristotle explores the implications of this argument in the remainder of Politics III, considering the rival claims of the rule of law and the rule of a supremely virtuous individual. Here absolute kingship is a limiting case of aristocracy. Again, in books VII-VIII, Aristotle describes the ideal constitution in which the citizens are fully virtuous.

Positive and Negative Liberty

Negative liberty is the absence of obstacles, barriers or constraints. One has negative liberty to the extent that actions are available to one in this negative sense. Positive liberty is the possibility of acting-or the fact of acting-in such a way as to take control of one's life and realize one's fundamental purposes. While negative liberty is usually attributed to individual agents, positive liberty is sometimes attributed to collectivities, or to individuals considered primarily as members of given collectivities.

The idea of distinguishing between a negative and a positive sense of the term 'liberty' goes back at least to Kant, and was examined and defended in depth by Isaiah Berlin in the 1950s and '60s. Discussions about positive and negative liberty normally take place within the context of political and social philosophy. They are distinct from, though sometimes related to, philosophical discussions about free will. Work on the nature of positive liberty often overlaps, however, with work on the nature of autonomy.

As Berlin showed, negative and positive liberty are not merely two distinct kinds of liberty; they can be seen as rival, incompatible interpretations of a single political ideal. Since few people claim to be against liberty, the way this term is interpreted and defined can have important political implications. Political liberalism tends to presuppose a negative definition of liberty: liberals generally claim that if one favours individual liberty one should place strong limitations on the activities of the state. Critics of liberalism often contest this implication by contesting the negative definition of liberty: they argue that the pursuit of liberty understood as self-realization or as self-determination (whether of the individual or of the collectivity) can require state intervention of a kind not normally allowed by liberals.

Many authors prefer to talk of positive and negative freedom. This is only a difference of style, and the terms 'liberty' and 'freedom' can be used interchangeably. Although some attempts have been made to distinguish between liberty and freedom, these have not caught on. Neither can they be translated into other European languages, which contain only the one term, of either Latin or Germanic origin (e.g. liberte, Freiheit), where English contains both.

Two Concepts of Liberty

Imagine you are driving a car through town, and you come to a fork in the road. You turn left, but no one was forcing you to go one way or the other. Next you come to a crossroads. You turn right, but no one was preventing you from going left or straight on. There is no traffic to speak of and there are no diversions or police roadblocks. So you seem, as a driver, to be completely free. But this picture of your situation might change quite dramatically if we consider that the reason you went left and then right is that you're addicted to cigarettes and you're desperate to get to the tobacconists before it closes. Rather than driving, you feel you are being driven, as your urge to smoke leads you uncontrollably to turn the wheel first to the left and then to the right. Moreover, you're perfectly aware that your turning right at the crossroads means you'll probably miss a train that was to take you to an appointment you care about very much. You long to be free of this irrational desire that is not only threatening your longevity but is also stopping you right now from doing what you think you ought to be doing.

This story gives us two contrasting ways of thinking of liberty. On the one hand, one can think of liberty as the absence of obstacles external to the agent. You are free if no one is stopping you from doing whatever you might want to do. In the above story you appear, in this sense, to be free. On the other hand, one can think of liberty as the presence of control on the part of the agent. To be free, you must be self-determined, which is to say that you must be able to control your own destiny in your own interests. In the above story you appear, in this sense, to be unfree: you are not in control of your own destiny, as you are failing to control a passion that you yourself would rather be rid of and which is preventing you from realizing what you recognize to be your true interests. One might say that while on the first view liberty is simply about how many doors are open to the agent, on the second view it is more about going through the right doors for the right reasons.

In a famous essay first published in 1958, Isaiah Berlin called these two concepts of liberty negative and positive respectively (Berlin 1969). The reason for using these labels is that in the first case liberty seems to be a mere absence of something (i.e. of obstacles, barriers, constraints or interference from others), whereas in the second case it seems to require the presence of something (i.e. of control, self-mastery, self-determination or self-realization). In Berlin's words, we use the negative concept of liberty in attempting to answer the question "What is the area within which the subject-a person or group of persons-is or should be left to do or be what he is able to do or be, without interference by other persons?", whereas we use the positive concept in attempting to answer the question "What, or who, is the source of control or interference that can determine someone to do, or be, this rather than that?"

It is useful to think of the difference between the two concepts in terms of the difference between factors that are external and factors that are internal to the agent. While theorists of negative freedom are primarily interested in the degree to which individuals or groups suffer interference from external bodies, theorists of positive freedom are more attentive to the internal factors affecting the degree to which individuals or groups act autonomously. Given this difference, one might be tempted to think that a political philosopher should concentrate exclusively on negative freedom, a concern with positive freedom being more relevant to psychology or individual morality than to political and social institutions. This, however, would be premature, for among the most hotly debated issues in political philosophy are the following: Is the positive concept of freedom a political concept? Can individuals or groups achieve positive freedom through political action? Is it possible for the state to promote the positive freedom of citizens on their behalf? And if so, is it desirable for the state to do so? The classic texts in the history of western political thought are divided over how these questions should be answered: theorists in the classical liberal tradition, like Constant, Humboldt, Spencer and Mill, are typically classed as answering 'no' and therefore as defending a negative concept of political freedom; theorists that are critical of this tradition, like Rousseau, Hegel, Marx and T.H. Green, are typically classed as answering 'yes' and as defending a positive concept of political freedom.

In its political form, positive freedom has often been thought of as necessarily achieved through a collectivity. Perhaps the clearest case is that of Rousseau's theory of freedom, according to which individual freedom is achieved through participation in the process whereby one's community exercises collective control over its own affairs in accordance with the 'general will'. Put in the simplest terms, one might say that a democratic society is a free society because it is a self-determined society, and that a member of that society is free to the extent that he or she participates in its democratic process. But there are also individualist applications of the concept of positive freedom. For example, it is sometimes said that a government should aim actively to create the conditions necessary for individuals to be self-sufficient or to achieve self-realization. The negative concept of freedom, on the other hand, is most commonly assumed in liberal defences of the constitutional liberties typical of liberal-democratic societies, such as freedom of movement, freedom of religion, and freedom of speech, and in arguments against paternalist or moralist state intervention. It is also often invoked in defences of the right to private property, although some have contested the claim that private property necessarily enhances negative liberty.

After Berlin, the most widely cited and best developed analyses of the negative concept of liberty include Hayek (1960), Day (1971), Oppenheim (1981), Miller (1983) and Steiner (1994). Among the most prominent contemporary analyses of the positive concept of liberty are Milne (1968), Gibbs (1976), C. Taylor (1979) and Christman (1991, 2005).

The Paradox of Positive Liberty

Many liberals, including Berlin, have suggested that the positive concept of liberty carries with it a danger of authoritarianism. Consider the fate of a permanent and oppressed minority. Because the members of this minority participate in a democratic process characterized by majority rule, they might be said to be free on the grounds that they are members of a society exercising self-control over its own affairs. But they are oppressed, and so are surely unfree. Moreover, it is not necessary to see a society as democratic in order to see it as self-controlled; one might instead adopt an organic conception of society, according to which the collectivity is to be thought of as a living organism, and one might believe that this organism will only act rationally, will only be in control of itself, when its various parts are brought into line with some rational plan devised by its wise governors (who, to extend the metaphor, might be thought of as the organism's brain). In this case, even the majority might be oppressed in the name of liberty.

Such justifications of oppression in the name of liberty are no mere products of the liberal imagination, for there are notorious historical examples of their endorsement by authoritarian political leaders. Berlin, himself a liberal and writing during the cold war, was clearly moved by the way in which the apparently noble ideal of freedom as self-mastery or self-realization had been twisted and distorted by the totalitarian dictators of the twentieth century-most notably those of the Soviet Union-so as to claim that they, rather than the liberal West, were the true champions of freedom. The slippery slope towards this paradoxical conclusion begins, according to Berlin, with the idea of a divided self. To illustrate: the smoker in our story provides a clear example of a divided self, for she is both a self that desires to get to an appointment and a self that desires to get to the tobacconists, and these two desires are in conflict.

We can now enrich this story in a plausible way by adding that one of these selves-the keeper of appointments-is superior to the other: the self that is a keeper of appointments is thus a 'higher' self, and the self that is a smoker is a 'lower' self. The higher self is the rational, reflecting self, the self that is capable of moral action and of taking responsibility for what she does. This is the true self, for rational reflection and moral responsibility are the features of humans that mark them off from other animals. The lower self, on the other hand, is the self of the passions, of unreflecting desires and irrational impulses. One is free, then, when one's higher, rational self is in control and one is not a slave to one's passions or to one's merely empirical self. The next step down the slippery slope consists in pointing out that some individuals are more rational than others, and can therefore know best what is in their and others' rational interests.

This allows them to say that by forcing people less rational than themselves to do the rational thing and thus to realize their true selves, they are in fact liberating them from their merely empirical desires.

Occasionally, Berlin says, the defender of positive freedom will take an additional step that consists in conceiving of the self as wider than the individual and as represented by an organic social whole-"a tribe, a race, a church, a state, the great society of the living and the dead and the yet unborn". The true interests of the individual are to be identified with the interests of this whole, and individuals can and should be coerced into fulfilling these interests, for they would not resist coercion if they were as rational and wise as their coercers. "Once I take this view", Berlin says, "I am in a position to ignore the actual wishes of men or societies, to bully, oppress, torture in the name, and on behalf, of their 'real' selves, in the secure knowledge that whatever is the true goal of man... must be identical with his freedom."

Those in the negative camp try to cut off this line of reasoning at the first step, by denying that there is any necessary relation between one's freedom and one's desires. Since one is free to the extent that one is externally unprevented from doing things, they say, one can be free to do what one does not desire to do. If being free meant being unprevented from realizing one's desires, then one could, again paradoxically, reduce one's unfreedom by coming to desire fewer of the things one is unfree to do. One could become free simply by contenting oneself with one's situation.

A perfectly contented slave is perfectly free to realize all of her desires. Nevertheless, we tend to think of slavery as the opposite of freedom. More generally, freedom is not to be confused with happiness, for in logical terms there is nothing to stop a free person from being unhappy or an unfree person from being happy. The happy person might feel free, but whether they are free is another matter (Day, 1971). Negative theorists of freedom therefore tend to say not that having freedom means being unprevented from doing as one desires, but that it means being unprevented from doing whatever one might desire to do.

Some theorists of positive freedom bite the bullet and say that the contented slave is indeed free-that in order to be free the individual must learn, not so much to dominate certain merely empirical desires, but to rid herself of them. She must, in other words, remove as many of her desires as possible. As Berlin puts it, if I have a wounded leg 'there are two methods of freeing myself from pain. One is to heal the wound. But if the cure is too difficult or uncertain, there is another method. I can get rid of the wound by cutting off my leg'. This is the strategy of liberation adopted by ascetics, stoics and Buddhist sages.

It involves a 'retreat into an inner citadel'-a soul or a purely noumenal self-in which the individual is immune to any outside forces. But this state, even if it can be achieved, is not one that liberals would want to call one of freedom, for it again risks masking important forms of oppression. It is, after all, often in coming to terms with excessive external limitations in society that individuals retreat into themselves, pretending to themselves that they do not really desire the worldly goods or pleasures they have been denied. Moreover, the removal of desires may also be an effect of outside forces, such as brainwashing, which we should hardly want to call a realization of freedom.

Because the concept of negative freedom concentrates on the external sphere in which individuals interact, it seems to provide a better guarantee against the dangers of paternalism and authoritarianism perceived by Berlin. To promote negative freedom is to promote the existence of a sphere of action within which the individual is sovereign, and within which she can pursue her own projects subject only to the constraint that she respect the spheres of others.

Humboldt and Mill, both defenders of the negative concept of freedom, compared the development of an individual to that of a plant: individuals, like plants, must be allowed to grow, in the sense of developing their own faculties to the full and according to their own inner logic. Personal growth is something that cannot be imposed from without, but must come from within the individual.

Two Attempts to Create a Third Way

Critics, however, have objected that the ideal described by Humboldt and Mill looks much more like a positive concept of liberty than a negative one. Positive liberty consists, they say, in exactly this growth of the individual: the free individual is one that develops, determines and changes her own desires and interests autonomously and from within. This is not liberty as the mere absence of obstacles, but liberty as self-realization. Why should the mere absence of state interference be thought to guarantee such growth? Is there not some third way between the extremes of totalitarianism and the minimal state of the classical liberals-some non-paternalist, non-authoritarian means by which positive liberty in the above sense can be actively promoted?

Much of the more recent work on positive liberty has been motivated by a dissatisfaction with the ideal of negative liberty combined with an awareness of the possible abuses of the positive concept so forcefully exposed by Berlin. John Christman (1991), for example, has argued that positive liberty concerns the ways in which desires are formed-whether as a result of rational reflection on all the options available, or as a result of pressure, manipulation or ignorance. What it does not regard, he says, is the content of an individual's desires. The promotion of positive freedom need not therefore involve the claim that there is only one right answer to the question of how a person should live, nor need it allow, or even be compatible with, a society forcing its members into given patterns of behaviour. Take the example of a Muslim woman who claims to espouse the fundamentalist doctrines generally followed by her family and the community in which she lives.

On Christman's account, this person is positively unfree if her desire to conform was somehow oppressively imposed upon her through indoctrination, manipulation or deceit. She is positively free, on the other hand, if she arrived at her desire to conform while aware of other reasonable options and she weighed and assessed these other options rationally. Even if this woman seems to have a preference for subservient behaviour, there is nothing necessarily freedom-enhancing or freedom-restricting about her having the desires she has, since freedom regards not the content of these desires but their mode of formation. On this view, forcing her to do certain things rather than others can never make her more free, and Berlin's paradox of positive freedom would seem to have been avoided.

It remains to be seen, however, just what a state can do, in practice, to promote positive liberty in Christman's sense without encroaching on any individual's sphere of negative liberty: the conflict between the two ideals seems to survive his alternative analysis, albeit in a milder form. Although not coercing individuals into specific patterns of behaviour, a state interested in promoting autonomy in Christman's sense might still be allowed considerable space for intervention of an informative and educational nature, perhaps subsidizing some activities (in order to encourage a plurality of genuine options) and financing this through taxation. Liberals might criticize this on anti-paternalist grounds, objecting that such measures will require the state to use resources in ways that the supposedly heteronomous individuals, if left to themselves, might have chosen to spend in other ways. Some liberals will make an exception in the case of the education of children (in such a way as to cultivate open minds and rational reflection), but even here other liberals will object that the right to negative liberty includes the right to decide how one's children should be educated. Other theorists of freedom have remained closer to the negative conception of freedom but have attempted to go beyond it, saying that freedom is not merely the enjoyment of a sphere of non-interference but the enjoyment of certain conditions in which such non-interference is guaranteed. These conditions may include the presence of a democratic constitution and a series of safeguards against a government wielding power arbitrarily, including the exercise of civic virtues on the part of citizens. As Berlin admits, on the negative view of freedom, I am free even if I live in a dictatorship just as long as the dictator happens, on a whim, not to interfere with me. There is no necessary connection between negative freedom and any particular form of government. On the alternative view sketched here, I am free only if I live in a society with the kinds of political institutions that guarantee the independence of each citizen from exercises of arbitrary power. Quentin Skinner has called this view of freedom 'neo-Roman', invoking ideas about freedom both of the ancient Romans and of a number of Renaissance and early modern writers. Philip Pettit has called the same view 'republican', and this label has tended to dominate in the recent literature.

Republican freedom can be thought of as a kind of status: to be a free person is to enjoy the rights and privileges attached to the status of republican citizenship, whereas the paradigm of the unfree person is the slave. Freedom is not simply a matter of non-interference, for a slave may enjoy a great deal of non-interference at the whim of her master. What makes her unfree is her status, such that she is permanently liable to interference of any kind. Even if the slave enjoys non-interference, she is, as Pettit puts it, 'dominated', because she is permanently subject to the arbitrary power of her owner.

Contemporary republicans therefore claim that their view of freedom is quite distinct from the negative view of freedom. As we have seen, one can enjoy non-interference without enjoying non-domination; conversely, according to Pettit, one can enjoy non-domination while nevertheless being interfered with, just as long as the interference in question is constrained, through republican power structures, to track one's interests. Only arbitrary power is inimical to freedom, not power as such. On the other hand, republican freedom is also distinct from positive freedom as expounded and criticized by Berlin. First, republican freedom does not consist in the activity of virtuous political participation; rather, that participation is seen as instrumentally related to freedom as non-domination. Secondly, the republican concept of freedom cannot lead to anything like the oppressive consequences feared by Berlin, because it has a commitment to non-domination and to liberal-democratic institutions already built into it.

It remains to be seen, however, whether the republican concept of freedom is ultimately distinguishable from the negative concept, or whether republican writers on freedom have not simply provided good arguments to the effect that negative freedom is best promoted, on balance and over time, through certain kinds of political institutions rather than others. While there is no necessary connection between negative liberty and democratic government, there may nevertheless be a strong empirical correlation between the two. Ian Carter and Matthew H. Kramer have argued, along these lines, that republican policies are best argued for empirically on the basis of the standard negative ideal of freedom, rather than on the basis of a conceptual challenge to that ideal. An important premise in their argument is that the degree to which a person is negatively free depends, in part, on the probability with which he or she will be constrained from performing future acts or act-combinations. People who are subject to arbitrary power are, according to Carter and Kramer, less free in the negative sense even if they do not actually suffer interference, because the probability of their suffering constraints is always greater (ceteris paribus, as a matter of empirical fact) than it would be if they were not subject to that arbitrary power.

One Concept of Liberty

The two sides identified by Berlin disagree over which of two different concepts best deserves the name of 'liberty'. Does this fact not denote the presence of some more basic agreement between the two sides? How, after all, could they see their disagreement as one about the definition of liberty if they did not think of themselves as in some sense talking about the same thing? In an influential article, the American legal philosopher Gerald MacCallum put forward the following answer: there is in fact only one basic concept of freedom, on which both sides in the debate converge. What the so-called negative and positive theorists disagree about is how this single concept of freedom should be interpreted. Indeed, in MacCallum's view, there are a great many different possible interpretations of freedom, and it is only Berlin's artificial dichotomy that has led us to think in terms of there being two. MacCallum defines the basic concept of freedom-the concept on which everyone agrees-as follows: a subject, or agent, is free from certain constraints, or preventing conditions, to do or become certain things. Freedom is therefore a triadic relation-that is, a relation between three things: an agent, certain preventing conditions, and certain doings or becomings of the agent. Any statement about freedom or unfreedom can be translated into a statement of the above form by specifying what is free or unfree, from what it is free or unfree, and what it is free or unfree to do or become. Any claim about the presence or absence of freedom in a given situation will therefore make certain assumptions about what counts as an agent, what counts as a constraint or limitation on freedom, and what counts as a purpose that the agent can be described as either free or unfree to carry out.

The definition of freedom as a triadic relation was first put forward in the seminal work of Felix Oppenheim in the 1950s and 60s. Oppenheim saw that an important meaning of 'freedom' in the context of political and social philosophy was as a relation between two agents and a particular (impeded or unimpeded) action. This interpretation of freedom remained, however, what Berlin would call a negative one. What MacCallum did was to generalize this triadic structure so that it would cover all possible claims about freedom, whether of the negative or the positive variety. In MacCallum's framework, unlike in Oppenheim's, the interpretation of each of the three variables is left open. In other words, MacCallum's position is a meta-theoretical one: his is a theory about the differences between theorists of freedom.

To illustrate MacCallum's point, let us return to the example of the smoker driving to the tobacconists. In describing this person as either free or unfree, we shall be making assumptions about each of MacCallum's three variables. If we say that the driver is free, what we shall probably mean is that an agent, consisting in the driver's empirical self, is free from external (physical or legal) obstacles to do whatever he or she might want to do. If, on the other hand, we say that the driver is unfree, what we shall probably mean is that an agent, consisting in a higher or rational self, is made unfree by internal, psychological constraints to carry out some rational, authentic or virtuous plan. Notice that in both claims there is a negative element and a positive element: each claim about freedom assumes both that freedom is freedom from something (i.e., preventing conditions) and that it is freedom to do or become something.

The dichotomy between 'freedom from' and 'freedom to' is therefore a false one, and it is misleading say that those who see the driver as free employ a negative concept and those who see the driver as unfree employ a positive one. What these two camps differ over is the way in which one should interpret each of the three variables in the triadic freedom-relation. More precisely, we can see that what they differ over is the extension to be assigned to each of the variables. Thus, those whom Berlin places in the negative camp typically conceive of the agent as having the same extension as that which it is generally given in ordinary discourse: they tend to think of the agent as an individual human being and as including all of the empirical beliefs and desires of that individual. Those in the so-called positive camp, on the other hand, often depart from the ordinary notion, in one sense imagining the agent as more extensive than in the ordinary notion, and in another sense imagining it as less extensive: they think of the agent as having a greater extension than in ordinary discourse in cases where they identify the agent's true desires and aims with those of some collectivity of which she is a member; and they think of the agent as having a lesser extension than in ordinary discourse in cases where they identify the true agent with only a subset of her empirical beliefs and desires-i.e., with those that are rational, authentic or virtuous.

Secondly, those in Berlin's positive camp tend to take a wider view of what counts as a constraint on freedom than those in his negative camp: the set of relevant obstacles is more extensive for the former than for the latter, since negative theorists tend to count only external obstacles as constraints on freedom, whereas positive theorists also allow that one may be constrained by internal factors, such as irrational desires, fears or ignorance. And thirdly, those in Berlin's positive camp tend to take a narrower view of what counts as a purpose one can be free to fulfill. The set of relevant purposes is less extensive for them than for the negative theorists, for we have seen that they tend to restrict the relevant set of actions or states to those that are rational, authentic or virtuous, whereas those in the negative camp tend to extend this variable so as to cover any action or state the agent might desire.

On MacCallum's analysis, then, there is no simple dichotomy between positive and negative liberty; rather, we should recognize that there is a whole range of possible interpretations or 'conceptions' of the single concept of liberty. Indeed, as MacCallum says and as Berlin seems implicitly to admit, a number of classic authors cannot be placed unequivocally in one or the other of the two camps.

Locke, for example, is normally thought of as one of the fathers or classical liberalism and therefore as a staunch defender of the negative concept of freedom. He indeed states explicitly that '[to be at] liberty is to be free from restraint and violence from others'. But he also says that liberty is not to be confused with 'license', and that "that ill deserves the name of confinement which hedges us in only from bogs and precipices." While Locke gives an account of constraints on freedom that Berlin would call negative, he seems to endorse an account of MacCallum's third freedom-variable that Berlin would call positive, restricting this to actions that are not immoral (liberty is not license) and to those that are in the agent's own interests (I am not unfree if prevented from falling into a bog). A number of contemporary libertarians have provided or assumed definitions of freedom that are similarly morally loaded (e.g. Nozick 1974; Rothbard 1982). This would seem to confirm MacCallum's claim that it is conceptually and historically misleading to divide theorists into two camps-a negative liberal one and a positive non-liberal one.

Analysis of Constraints

To illustrate the range of interpretations of the concept of freedom made available by MacCallum's analysis, let us now take a closer look at his second variable-that of constraints on freedom. We have seen that for those theorists Berlin places in the negative camp, only obstacles external to the agent tend to count as constraints on her freedom. We should now note that these theorists usually distinguish between different kinds of external obstacle, restricting the range of obstacles that count as constraints on freedom to those that are brought about by other agents. For theorists who conceive of constraints on freedom in this way, I am only unfree to the extent that other people prevent me from doing certain things.

If I am incapacitated by natural causes-by a genetic handicap, say, or by a virus or by certain climatic conditions-I may be rendered unable to do certain things, but I am not, for that reason, rendered unfree to do them. Thus, if you lock me in my house, I shall be both unable and unfree to leave. But if I am unable to leave because I suffer from a debilitating illness or because a snow drift has blocked my exit, I am nevertheless free, or am at least not unfree, to leave. The reason such theorists give, for restricting the set of relevant preventing conditions in this way, is that they see freedom as a social relation-a relation between persons. Freedom as a non-social relation is more the concern of engineers and medics than of political and social philosophers.

In attempting to distinguish between natural and social obstacles we shall inevitably come across gray areas. An important example is that of obstacles created by impersonal economic forces. Do economic constraints like recession, poverty and unemployment merely incapacitate people, or do they also render them unfree? One way of supplying a clear answer to this question is by taking an even more restrictive view of what counts as a constraint on freedom, and saying that only a subset of the set of obstacles brought about by other persons counts as a restriction of freedom: those brought about intentionally. In this case, impersonal economic forces, being brought about unintentionally, do not restrict people's freedom, even though they undoubtedly make many people unable to do many things. This last view has been taken by a number of market-oriented libertarians, including, most famously, Friedrich von Hayek, according to whom freedom is the absence of coercion, where to be coerced is to be subject to the arbitrary will of another. Critics of libertarianism, on the other hand, typically endorse a wider conception of constraints on freedom that includes not only intentionally imposed obstacles but also unintended obstacles for which someone may nevertheless be held responsible, or indeed obstacles of any kind whatsoever.

Thus, socialists and egalitarians have tended to claim that the poor in a capitalist society are as such unfree, or that they are less free than the rich, in contrast to libertarians, who have tended to claim that the poor in a capitalist society are no less free than the rich. Egalitarians typically (though not always) assume a broader notion than libertarians of what counts as a constraint on freedom. Although this view does not necessarily imply what Berlin would call a positive notion of freedom, egalitarians often call their own definition a positive one, in order to convey the sense that freedom requires the presence of abilities, or what Amartya Sen has influentially called 'capabilities'. If we take an even closer look at the different notions of constraint employed, we can see that there are in fact two different dimensions along which one's notion of a constraint might be broader or narrower. A first dimension is that of the source of a constraint on freedom-in other words, what it is that brings about a constraint on freedom. We have seen, for example, that some include as constraints on freedom only obstacles brought about by human action, whereas others also include obstacles with a natural origin. A second dimension is that of the type of constraint involved. We have seen, for example, that some include only physical barriers or coercion as relevant types of preventing factors, whereas others recognize as constraints on freedom more subtle forms of impediment, such as disincentives, psychological difficulties, or the distorted views that can be brought about by ideological manipulation.

To see the difference between the two dimensions of source and type, consider the case of internal constraints. An internal constraint is a type of constraint, defined by reference to its location inside the agent. It is a category that covers various psychological phenomena such as ignorance, irrational desires, illusions and phobias. Such a constraint can be caused in various ways: for example, it might have a genetic origin, or it might be brought about intentionally by others, as in the case of brainwashing or manipulation. In the first case we have an internal constraint brought about by natural causes; in the second, an internal constraint intentionally imposed by another human agent. Given the independence of these two dimensions, one might want to combine a narrow view of what counts as a source of a constraint with a broad view of what types of obstacle count as constraints, or vice versa. To illustrate the independence of these two dimensions, consider the case of the unorthodox libertarian Hillel Steiner.

On the one hand, Steiner has a much broader view than Hayek of the possible sources of constraints on freedom: he does not limit the set of such sources to intentional human actions, but extends it to cover all kinds of human cause, whether or not any humans intend such causes and whether or not they can be held morally accountable for them, believing that any restriction of such non-natural sources can only be an arbitrary stipulation, usually arising from some more or less conscious ideological bias. On the other hand, Steiner has an even narrower view than Hayek of what counts as a type of constraint: for Steiner, an agent only counts as unfree to do something if it is physically impossible for her to do that thing.

Any extension of the constraint variable to include other types of obstacle, such as those brought about by coercive threats, would, in his view, necessarily involve a reference to the agent's desires, and we have seen that for those liberals in the negative camp there is no necessary relation between an agent's freedom and her desires. Consider the coercive threat 'Your money or your life!'. This does not make it impossible for you to refuse to hand over your money, only much less desirable for you to do so. If you decide not to hand over the money, you will of course be killed. That will count as a restriction of your freedom, because it will render physically impossible a great number of actions on your part.

But it is not the issuing of the threat that creates this unfreedom, and you are not unfree until the sanction (described in the threat) is carried out. For this reason, Steiner excludes threats-and with them all other kinds of imposed costs-from the set of obstacles that count as freedom-restricting. This conception of freedom derives from Hobbes, and its defenders often call it the 'pure' negative conception to distinguish it from those 'impure' negative conceptions that make at least minimal references to the agent's beliefs, desires or values.

Steiner's account of the relation between freedom and coercive threats might be thought to have counterintuitive implications, even from the liberal point of view. Many laws that are normally thought to restrict negative freedom do not physically prevent people from doing what is prohibited, but deter them from doing so by threatening punishment. Are we to say, then, that these laws do not restrict the negative freedom of those who obey them?

A solution to this problem may consist in saying that although a law against doing some action, x, does not remove the freedom to do x, it nevertheless renders physically impossible certain combinations of actions that include doing x and doing what would be precluded by the punishment. There is a restriction of the person's overall negative freedom—i.e. a reduction in the overall number of act-combinations available to her—even though she does not lose the freedom to do any specific thing taken in isolation.

The Concept of Overall Freedom

The concept of overall freedom appears to play an important role both in everyday discourse and in contemporary political philosophy. It is only recently, however, that philosophers have stopped concentrating exclusively on the meaning of a particular freedom-the freedom to do or become this or that particular thing-and have started asking whether we can also make sense of descriptive claims to the effect that one person or society is freer than another or of liberal normative claims to the effect that freedom should be maximized or that people should enjoy equal freedom or that they each have a right to a certain minimum level of freedom. The literal meaningfulness of such claims depends on the possibility of gauging degrees of overall freedom, sometimes comparatively, sometimes absolutely.

Theorists disagree, however, about the importance of the notion of overall freedom. For some libertarian and liberal egalitarian theorists, freedom is valuable as such. This suggests that more freedom is better than less (at least ceteris paribus), and that freedom is one of those goods that a liberal society ought to distribute in a certain way among individuals. For other liberal theorists, like Ronald Dworkin (1977) and the later Rawls (1991), freedom is not valuable as such, and all claims about maximal or equal freedom ought to be interpreted not as literal references to a quantitative good called 'liberty' but as elliptical references to the adequacy of lists of certain particular liberties, or types of liberties, selected on the basis of values other than liberty itself. Generally speaking, only the first group of theorists finds the notion of overall freedom interesting.

The theoretical problems involved in measuring overall freedom include that of how an agent's available actions are to be individuated, counted and weighted, and that of comparing and weighting different types (but not necessarily different sources) of constraints on freedom (such as physical prevention, punishability, threats and manipulation).

How are we to make sense of the claim that the number of options available to a person has increased? Should all options count for the same in terms of degrees of freedom, or should they be weighted according to their importance in terms of other values?

And how are we to compare the unfreedom created by the physical impossibility of an action with, say, the unfreedom created by the difficulty or costliness or punishability of an action? It is only by comparing these different kinds of actions and constraints that we shall be in a position to compare individuals' overall degrees of freedom. These problems have been addressed, with differing degrees of optimism, not only by political philosophers but also, and increasingly, by social choice theorists interested in finding a freedom-based alternative to the standard utilitarian or 'welfarist' framework that has tended to dominate their discipline.

MacCallum's framework is particularly well suited to the clarification of such issues. For this reason, theorists working on the measurement of freedom tend not to refer a great deal to the distinction between positive and negative freedom. This said, most of them (e.g. Steiner, Carter, Kramer, Sen, Sugden) are concerned with freedom as the availability of options. And the notion of freedom as the availability of options is unequivocally negative in Berlin's sense at least where two conditions are met: first, the source of unfreedom-creating constraints is limited to the actions of other agents, so that natural or self-inflicted obstacles are not seen as decreasing an agent's freedom; secondly, the actions one is free or unfree to perform are weighted in some value-neutral way, so that one is not seen as freer simply because the options available to one are more valuable or conducive to one's self-realization. Of the above-mentioned authors, only Steiner embraces both conditions explicitly. Sen rejects both of them, despite not endorsing anything like positive freedom in Berlin's sense.

3

Niccolo Machiavelli

Niccolo di Bernardo di Machiavelli (May 3, 1469 – June 21, 1527) was an Italian diplomat, political philosopher, musician, poet and playwright. Machiavelli was a figure of the Italian Renaissance, and a central figure of its political scene. In June of 1498, following the ouster and execution of Savonarola, the Great Council elected Machiavelli as the Secretary to the second Chancery of the Republic of Florence. He is best known for his treatises on realist political theory (*The Prince*, which he considered his *Magnum opus*) on the one hand and republicanism (*Discourses on Livy*) on the other. These two written works, in addition to his *History of Florence* (which was commissioned by the Medici family), were published posthumously in 1531. His philosophical views on politics were such that his surname has since passed into common dialect, referring to any political move that is devious or cunning in nature.

Life

Machiavelli was born in Florence, the second son of Bernardo di Niccolo Machiavelli, a lawyer, and of Bartolommea di Stefano Nelli. His family were believed to be descendants of the old marquesses of Tuscany, and to have included 13 Florentine gonfaloniers of justice.

His education left him with a thorough knowledge of the Latin and Italian classics. Machiavelli was born into a tumultuous era in which Popes were leading armies, and wealthy city-states of Italy would fall one after another into the hands of foreign powers — France, Spain and the Holy Roman Empire. It was a time of constantly shifting alliances, condottieri who changed sides without warning, and governments rising and falling in the space of weeks. Perhaps most significant during this erratic upheaval was the sack of Rome in 1527 by rampaging soldiers of the Holy Roman Empire, the first time that Rome had been sacked by a Germanic army in nearly twelve centuries. Rich cities such as Florence and Genoa suffered a similar fate during these years.

Machiavelli, trained as a man with great nobility and severe rigor from his father, entered governmental service as a clerk and ambassador in 1494; that same year, Florence had restored the republic and expelled the Medici family, rulers of the city for nearly sixty years.

Machiavelli was placed as a member of a Council responsible for diplomatic negotiations and military matters. Between 1499 and 1512, he undertook a number of diplomatic missions to the court of Louis XII in France, Ferdinand II of Aragon, and the Papacy in Rome. From 1502 to 1503, he was a witness to the effective statebuilding methods of the soldier/churchman Cesare Borgia, who was at that time enlarging his territories in central Italy through a mixture of audacity, prudence, self-reliance, firmness and, not infrequently, cruelty.

Between 1503 to 1506, Machiavelli was responsible for the Florentine militia including the defense of the city. He distrusted mercenaries (a philosophy expounded at length in the *Discorsi* and in *Il Principe*) and much preferred a citizen militia. This philosophy bore fruit when, in 1509, Florence's citizen forces defeated Pisa under Machiavelli's direction. However, in August 1512, the Medici with the help of Pope Julius II used Spanish troops to defeat the Florentine forces at Prato.

The Florentine head of state, Piero Soderini, resigned and went into exile, and Florence and the republic was subsequently dissolved. Machiavelli, having played a significant role in the republic's anti-Medici government, was removed from office and in 1513 he was accused of conspiracy and arrested. Although tortured "by the rope" (a practice wherein one's hands were bound behind one's back and connected to a pulley which would lift the victim off the ground, dislocating one's shoulders), he denied his involvement and was eventually released.

He retired to his estate at Sant'Andrea in Percussina near Florence and began writing the treatises that would ensure his place in the development of political philosophy and conduct. In a famous letter to his friend Francesco Vettori, he described how he spent his days in exile:

> When evening comes, I return home [from work and from the local tavern and go to my study. On the threshold I strip naked, taking off my muddy, sweaty workday clothes, and put on the robes of court and palace, and in this graver dress I enter the courts of the ancients and am welcomed by them, and there I taste the food that alone is mine, and for which I was born. And there I make bold to speak to them and ask the motives of their actions, and they, in their humanity reply to me. And for the space of four hours I forget the world, remember no vexation, fear poverty no more, tremble no more at death; I pass indeed into their world.

Machiavelli himself identified a unifying theme in *The Prince* and the Discorsi:

> All cities that ever at any time have been ruled by an absolute prince, by aristocrats or by the people, have had for their protection force combined with prudence, because the latter is not enough alone, and the first either does not produce things, or when they are produced, does not maintain them. Force and prudence, then, are the might of all the governments that ever have been or will be in the world.

Machiavelli died in San Casciano, a few miles outside of Florence, in 1527. His resting place is unknown; however a cenotaph in his honour was placed at the Church of Santa Croce in Florence. The Latin sentence on the tomb — TANTO NOMINI NULLUM PAR ELOGIUM — is translated as either 'for so great a name, no praise is adequate' or 'No elegy is equal to such a name'.

Works

Il Principe: Machiavelli's best known book is *The Prince*, in which he describes the arts by which a Prince (a ruler) can retain control of his realm. He focuses primarily on what he calls the "new prince", under the assumption that a hereditary prince has an easier task since the people are accustomed to him. All a hereditary prince needs to do is carefully maintain the institutions that the people are used to; a new prince has a much more difficult task since he must stabilize his newfound power and build a structure that will endure. This task requires the Prince to be publicly above reproach but privately may require him to do immoral things in order to achieve his goals. Machiavelli explains through examples which princes are the most successful in obtaining and maintaining power. He draws his examples from personal observations made while he was on diplomatic missions for Florence and from his readings in ancient history. He periodically uses Latin phrases, and many examples are drawn from Classical sources. Machiavelli does not dispense entirely with morality nor advocate wholesale selfishness or degeneracy. Instead he outlines his definition of, for example, the criteria for acceptable cruel actions (it must be swift, effective, and short-lived). Machiavelli also does not miss the irony in the fact that good can come from evil actions. Notwithstanding the mitigating themes in *The Prince*, the Catholic Church put the work in its Index Librorum Prohibitorum and it was viewed in a negative light by many Humanists such as Erasmus.

The primary contribution of *The Prince* to the history of political thought is its fundamental break between realism and idealism. "The end justifies the means," though never directly stated in the book, is often quoted as indicative of the pragmatism that can be said to undergird Machiavelli's philosophy. *The Prince* should be read strictly as a guidebook on getting to and preserving power. In contrast with Plato and Aristotle, the ideal society is not the aim. In fact, Machiavelli emphasizes the need for the exercise of brute power where necessary and rewards, patron-clientelism etc. to preserve the status quo.

The term "Machiavellian" was adopted by some of Machiavelli's contemporaries, often used in the introductions of political tracts of the sixteenth century that offered more 'just' reasons of state, most notably those of Jean Bodin and Giovanni Botero. The pejorative term Machiavellian as it is used today (or anti-Machiavellism as it was used from the sixteenth century) is thus a misnomer, as it describes one who deceives and manipulates others for gain; whether the gain is personal or not is of no relevance, only that any actions taken are only important insofar as they affect the results. It fails to include some of the more moderating themes found in Machiavelli's works and the name is now associated with the extreme viewpoint.

Discorsi

Machiavelli's *Discourse on the First Ten Books of Titus Livy* comprises the early history of Rome. It constitutes a series of lessons on how a republic should be started and structured, including the concept of checks and balances, the strength of a tripartite structure and the superiority of a republic over a principality.

From *The Discourses*:

> "In fact, when there is combined under the same constitution a prince, a nobility, and the power of the people, then these three powers will watch and keep each other reciprocally in check." Book I, Chapter II

> "Doubtless these means [of attaining power are cruel and destructive of all civilized life, and neither Christian nor even human, and should be avoided by every one. In fact, the life of a private citizen would be preferable to that of a king at the expense of the ruin of so many human beings." Book I, Chapter XXVI

> "Now in a well-ordered republic it should never be necessary to resort to extra-constitutional measures...." Book I, Chapter XXXIV

> "...the governments of the people are better than those of princes." Book I, Chapter LVIII

> "...if we compare the faults of a people with those of princes, as well as their respective good qualities, we shall find the people vastly superior in all that is good and glorious." Book I, Chapter LVIII

> "For government consists mainly in so keeping your subjects that they shall be neither able nor disposed to injure you...." Book II, Chapter XXIII

"...no prince is ever benefited by making himself hated." Book III, Chapter XIX

"Let not princes complain of the faults committed by the people subjected to their authority, for they result entirely from their own negligence or bad example." Book III, Chapter XXIX

Power, *Virtu,* and *Fortuna*

Machiavelli presents to his readers a vision of political rule purged of extraneous moralizing influences and fully aware of the foundations of politics in the effective exercise of power. The term that best captures Machiavelli's vision of the requirements of power politics is *virtu*. While the Italian word would normally be translated into English as "virtue," and would ordinarily convey the conventional connotation of moral goodness, Machiavelli obviously means something very different when he refers to the virtu of the prince. In particular, Machiavelli employs the concept of *virtu* to refer to the range of personal qualities that the prince will find it necessary to acquire in order to "maintain his state" and to "achieve great things," the two standard markers of power for him. This makes it brutally clear there can be no equivalence between the conventional virtues and Machiavellian *virtu.*

Machiavelli expects princes of the highest *virtu* to be capable, as the situation requires, of behaving in a completely evil fashion. For the circumstances of political rule are such that moral viciousness can never be excluded from the realm of possible actions in which the prince may have to engage. Machiavelli's sense of what it is to be a person of *virtu* can thus be summarized by his recommendation that the prince above all else must acquire a "flexible disposition." That ruler is best suited for office, on Machiavelli's account, who is capable of varying her/his conduct from good to evil and back again "as fortune and circumstances dictate." It is not a coincidence that Machiavelli also uses the term virtu in his book *The Art of War* in order to describe the strategic prowess of the general who adapts to different battlefield conditions as the situation dictates. Machiavelli sees politics to be a sort of a battlefield on a different scale. Hence, the prince just like the general needs to be in possession of *virtu,* that is, to know which strategies and techniques are appropriate to what particular circumstances. Thus, *virtu* winds up being closely connected to Machiavelli's notion of the power. The ruler of *virtu* is bound to be competent in the application of power; to possess *virtu* is indeed to have mastered all the rules connected with the effective application of power. *Virtu* is to power politics what conventional virtue is to those thinkers who suppose that moral goodness is sufficient to be a legitimate ruler: it is the touchstone of political success.

What is the conceptual link between virtu and the effective exercise of power for Machiavelli? The answer lies with another central Machiavellian concept, *Fortuna* (usually translated as "fortune"). *Fortuna* is the enemy of political order, the ultimate threat to the safety and security of the state. Machiavelli's use of the concept has been widely debated without a very satisfactory resolution. Suffice it to say that, as with virtu, *Fortuna* is employed by him in a distinctive way. Where conventional representations treated *Fortuna* as a mostly benign, if fickle, goddess, who is the source of human goods as well as evils, Machiavelli's fortune is a malevolent and uncompromising fount of human misery, affliction, and disaster. While human *Fortuna* may be responsible for such success as human beings achieve, no man can act effectively when directly opposed by the goddess.

Machiavelli's most famous discussion of *Fortuna* occurs in Chapter 25 of *The Prince*, in which he proposes two analogies for understanding the human situation in the face of events. Initially, he asserts that fortune resembles "one of our destructive rivers which, when it is angry, turns the plains into lakes, throws down the trees and buildings, takes earth from one spot, puts it in another; everyone flees before the flood; everyone yields to its fury and nowhere can repel it." Yet the furor of a raging river does not mean that its depredations are beyond human control: before the rains come, it is possible to take precautions to divert the worst consequences of the natural elements. "The same things happen about *Fortuna*," Machiavelli observes, "She shows her power where virtu and wisdom do not prepare to resist her, and directs her fury where she knows that no dykes or embankments are ready to hold her." *Fortuna* may be resisted by human beings, but only in those circumstances where "*virtu* and wisdom" have already prepared for her inevitable arrival.

Machiavelli reinforces the association of *Fortuna* with the blind strength of nature by explaining that political success depends upon appreciation of the operational principles of Fortuna. His own experience has taught him that "it is better to be impetuous than cautious, because *Fortuna* is a woman and it is necessary, in order to keep her under, to beat and maul her." In other words, Fortuna demands a violent response of those who would control her. "She more often lets herself be overcome by men using such methods than by those who proceed coldly," Machiavelli continues, "therefore always, like a woman, she is the friend of young men, because they are less cautious, more spirited, and with more boldness master her." The wanton behaviour of *Fortuna* demands an aggressive, even violent response, lest she take advantage of those men who are too retiring or "effeminate" to dominate her. Machiavelli's remarks point toward several salient conclusions about Fortuna and her place in his intellectual universe. Throughout his corpus, *Fortuna* is depicted as a primal source of violence (especially as directed against humanity) and as antithetical to reason. Thus, Machiavelli realizes that only preparation to pose an extreme response to the vicissitudes of *Fortuna* will ensure victory against her. This is what *virtu* provides: the ability to respond to fortune at any time and in any way that is necessary.

Morality, Religion, and Politics

These basic building blocks of Machiavelli's thought have induced considerable controversy among his readers going back to the sixteenth century, when he was denounced as an apostle of the Devil, but also was read and applied sympathetically by authors (and politicians) enunciating the doctrine of "reason of state" (Viroli 1992). The main source of dispute concerned Machiavelli's attitude toward conventional moral and religious standards of human conduct, mainly in connection with *The Prince*. For many, his teaching adopts the stance of immoralism or, at least, amoralism. The most extreme versions of this reading find Machiavelli to be a "teacher of evil," in the famous words of Leo Strauss, on the grounds that he counsels leaders to avoid the common values of justice, mercy, temperance, wisdom, and love of their people in preference to the use of cruelty, violence, fear, and deception. A more moderate school of thought, associated with the name of Benedetto Croce (1925), views Machiavelli as simply a "realist" or a "pragmatist" advocating the suspension of commonplace ethics in matters of politics.

Moral values have no place in the sorts of decisions that political leaders must make, and it is a category error of the gravest sort to think otherwise. Weaker still is the claim pioneered by Ernst Cassirer (1946) that Machiavelli simply adopts the stance of a scientist-a kind of "Galileo of politics" in distinguishing between the "facts" of political life and the "values" of moral judgment. Thus, Machiavelli lays claim to the mantle of the founder of "modern" political science, in contrast with Aristotle's classical norm-laden vision of a political science of virtue. Perhaps, the mildest version of the amoral hypothesis has been proposed by Quentin Skinner (1978), who claims that the ruler's commission of acts deemed vicious by convention is a "last best" option. Concentrating on the claim in *The Prince* that a head of state ought to do good if he can, but must be prepared to commit evil if he must, Skinner argues that Machiavelli prefers conformity to moral virtue *ceteris paribus.*

In direct contrast, some of Machiavelli's readers have found no taint of immoralism in his thought whatsoever. Jean-Jacques Rousseau long ago held that the real lesson of The Prince is to teach the people the truth about how princes behave and thus to expose, rather than celebrate, the immorality at the core of one-man rule. Various versions of this thesis have been disseminated more recently. Some scholars, such as Garrett Mattingly (1958), have pronounced Machiavelli the supreme satirist, pointing out the foibles of princes and their advisors. The fact that Machiavelli later wrote biting popular stage comedies is cited as evidence in support of his strong satirical bent. Thus, we should take nothing Machiavelli says about moral conduct at face value, but instead should understood his remarks as sharply humorous commentary on public affairs. Alternatively, Mary Deitz (1986) asserts that Machiavelli's agenda was driven by a desire to "trap" the prince by offering carefully crafted advice (such as arming the people) designed to undo the ruler if taken seriously and followed. A similar range of opinions exists in connection with Machiavelli's attitude toward religion in general, and Christianity in particular. Machiavelli was no friend of the institutionalized Christian Church as he knew it. The *Discourses* makes clear that conventional Christianity saps from human beings the vigor required for active civil life. And *The Prince* speaks with equal parts disdain and admiration about the contemporary condition of the Church and its Pope. Many scholars have taken such evidence to indicate that Machiavelli was himself profoundly anti-Christian, preferring the pagan civil religions of ancient societies such as Rome, which he regarded to be more suitable for a city endowed with virtu.

Anthony Parel (1992) argues that Machiavelli's cosmos, governed by the movements of the stars and the balance of the humors, takes on an essentially pagan and pre-Christian cast. For others, Machiavelli may best be described as a man of conventional, if unenthusiastic, piety, prepared to bow to the externalities of worship but not deeply devoted in either soul or mind to the tenets of Christian faith. A few dissenting voices, most notably Sebastian de Grazia (1989), have attempted to rescue Machiavelli's reputation from those who view him as hostile or indifferent to Christianity.

Grazia demonstrates how central biblical themes run throughout Machiavelli's writings, finding there a coherent conception of a divinely-centered and ordered cosmos in which other forces ("the heavens," "fortune," and the like) are subsumed under a divine will and plan. Cary Nederman (1999) extends and systematizes Grazia's insights by showing how such central Christian theological doctrines as grace and free will form important elements of Machiavelli's conceptual structure.

Language and Concepts

Machiavelli has also been credited (most recently by Skinner 1978) with formulating for the first time the "modern concept of the state," understood in the broadly Weberian sense of an impersonal form of rule possessing a monopoly of coercive authority within a set territorial boundary. Certainly, the term *lo stato* appears widely in Machiavelli's writings, especially in

The Prince, in connection with the acquisition and application of power in a coercive sense, which renders its meaning distinct from the Latin term status (condition or station) from which it is derived. Moreover, scholars cite Machiavelli's influence in shaping the early modern debates surrounding "reason of state"-the doctrine that the good of the state itself takes precedence over all other considerations, whether morality or the good of citizens-as evidence that he was received by his near-contemporaries as a theorist of the state. Machiavelli's name and doctrines were widely invoked to justify the priority of the interests of the state in the age of absolutism.

Yet, as Harvey Mansfield (1996) has shown, a careful reading of Machiavelli's use of *lo stato* in The Prince and elsewhere does not support this interpretation. Machaivelli's "state" remains a personal patrimony, a possession more in line with the medieval conception of dominium as the foundation of rule. (Dominium is a Latin term that may be translated with equal force as "private property" and as "political dominion.") Thus, the "state" is literally owned by whichever prince happens to have control of it. Moreover, the character of governance is determined by the personal qualities and traits of the ruler-hence, Machiavelli's emphasis on *virtu* as indispensable for the prince's success. These aspects of the deployment of *lo stato* in *The Prince* mitigate against the "modernity" of his idea. Machiavelli is at best a transitional figure in the process by which the language of the state emerged in early modern Europe, as Mansfield concludes.

Another factor that must be kept in mind when evaluating the general applicability of Machiavelli's theory in *The Prince* stems from the very situation in which his prince of *virtu* operates. Such a ruler comes to power not by dynastic inheritance or on the back of popular support, but purely as a result of his own initiative, skill, talent, and/or strength (all words that may be translated for virtu). Thus, the Machiavellian prince can count on no pre-existing structures of legitimation, as discussed above. In order to "maintain his state," then, he can only rely upon his own fount of personal characteristics to direct the use of power and establish his claim on rulership. This is a precarious position, since Machiavelli insists that the throes of fortune and the conspiracies of other men render the prince constantly vulnerable to the loss of his state. The idea of a stable constitutional regime that reflects the tenor of modern political thought (and practice) is nowhere to be seen in Machiavelli's conception of princely government. Indeed, one might wonder whether Machiavelli, for all of his alleged realism, actually believed that a prince of complete *virtu* could in fact exist. He sometimes seems to imagine that a successful prince would have to develop a psychology entirely different from that known hitherto to mankind, inasmuch as this "new" prince is "prepared to vary his conduct as the winds of fortune and changing circumstances constrain him and ... not deviate from right conduct if possible, but be capable of entering upon the path of wrongdoing when this becomes necessary." This flexibility yields the core of the "practical" advice that Machiavelli offers to the ruler seeking to maintain his state: exclude no course of action out of hand, but be ready always to perform whatever acts are required by political circumstance.

Yet Machiavelli himself apparently harboured severe doubts about whether human beings were psychologically capable of generating such flexible dispositions within themselves. In spite of the great number of his historical examples, Machiavelli can point in *The Prince* to no single ruler who evinced the sort of variable *virtu* that he deems necessary for the complete control of fortune. Rather, his case studies of successful rulers repeatedly point to the situation of a prince whose characteristics suited his times but whose consistency of conduct (as in the case of Pope Julius II) "would have brought about his downfall" if circumstances had changed. Even the Emperor Severus, whose techniques Machiavelli lauds, succeeded because he employed "the courses of action that are necessary for establishing himself in power"; he is not, however, to be imitated universally. Machiavelli's evaluation of the chances for creating a new, psychologically flexible type of character is extremely guarded, and tends to be worded in conditional form and in the subjective mood: "If it were possible to change one's nature to suit the times and circumstances, one would always be successful." Such observations must make us wonder whether Machiavelli's advice that princes acquire dispositions which vary according to circumstance was so "practical" (even in his own mind) as he had asserted.

Liberty and Conflict

While *The Prince* is doubtless the most widely read of his works, the *Discourses* on the Ten Books of Titus Livy perhaps most honestly expresses Machiavelli's personal political beliefs and commitments, in particular, his republican sympathies. The Discourses certainly draw upon the same reservoir of language and concepts that fed *The Prince*, but the former treatise leads us to draw conclusions quite different from-many scholars have said contradictory to-the latter. In particular, across the two works, Machiavelli consistently and clearly distinguishes between a minimal and a full conception of "political" or "civil" order, and thus constructs a hierarchy of ends within his general account of communal life.

A minimal constitutional order is one in which subjects live securely (*vivere sicuro*), ruled by a strong government which holds in check the aspirations of both nobility and people, but is in turn balanced by other legal and institutional mechanisms. In a fully constitutional regime, however, the goal of the political order is the freedom of the community (*vivere libero*), created by the active participation of, and contention between, the nobility and the people. As Quentin Skinner has argued, liberty forms a value that anchors Machiavelli's political theory and guides his evaluations of the worthiness of different types of regimes. Only in a republic, for which Machiavelli expresses a distinct preference, may this goal be attained. Machiavelli adopted this position on both pragmatic and principled grounds. During his career as a secretary and diplomat in the Florentine republic, Machiavelli came to acquire vast experience of the inner workings of French government, which became his model for the "secure" (but not free) polity. Although Machiavelli makes relatively little comment about the French monarchy in *The Prince*, he devotes a great deal of attention to France in the *Discourses*. Why would Machiavelli effusively praise (let alone even analyze) a hereditary monarchy in a work supposedly designed to promote the superiority of republics? The answer stems from Machiavelli's aim to contrast the best case scenario of a monarchic regime with the institutions and organization of a republic. Even the most excellent monarchy, in Machiavelli's view, lacks certain salient qualities that are endemic to properly constituted republican government and that make the latter constitution more desirable than the former.

Machiavelli asserts that the greatest virtue of the French kingdom and its king is the dedication to law. "The kingdom of France is moderated more by laws than any other kingdom of which at our time we have knowledge," Machiavelli declares. The explanation for this situation Machiavelli refers to the function of the Parliament. "The kingdom of France," he states, "lives under laws and orders more than any other kingdom. These laws and orders are maintained by Parliaments, notably that of Paris: by it they are renewed any time it acts against a prince of the kingdom or in its sentences condemns the king. And up to now it has maintained itself by having been a persistent executor against that nobility." These passages of the *Discourses* seem to suggest that Machiavelli has great admiration for the institutional arrangements that obtain in France. Specifically, the French king and the nobles, whose power is such that they would be able to oppress the populace, are checked by the laws of the realm which are enforced by the independent authority of the Parliament. Thus, opportunities for unbridled tyrannical conduct are largely eliminated, rendering the monarchy temperate and "civil."

Yet such a regime, no matter how well ordered and law-abiding, remains incompatible with *vivere libero*. Discussing the ability of a monarch to meet the people's wish for liberty, Machiavelli comments that "as far as the ... popular desire of recovering their liberty, the prince, not being able to satisfy them, must examine what the reasons are that make them desire being free." He concludes that a few individuals want freedom simply in order to command others; these, he believes, are of sufficiently small number that they can either be eradicated or bought off with honours. By contrast, the vast majority of people confuse liberty with security, imagining that the former is identical to the latter: "But all the others, who are infinite, desire liberty in order to live securely (*vivere sicuro*)." Although the king cannot give such liberty to the masses, he can provide the security that they crave:

> As for the rest, for whom it is enough to live securely (*vivere sicuro*), they are easily satisfied by making orders and laws that, along with the power of the king,

> comprehend everyone's security. And once a prince does this, and the people see that he never breaks such laws, they will shortly begin to live securely (*vivere sicuro*) and contentedly.

Machiavelli then applies this general principle directly to the case of France, remarking that "the people live securely (*vivere sicuro*) for no other reason than that its kings are bound to infinite laws in which the security of all their people is comprehended." The law-abiding character of the French regime ensures security, but that security, while desirable, ought never to be confused with liberty. This is the limit of monarchic rule: even the best kingdom can do no better than to guarantee to its people tranquil and orderly government.

Machiavelli holds that one of the consequences of such *vivere sicuro* is the disarmament of the people. He comments that regardless of "how great his kingdom is," the king of France "lives as a tributary" to foreign mercenaries. This all comes from having disarmed his people and having preferred ... to enjoy the immediate profit of being able to plunder the people and of avoiding an imaginary rather than a real danger, instead of doing things that would assure them and make their states perpetually happy. This disorder, if it produces some quiet times, is in time the cause of straitened circumstances, damage and irreparable ruin. A state that makes security a priority cannot afford to arm its populace, for fear that the masses will employ their weapons against the nobility (or perhaps the crown). Yet at the same time, such a regime is weakened irredeemably, since it must depend upon foreigners to fight on its behalf. In this sense, any government that takes *vivere sicuro* as its goal generates a passive and impotent populace as a inescapable result. By definition, such a society can never be free in Machiavelli's sense of *vivere libero,* and hence is only minimally, rather than completely, political or civil. Confirmation of this interpretation of the limits of monarchy for Machiavelli may be found in his further discussion of the disarmament of the people, and its effects, in *The Art of War*. Addressing the question of whether a citizen army is to be preferred to a mercenary one, he insists that the liberty of a state is contingent upon the military preparedness of its subjects. Acknowledging that "the king [of France] has disarmed his people in order to be able to command them more easily," Machiavelli still concludes "that such a policy is ... a defect in that kingdom, for failure to attend to this matter is the one thing that makes her weak." In his view, whatever benefits may accrue to a state by denying a military role to the people are of less importance than the absence of liberty that necessarily accompanies such disarmament. The problem is not merely that the ruler of a disarmed nation is in thrall to the military prowess of foreigners.

More crucially, Machiavelli believes, a weapons-bearing citizen militia remains the ultimate assurance that neither the government nor some usurper will tyrannize the populace. "So Rome was free four hundred years and was armed; Sparta, eight hundred; many other cities have been unarmed and free less than forty years." Machiavelli is confident that citizens will always fight for their liberty-against internal as well as external oppressors. Indeed, this is precisely why successive French monarchs have left their people disarmed: they sought to maintain public security and order, which for them meant the elimination of any opportunities for their subjects to wield arms. The French regime, because it seeks security above all else (for the people as well as for their rulers), cannot permit what Machiavelli takes to be a primary means of promoting liberty.

The case of disarmament is an illustration of a larger difference between minimally constitutional systems such as France and fully political communities such as the Roman Republic, namely, the status of the classes within the society. In France, the people are entirely passive and the nobility is largely dependent upon the king, according to Machiavelli's own observations. By contrast, in a republic, where the realization of liberty is paramount, both the people and the nobility must take an active (and sometimes clashing) role in self-government. The liberty of the whole, for Machiavelli, depends upon the liberty of its component parts. In his famous discussion of this subject in the *Discourses*, he remarks, To me those who condemn the tumults between the Nobles and the Plebs seem to be caviling at the very thing that was the primary cause of Rome's retention of liberty.... And they do not realize that in every republic there are two different dispositions, that of the people and that of the great men, and that all legislation favoring liberty is brought about by their dissension.

Machiavelli knows that he is adopting an unusual perspective here, since customarily the blame for the collapse of the Roman Republic has been assigned to warring factions that eventually ripped it apart. But Machiavelli holds that precisely the same conflicts generated a "creative tension" that was the source of Roman liberty. For "those very tumults that so many inconsiderately condemn" directly generated the good laws of Rome and the virtuous conduct of its citizens. Hence, "Enmities between the people and the Senate should, therefore, be looked upon as an inconvenience which it is necessary to put up with in order to arrive at the greatness of Rome." Machiavelli thinks that other republican models (such as those adopted by Sparta or Venice) will produce weaker and less successful political systems, ones that are either stagnant or prone to decay when circumstances change.

Popular Liberty and Popular Speech

Machiavelli evinces particular confidence in the capacity of the people to contribute to the promotion of communal liberty. In the Discourses, he ascribes to the masses a quite extensive competence to judge and act for the public good in various settings, explicitly contrasting the "prudence and stability" of ordinary citizens with the unsound discretion of the prince. Simply stated, "A people is more prudent, more stable, and of better judgment than a prince." This is not an arbitrary expression of personal preference on Machiavelli's part. He maintains that the people are more concerned about, and more willing to defend, liberty than either princes or nobles. Where the latter tend to confuse their liberty with their ability to dominate and control their fellows, the masses are more concerned with protecting themselves against oppression and consider themselves "free" when they are not abused by the more powerful or threatened with such abuse. In turn, when they fear the onset of such oppression, ordinary citizens are more inclined to object and to defend the common liberty. Such an active role for the people, while necessary for the maintenance of vital public liberty, is fundamentally antithetical to the hierarchical structure of subordination-and-rule on which monarchic vivere sicuro rests.

The preconditions of *vivere libero* simply do not favour the security that is the aim of constitutional monarchy. One of the main reasons that security and liberty remain, in the end, incompatible for Machiavelli-and that the latter is to be preferred-may surely be traced to the "rhetorical" character of his republicanism.

Machiavelli clearly views speech as the method most appropriate to the resolution of conflict in the republican public sphere; throughout the *Discourses,* debate is elevated as the best means for the people to determine the wisest course of action and the most qualified leaders. The tradition of classical rhetoric, with which he was evidently familiar, directly associated public speaking with contention: the proper application of speech in the realms of forensic and deliberative genres of rhetoric is an adversarial setting, with each speaker seeking to convince his audience of the validity of his own position and the unworthiness of his opponents'.

This theme was taken up, in turn, by late medieval Italian practitioners and theorists of rhetoric, who emphasized that the subject matter of the art was lite (conflict). Thus, Machiavelli's insistence upon contention as a prerequisite of liberty also reflects his rhetorical predilections (Viroli 1998). By contrast, monarchic regimes-even the most secure constitutional monarchies such as France-exclude or limit public discourse, thereby placing themselves at a distinct disadvantage. It is far easier to convince a single ruler to undertake a disastrous or ill-conceived course of action than a multitude of people. The apparent "tumult" induced by the uncertain liberty of public discussion eventually renders more likely a decision conducive to the common good than does the closed conversation of the royal court.

This connects to the claim in the *Discourses* that the popular elements within the community form the best safeguard of civic liberty as well as the most reliable source of decision-making about the public good. Machiavelli's praise for the role of the people in securing the republic is supported by his confidence in the generally illuminating effects of public speech upon the citizen body. Near the beginning of the first *Discourse,* he notes that some may object to the extensive freedom enjoyed by the Roman people to assemble, to protest, and to veto laws and policies.

But he responds that the Romans were able to maintain liberty and order because of the people's ability to discern the common good when it was shown to them. At times when ordinary Roman citizens wrongly supposed that a law or institution was designed to oppress them, they could be persuaded that their beliefs are mistaken ... [through] the remedy of assemblies, in which some man of influence gets up and makes a speech showing them how they are deceiving themselves. And as Tully says, the people, although they may be ignorant, can grasp the truth, and yield easily when told what is true by a trustworthy man. The reference to Cicero (one of the few in the *Discourses*) confirms that Machiavelli has in mind here a key feature of classical republicanism: the competence of the people to respond to and support the words of the gifted orator when he speaks truly about the public welfare.

Machiavelli returns to this theme and treats it more extensively at the end of the first Discourse. In a chapter intended to demonstrate the superiority of popular over princely government, he argues that the people are well ordered, and hence "prudent, stable and grateful," so long as room is made for public speech and deliberation within the community. Citing the formula *vox populi, vox dei*, Machiavelli insists that public opinion is remarkably accurate in its prognostications.... With regard to its judgment, when two speakers of equal skill are heard advocating different alternatives, very rarely does one find the people failing to adopt the better view or incapable of appreciating the truth of what it hears.

Not only are the people competent to discern the best course of action when orators lay out competing plans, but they are in fact better qualified to make decisions, in Machiavelli's view, than are princes. For example, "the people can never be persuaded that it is good to appoint to an office a man of infamous or corrupt habits, whereas a prince may easily and in a vast variety of ways be persuaded to do this." Likewise, should the people depart from the law-abiding path, they may readily be convinced to restore order: "For an uncontrolled and tumultuous people can be spoken to by a good man and easily led back into a good way. But no one can speak to a wicked prince, and the only remedy is steel.... To cure the malady of the people words are enough." The contrast Machiavelli draws is stark. The republic governed by words and persuasion-in sum, ruled by public speech-is almost sure to realize the common good of its citizens; and even should it err, recourse is always open to further discourse. Non-republican regimes, because they exclude or limit discursive practices, ultimately rest upon coercive domination and can only be corrected by violent means.

Place in Western Political Thought

What is "modern" or "original" in Machiavelli's thought? What is Machiavelli's "place" in the history of Western ideas? The body of literature debating this question, especially in connection with The Prince and Discourses, has grown to truly staggering proportions. John Pocock (1975), for example, has traced the diffusion of Machiavelli's republican thought throughout the so-called Atlantic world and, specifically, into the ideas that guided the framers of the American constitution. Paul Rahe (1992) argues for a similar set of influences, but with an intellectual substance and significance different than Pocock. For Pocock, Machiavelli's republicanism is of a civic humanist variety whose roots are to be found in classical antiquity; for Rahe, Machiavelli's republicanism is entirely novel and modern. Likewise, cases have been made for Machiavelli's political morality, his conception of the state, his religious views, and many other features of his work as the distinctive basis for the originality of his contribution.

Yet few firm conclusions have emerged within scholarship. One plausible explanation for the inability to resolve these issues of "modernity" and "originality" is that Machiavelli was in a sense trapped between innovation and tradition, between via antiqua and via moderna (to adopt the usage of Janet Coleman 1995), in a way that generated internal conceptual tensions within his thought as a whole and even within individual texts. This historical ambiguity permits scholars to make equally convincing cases for contradictory claims about his fundamental stance without appearing to commit egregious violence to his doctrines. This point differs from the accusation made by certain scholars that Machiavelli was fundamentally "inconsistent."

Rather, salient features of the distinctively Machiavellian approach to politics should be credited to an incongruity between historical circumstance and intellectual possibility. What makes Machiavelli a troubling yet stimulating thinker is that, in his attempt to draw different conclusions from the commonplace expectations of his audience, he still incorporated important features of precisely the conventions he was challenging. In spite of his repeated assertion of his own originality, his careful attention to preexisting traditions meant that he was never fully able to escape his intellectual confines.

Thus, Machiavelli ought not really to be classified as either purely an "ancient" or a "modern," but instead deserves to be located in the interstices between the two. Among the most original thinkers of the Renaissance is a brilliant and slightly tragic figure, Niccolo Machiavelli. Throughout the sixteenth and seventeenth centuries, his name would be synonymous with deviousness, cruelty, and wilfully destructive rationality; no thinker was every so demonized or misunderstood than Machiavelli. The source of this misunderstanding is his most influential and widely read treatise on government, *The Prince,* a remarkably short book that attempts to lay out methods to secure and maintain political power.

His life spanned the greatest period of cultural achievement in Florence to its ultimate downfall. This period was marked by political instability, fear, invasion, intrigue, and high cultural achievement as the tiny states of Italy, including the Papal States, were pulled into the politics and wars of Europe by the immense gravity of two large states, Spain and France. His life began at the very start of this process: in 1469, when Ferdinand and Isabella married and through this marriage created a new, large kingdom of Spain composed of Castile and Aragon, Machiavelli was born to a wealthy Florentine lawyer. In his lifetime, he would see the efflorescence of Florentine culture and political power under the brilliant political genius of Lorenzo de'Medici. He would also see the twilight of the Medici power as Lorenzo's son and successor, Piero de'Medici, was thrown from power by the Dominican monk, Savonarola, who set up a true Florentine Republic. When

Savonarola, fanatic about reform, was himself thrown from power and burned, a second Republic was set up under Soderini in 1498. Machiavelli was the secretary of this new Republic, an important and distinguished position. *The Republic*, however, was crushed in 1512 by the Spanish who installed the Medici's as rulers of Florence once again.

It seems that Machiavelli really had no political commitments or political stripe: he seems to have been on nobody's side politically. For when the Medici came to power, he began to work overtime to get in good with them. It seems that either he was ruthlessly ambitious or believed in serving in government no matter what political group or party was in charge. The Medici, however, never fully trusted him since he had been an important official in the Republic. They imprisoned and tortured him in 1513 and eventually banished him to his country estate at San Casciano (all this torture and imprisonment, however, didn't stop him from trying to get in good with the Medicis).

It was during his exile in San Casciano, when he was desparate to get back into government, that he wrote his principle works: the *Discourse on Livy, The Prince, The History of Florence*, and two plays. Many of these works, such as The Prince, were written for the express purpose of getting a job in the Medici government. The tremendous innovation of both the Discourses on Livy and *The Prince* was Machiavelli's uncoupling of political theory from ethics. Throughout the Western tradition, as in the Chinese tradition, political theory and policy was closely linked to ethics. Aristotle summed up this connection when he defined politics as merely an extension of ethics. Throughout the Western tradition, then, politics had been understood in terms of right and wrong, just and unjust, temperate and intemperate, and so on. The moral terms used to evaluate human actions were employed to evaluate political actions.

Machiavelli was the first to discuss politics and social phenomena in their own terms without recourse to ethics or jurisprudence. In many ways you could consider Machiavelli to be the first major Western thinker to apply the strictly scientific method of Aristotle and Averroes to politics. He did so by observing the phenomena of politics, reading all that's been written on the subject, and describing political systems in their own terms. For Machiavelli, politics was about one and only one thing: getting and keeping power or authority. Everything else-religion, morality, etc-that people associate with politics has nothing to do with this fundamental aspect of politics-unless being moral helps one get and keep power. The only skill that counts in getting and maintaining power is calculation; the successful politician knows what to do or what to say for every situation.

With this insight, Machiavelli in *The Prince* simply describes the means by which individuals have tried to seize and to maintain power. Most of the examples he gives are failures; the entire book is suffused with tragedy for at any moment, if the ruler makes one miscalculation, all the authority he has so assiduously cultivated will dry up like the morning dew. The social and political world of the *The Prince* is monstrously unpredictable and volatile; only the most superhuman calculative mind can overcome this social and political volatility.

Throughout *The Prince* and the *Discourses* , it's clear that Machiavelli has praise only for the winners. For this reason, he admires figures such as Alexander VI and Julius II, universally hated throughout Europe as ungodly popes, for their astonishing military and political success. His refusal to allow ethical judgements enter into political theory branded him throughout the Renaissance as a kind of anti-Christ. In chapters such as "Whether a Prince Should Be True to his Word," Machiavelli argues that any moral judgment should be secondary to getting, increasing and maintaining power. The answer to the above question, for instance, is "it's good to be true to your word, but you should lie whenever it advances your power or security-not only that, it's necessary." It might help to understand Machiavelli to imagine that he's not talking about the state so much in ethical terms but in medical terms. For Machiavelli believed that the Italian situation was desperate and that the Florentine state was in grave danger. Rather than approach the question from an ethical point of view, Machiavelli was genuinely concerned with healing the state to make it stronger.

For instance, in talking about seditious points of view, Machiavelli doesn't make an ethical argument, but rather a medical one-"seditious people should be amputated before they infect the whole state." The single most articulated value in the work of Machiavelli is *virtu* (Latin *virtus*), which is related to our word, "virtue." Machiavelli means it more in its Latin sense of "manly," but individuals with virtu are primarily marked by their ability to enforce their will on volatile social situations. They do this through a combination of strong will, strength, and brilliant and strategic calculation. In one of the most famous passages from *The Prince*, Machiavelli describes the proper orientation towards the volatility of the world, or Fortune, by comparing Fortune to a lady: "la fortuna e donna," or "Fortune is a Lady."

Machiavelli is referring to the courtly love tradition, where the lady that constitutes the object of desire is approached and entreated and begged. The ideal Prince, however, for Machiavelli does not entreat or beg Lady Fortune, but rather physically grabs her and takes whatever he wants. This was a scandalous passage and still is today, but it represents a powerful translation of the Renaissance idea of human potential to the area of politics.

For if, according to Pico della Mirandola, a human being can self-transform into anything it wants, then it must be possible for a single, strong-willed individual to order the chaos of political life. Despite his hopes that the Medicis might prove to be those ideal rulers that could unite Italy, they did not remain in power for long. When Guilio de'Medici left Firenze to become Pope Clement VII, the subalterns that he left in charge of the city managed it very poorly. The people soon overthrew the Medici rule and established the Third Republic of Firenze in 1527. Machiavelli saw his chance and tried to get a position in the new republic, but the new rulers distrusted him because of his long association with the Medici. So on June 22, 1527, only a few months after the establishment of the Third Republic, Machiavelli died. That same year, Rome was sacked by Emperor Charles VII and the pope was forced to ally with Charles. In 1530, the pope and Charles led a punitive expedition against Firenze and crushed it as an independent state. Three years after the death of Machiavelli and two years before the publication of *The Prince*, the state that Machiavelli worked so hard to help and believed so much in blinked out of existence.

4

Thomas Hobbes

Thomas Hobbes (5 April 1588 – 4 December 1679) was an English philosopher, whose famous 1651 book *Leviathan* established the foundation for most of Western political philosophy from the perspective of social contract theory and classical republicanism. Hobbes is remembered today for his work on political philosophy, although he contributed to a diverse array of fields, including history, geometry, physics of gases, theology, ethics, general philosophy, and political science. But nonetheless Hobbes's account of human nature as self-interested cooperation has proved to be an enduring theory in the field of philosophical anthropology.

Early Life and Education

Thomas Hobbes was born in Wiltshire, England on 5 April 1588 (some sources say Malmesbury). Born prematurely on April 5, 1588, when his mother heard of the coming invasion of the Spanish Armada, Thomas Hobbes later reported that "my mother gave birth to twins: myself and fear." His childhood is almost a complete blank, and his mother's name is unknown. His father, also Thomas, the vicar of Charlton and Westport, abandoned his three children to the care of an older brother (Thomas junior's uncle), Francis, when forced to flee to London after being involved in a fight with a clergyman outside his own church.

Hobbes was educated at Westport church from the age of four, passed to the Malmesbury school and then to a private school kept by a young man named Robert Latimer, a graduate of Oxford University. Hobbes was a good pupil, and around 1603 he went up to Magdalen Hall, which is most closely related to Hertford

College, Oxford. The principal was a puritan called John Wilkinson, and he had some influence on Hobbes.

At university, Hobbes appears to have followed his own curriculum; he was "little attracted by the scholastic learning". He did not complete his B.A. degree until 1608, but he was recommended by Sir James Hussey, his master at Magdalen, as tutor to William, the son of William Cavendish, Baron of Hardwick (and later Earl of Devonshire), and began a life-long connection with that family.

Hobbes became a companion to the younger William and they both took part in a grand tour in 1610. Hobbes was exposed to European scientific and critical methods during the tour in contrast to the scholastic philosophy which he had learned in Oxford. His scholarly efforts at the time were aimed at a careful study of classic Greek and Latin authors, the outcome of which was, in 1628, his great translation of Thucydides' *History of the Peloponnesian War*, the first translation of that work into English from a Greek manuscript.

Although he associated with literary figures like Ben Jonson and thinkers such as Francis Bacon, he did not extend his efforts into philosophy until after 1629. His employer Cavendish, then the Earl of Devonshire, died of the plague in June 1628. The widowed countess dismissed Hobbes but he soon found work, again as a tutor, this time to the son of Sir Gervase Clifton. This task, chiefly spent in Paris, ended in 1631 when he again found work with the Cavendish family, tutoring the son of his previous pupil. Over the next seven years as well as tutoring he expanded his own knowledge of philosophy, awakening in him curiosity over key philosophic debates. He visited Florence in 1636 and later was a regular debater in philosophic groups in Paris, held together by Marin Mersenne. From 1637 he considered himself a philosopher and scholar.

Moral and Political Philosophy

We can see Hobbes's importance if we briefly compare him with the most famous political thinkers before and after him. A century before, Nicolo Machiavelli had emphasized the harsh realities of power, as well as recalling ancient Roman experiences of political freedom. Machiavelli appears as the first modern political thinker, because like Hobbes he was no longer prepared to talk about politics in terms set by religious faith (indeed, he was still more offensive than Hobbes to many orthodox believers), instead, he looked upon politics as a secular discipline divorced from theology. But unlike Hobbes, Machiavelli offers us no comprehensive philosophy: we have to reconstruct his views on the importance and nature of freedom; it remains uncertain which, if any, principles Machiavelli draws on in his apparent praise of amoral power politics. Writing a few years after Hobbes, John Locke had definitely accepted the terms of debate Hobbes had laid down: how can human beings live together, when religious or traditional justifications of authority are no longer effective or persuasive? How is political authority justified and how far does it extend? In particular, are our political rulers properly as unlimited in their powers as Hobbes had suggested? And if they are not, what system of politics will ensure that they do not overstep the mark, do not trespass on the rights of their subjects?

So, in assessing Hobbes's political philosophy, our guiding questions can be: What did Hobbes write that was so important? How was he able to set out a way of thinking about politics and power that remains decisive nearly four centuries afterwards? We can get some clues to this second question if we look at Hobbes's life and times.

Life and Times

Hobbes's biography is dominated by the political events in England and Scotland during his long life. Born in 1588, the year the Spanish Armada made its ill-fated attempt to invade England, he lived to the exceptional age of 91, dying in 1679. He was not born to power or wealth or influence: the son of a disgraced village vicar, he was lucky that his uncle was wealthy enough to provide for his education and that his intellectual talents were soon recognized and developed (through thorough training in the classics of Latin and Greek). Those intellectual abilities, and his uncle's support, brought him to university at Oxford. And these in turn-together with a good deal of common sense and personal maturity-won him a place tutoring the son of an important noble family, the Cavendishes. This meant that Hobbes entered circles where the activities of the King, of Members of Parliament, and of other wealthy landowners were known and discussed, and indeed influenced. Thus intellectual and practical ability brought Hobbes to a place close to power-later he would even be math tutor to the future King Charles II. Although this never made Hobbes powerful, it meant he was acquainted with and indeed vulnerable to those who were. As the scene was being set for the Civil Wars of 1642-46 and 1648-51-wars that would lead to the King being executed and a republic being declared-Hobbes felt forced to leave the country for his personal safety, and lived in France from 1640 to 1651. Even after the monarchy had been restored in 1660, Hobbes's security was not always certain: powerful religious figures, critical of his writings, made moves in Parliament that apparently led Hobbes to burn some of his papers for fear of prosecution.

Thus Hobbes lived in a time of upheaval, sharper than any England has since known. This turmoil had many aspects and causes, political and religious, military and economic. England stood divided against itself in several ways. The rich and powerful were divided in their support for the King, especially concerning the monarch's powers of taxation. Parliament was similarly divided concerning its own powers vis-a-vis the King. Society was divided religiously, economically, and by region. Inequalities in wealth were huge, and the upheavals of the Civil Wars saw the emergence of astonishingly radical religious and political sects. (For instance, "the Levellers" called for much greater equality in terms of wealth and political rights; "the Diggers," more radical still, fought for the abolition of wage labour.) Civil war meant that the country became militarily divided. And all these divisions cut across one another: for example, the army of the republican challenger, Cromwell, was the main home of the Levellers, yet Cromwell in turn would act to destroy their power within the army's ranks. In addition, England's recent union with Scotland was fragile at best, and was almost destroyed by King Charles I's attempts to impose consistency in religious practices. We shall see that Hobbes's greatest fear was social and political chaos-and he had ample opportunity both to observe it and to suffer its effects.

Although social and political turmoil affected Hobbes's life and shaped his thought, it never hampered his intellectual development. His early position as a tutor gave him the scope to read, write and publish, and brought him into contact with notable English intellectuals such as Francis Bacon. His self-imposed exile in France, along with his emerging reputation as a scientist and thinker, brought him into contact with major European intellectual figures of his time, leading to exchange and controversy with figures such as Descartes, Mersenne and Gassendi. Intensely disputatious, Hobbes repeatedly embroiled himself in prolonged arguments with clerics, mathematicians, scientists and philosophers-sometimes to the cost of his intellectual reputation. His writing was as undaunted by age and ill health as it was by the events of his times. Though his health slowly failed-from about sixty, he began to suffer "shaking palsy," probably Parkinson's disease, which steadily worsened-even in his eighties he continued to dictate his thoughts to a secretary, and to defend his quarter in various controversies.

Hobbes gained a reputation in many fields. He was known as a scientist (especially in optics), as a mathematician (especially in geometry), as a translator of the classics, as a writer on law, as a disputant in metaphysics and epistemology; not least, he became notorious for his writings and disputes on religious questions. But it is for his writings on morality and politics that he has, rightly, been most remembered. Without these, scholars might remember Hobbes as an interesting intellectual of the seventeenth century; but few philosophers would even recognize his name.

Two Intellectual Influences

As well as the political background just stressed, two influences are extremely marked in Hobbes's work. The first is a reaction against religious authority as it had been known, and especially against the scholastic philosophy that accepted and defended such authority. The second is a deep admiration for (and involvement in) the emerging scientific method, alongside an admiration for a much older discipline, geometry. Both influences affected how Hobbes expressed his moral and political ideas. In some areas it's also clear that they significantly affected the ideas themselves.

Hobbes's contempt for scholastic philosophy is boundless. Leviathan and other works are littered with references to the "frequency of insignificant speech" in the speculations of the scholastics, with their combinations of Christian theology and Aristotelian metaphysics. Hobbes's reaction, apart from much savage and sparkling sarcasm, is twofold. In the first place, he makes very strong claims about the proper relation between religion and politics. He was not (as many have charged) an atheist, but he was deadly serious in insisting that theological disputes should be kept out of politics. (He also adopts a strongly materialist metaphysics, that-as his critics were quick to charge-makes it difficult to account for God's existence as a spiritual entity.)

For Hobbes, the sovereign should determine the proper forms of religious worship, and citizens never have duties to God that override their duty to obey political authority. Second, this reaction against scholasticism shapes the presentation of Hobbes's own ideas. He insists that terms be clearly defined and relate to actual concrete experiences-part of his empiricism. Commentators debate how seriously to take Hobbes's stress on the importance of definition, and whether it embodies a definite philosophical doctrine.

What is certain, and more important from the point of view of his moral and political thought, is that he tries extremely hard to avoid any metaphysical categories that don't relate to physical realities (especially the mechanical realities of matter and motion). Commentators further disagree whether Hobbes's often mechanical sounding definitions of human nature and human behaviour are actually important in shaping his moral and political ideas-see Materialism versus self-knowledge below.

Hobbes's determination to avoid the "insignificant" (that is, meaningless) speech of the scholastics also overlaps with his admiration for the emerging physical sciences and for geometry. His admiration is not so much for the emerging method of experimental science, but rather for deductive science-science that deduces the workings of things from basic first principles and from true definitions of the basic elements. Hobbes therefore approves a mechanistic view of science and knowledge, one that models itself very much on the clarity and deductive power exhibited in proofs in geometry. It is fair to say that this a priori account of science has found little favour after Hobbes's time.

It looks rather like a dead-end on the way to the modern idea of science based on patient observation, theory-building and experiment. Nonetheless, it certainly provided Hobbes with a method that he follows in setting out his ideas about human nature and politics. As presented in Leviathan, especially, Hobbes seems to build from first elements of human perception and reasoning, up to a picture of human motivation and action, to a deduction of the possible forms of political relations and their relative desirability. Once more, it can be disputed whether this method is significant in shaping those ideas, or merely provides Hobbes with a distinctive way of presenting them.

Ethics and Human Nature

Hobbes's moral thought is difficult to disentangle from his politics. On his view, what we ought to do depends greatly on the situation in which we find ourselves. Where political authority is lacking (as in his famous natural condition of mankind), our fundamental right seems to be to save our skins, by whatever means we think fit. Where political authority exists, our duty seems to be quite straightforward: to obey those in power. But we can usefully separate the ethics from the politics if we follow Hobbes's own division. For him ethics is concerned with human nature, while political philosophy deals with what happens when human beings interact. What, then, is Hobbes's view of human nature?

Materialism Versus Self-Knowledge

Reading the opening chapters of Leviathan is a confusing business, and the reason for this is already apparent in Hobbes's very short "Introduction." He begins by telling us that the human body is like a machine, and that political organization ("the commonwealth") is like an artificial human being. He ends by saying that the truth of his ideas can be gauged only by self-examination, by looking into our selves to adjudge our characteristic thoughts and passions, which form the basis of all men's actions. But what is the relationship between these two very different claims? For obviously when we look into ourselves we do not see mechanical pushes and pulls. This mystery is hardly answered by Hobbes's method in the opening chapters, where he persists in talking about all manner of psychological phenomena-from emotions to thoughts to whole trains of reasoning-as products of mechanical interactions. (As to what he will say about successful political organization, the resemblance between the commonwealth and a functioning human being is slim indeed. Hobbes's only real point seems to be that there should be a "head" that decides most of the important things that the "body" does.)

Most commentators now agree with an argument made in the 1960's by the political philosopher Leo Strauss. Hobbes draws on his notion of a mechanistic science, that works deductively from first principles, in setting out his ideas about human nature. Science provides him with a distinctive method and some memorable metaphors and similes. What it does not provide-nor could it, given the rudimentary state of physiology and psychology in Hobbes's day-are any decisive or substantive ideas about what human nature really is. Those ideas may have come, as Hobbes also claims, from self-examination. In all likelihood, they actually derived from his reflection on contemporary events and his reading of classics of political history such as Thucydides.

This is not to say that we should ignore Hobbes's ideas on human nature-far from it. But it does mean we should not be misled by scientific imagery that stems from an infact non-existent science (and also, to some extent, from an unproven and uncertain metaphysics). The point is important mainly when it comes to a central interpretative point in Hobbes's work: whether or not he thinks of human beings as mechanical objects, programmed as it were to pursue their self-interest. Some have suggested that Hobbes's mechanical world-view leaves no room for the influence of moral ideas, that he thinks the only effective influence on our behaviour will be incentives of pleasure and pain. But while it is true that Hobbes sometimes says things like this, we should be clear that the ideas fit together only in a metaphorical way. For example, there's no reason why moral ideas shouldn't "get into" the mechanisms that drive us round (like so many clock-work dolls perhaps?).

Likewise, there's no reason why pursuing pleasure and pain should work in our self-interest. (What self-interest is depends on the time-scale we adopt, and how effectively we might achieve this goal also depends on our insight into what harms and benefits us). If we want to know what drives human beings, on Hobbes's view, we must read carefully all he says about this, as well as what he needs to assume if the rest of his thought is to make sense. The mechanistic metaphor is something of a red herring and, in the end, probably less useful than his other starting point in Leviathan, the Delphic epithet: nosce teipsum, "know thyself."

This is Hobbes's picture of man. We are needy and vulnerable. We are easily led astray in our attempts to know the world around us. Our capacity to reason is as fragile as our capacity to know; it relies upon language and is prone to error and undue influence. When we act, we may do so selfishly or impulsively or in ignorance, on the basis of faulty reasoning or bad theology or others' emotive speech.

What is the political fate of this rather pathetic sounding creature-that is, of us? Unsurprisingly, Hobbes thinks little happiness can be expected of our lives together. The best we can hope for is peaceful life under an authoritarian-sounding sovereign. The worst, on Hobbes's account, is what he calls the "natural condition of mankind," a state of violence, insecurity and constant threat. In outline, Hobbes's argument is that the alternative to government is a situation no one could reasonably wish for, and that any attempt to make government accountable to the people must undermine it, so threatening the situation of non-government that we must all wish to avoid. Our only reasonable option, therefore, is a "sovereign" authority that is totally unaccountable to its subjects. Let us deal with the "natural condition" of non-government, also called the "state of nature," first of all.

The Natural Condition of Mankind

The state of nature is "natural" in one specific sense only. For Hobbes political authority is artificial: in the "natural" condition human beings lack government, which is an authority created by men. What is Hobbes's reasoning here? He claims that the only authority that naturally exists among human beings is that of a mother over her child, because the child is so very much weaker than the mother (and indebted to her for its survival). Among adult human beings this is invariably not the case. Hobbes concedes an obvious objection, admitting that some of us are much stronger than others. And although he's very sarcastic about the idea that some are wiser than others, he doesn't have much difficulty with the idea that some are fools and others are dangerously cunning. Nonetheless, it's almost invariably true that every human being is capable of killing any other. Even the strongest must sleep; even the weakest might persuade others to help him kill another. Because adults are "equal" in this capacity to threaten one another's lives, Hobbes claims there is no natural source of authority to order their lives together.

Thus, as long as human beings have not successfully arranged some form of government, they live in Hobbes's state of nature. Such a condition might occur at the "beginning of time," or in "primitive" societies (Hobbes thought the American Indians lived in such a condition). But the real point for Hobbes is that a state of nature could just as well occur in seventeenth century England, should the King's authority be successfully undermined. It could occur tomorrow in every modern society, for example, if the police and army suddenly refused to do their jobs on behalf of government. Unless some effective authority stepped into the King's place (or the place of army and police and government), Hobbes argues the result is doomed to be deeply awful, nothing less than a state of war.

Why should peaceful cooperation be impossible without an overarching authority? Hobbes provides a series of powerful arguments that suggest it is extremely unlikely that human beings will live in security and peaceful cooperation without government. (Anarchism, the thesis that we should live without government, of course disputes these arguments.) His most basic argument is threefold. (i) He thinks we will compete, violently compete, to secure the basic necessities of life and perhaps to make other material gains. (ii) He argues that we will challenge others and fight out of fear ("diffidence"), so as to ensure our personal safety. (iii) And he believes that we will seek reputation ("glory"), both for its own sake and for its protective effects (for example, so that others will be afraid to challenge us). This is a more difficult argument than it might seem. Hobbes does not suppose that we are all selfish, that we are all cowards, or that we are all desperately concerned with how others see us. Two points, though. First, he does think that some of us are selfish, some of us cowardly, and some of us "vainglorious" (perhaps some people are of all of these!). Moreover, many of these people will be prepared to use violence to attain their ends-especially if there's no government or police to stop them. In this Hobbes is surely correct. Second, in some situations it makes good sense, at least in the short term, to use violence and to behave selfishly, fearfully or vaingloriously.

If our lives seem to be at stake, after all, we're unlikely to have many scruples about stealing a loaf of bread; if we perceive someone as a deadly threat, we may well want to attack first, while his guard is down; if we think that there are lots of potential attackers out there, it's going to make perfect sense to get a reputation as someone who shouldn't be messed with. In Hobbes's words, "the wickedness of bad men also compels good men to have recourse, for their own protection, to the virtues of war, which are violence and fraud." (De Cive, Epistle Dedicatory) As well as being more complex than first appears, Hobbes's argument becomes very difficult to refute.

Underlying this most basic argument is an important consideration about insecurity. As we shall see Hobbes places great weight on contracts. In particular, he often speaks of "covenants," by which he means a contract where one party performs his part of the bargain later than the other. In the state of nature such agreements aren't going to work. Only the weakest will have good reason to perform the second part of a covenant, and then only if the stronger party is standing over them. Yet a huge amount of human cooperation relies on trust, that others will return their part of the bargain over time. A similar point can be made about property, most of which we can't carry about with us and watch over. This means we must rely on others respecting our possessions over extended periods of time. If we can't do this, then many of the achievements of human society that involve putting hard work into land (farming, building) or material objects (the crafts, or modern industrial production, still unknown in Hobbes's time) will be near impossible. One can reasonably object to such points: Surely there are basic duties to reciprocate fairly and to behave in a trustworthy manner? Even if there's no government providing a framework of law, judgment and punishment, don't most people have a reasonable sense of what is right and wrong, which will prevent the sort of contract-breaking and generalized insecurity that Hobbes is concerned with?

Indeed, shouldn't our basic sense of morality prevent much of the greed, pre-emptive attack and reputation-seeking that Hobbes stressed in the first place? This is the crunch point of Hobbes's argument, and it is here (if anywhere) that one can accuse Hobbes of "pessimism." He makes two claims. The first concerns our duties in the state of nature (that is, the so-called "right of nature"). The second follows from this, and is less often noticed: it concerns the danger posed by our different and variable judgments of what is right and wrong.

On Hobbes's view the right of nature is quite simple to define. Naturally speaking-that is, outside of civil society-we have a right to do whatever we think will ensure our self-preservation. The worst that can happen to us is violent death at the hands of others. If we have any rights at all, if (as we might put it) nature has given us any rights whatsoever, then the first is surely this: the right to prevent violent death befalling us. But Hobbes says more than this, and it is this point that makes his argument so powerful.

We do not just have a right to ensure our self-preservation: we each have a right to judge what will ensure our self-preservation. And this is where Hobbes's picture of man becomes important. Hobbes has given us good reasons to think that human beings rarely judge wisely. Yet in the state of nature no one is in a position to successfully define what is good judgment. If I judge that killing you is a sensible or even necessary move to safeguard my life, then-in Hobbes's state of nature-I have a right to kill you. Others might judge the matter differently, of course. Almost certainly you'll have quite a different view of things (perhaps you were just stretching your arms, not raising a musket to shoot me). Because we're all insecure, because trust is more-or-less absent, there's little chance of our sorting out misunderstandings peacefully, nor can we rely on some (trusted) third party to decide whose judgment is right. We all have to be judges in our own causes, and the stakes are very high indeed: life or death.

For this reason Hobbes makes very bold claims that sound totally amoral. "To this war of every man against every man," he says, "this also is consequent [i.e., it follows]: that nothing can be unjust. The notions of right and wrong, justice and injustice have no place [in the state of nature]." He further argues that in the state of nature we each have a right to all things, "even to one another's body.' Hobbes is dramatizing his point, but the core is defensible. If I judge that I need such and such-an object, another person's labour, another person's death-to ensure my continued existence, then in the state of nature, there is no agreed authority to decide whether I'm right or wrong. New readers of Hobbes often suppose that the state of nature would be a much nicer place, if only he were to picture human beings with some basic moral ideas. But this is naïve: unless people share the same moral ideas, not just at the level of general principles but also at the level of individual judgment, then the challenge he poses remains unsolved: human beings who lack some shared authority are almost certain to fall into dangerous and deadly conflict.

There are different ways of interpreting Hobbes's view of the absence of moral constraints in the state of nature. Some think that Hobbes is imagining human beings who have no idea of social interaction and therefore no ideas about right and wrong. In this case, the natural condition would be a purely theoretical construction, and would demonstrate what both government and society do for human beings. (A famous statement about the state of nature in De Cive might support this interpretation: "looking at men as if they had just emerged from the earth like mushrooms and grown up without any obligation to each other...") Another, complementary view reads Hobbes as a psychological egoist, so that-in the state of nature as elsewhere-he is merely describing the interaction of selfish and amoral human beings.

Others suppose that Hobbes has a much more complex picture of human motivation, so that there is no reason to think moral ideas are absent in the state of nature. In particular, it's historically reasonable to think that Hobbes invariably has civil war in mind, when he describes our "natural condition." If we think of civil war, we need to imagine people who've lived together and indeed still do live together-huddled together in fear in their houses, banded together as armies or guerrillas or groups of looters. The problem here isn't a lack of moral ideas-far from it-rather that moral ideas and judgments differ enormously. This means (for example) that two people who are fighting tooth and nail over a cow or a gun can both think they're perfectly entitled to the object and both think they're perfectly right to kill the other-a point Hobbes makes explicitly and often. It also enables us to see that many Hobbesian conflicts are about religious ideas or political ideals (as well as self-preservation and so on)-as in the British Civil War raging while Hobbes wrote Leviathan, and in the many violent sectarian conflicts throughout the world today.

In the end, though, whatever account of the state of nature and its (a) morality we attribute to Hobbes, we must remember that it is meant to function as a powerful and decisive threat: if we do not heed Hobbes's teachings and fail to respect existing political authority, then the natural condition and its horrors of war await us.

The Laws of Nature and the Social Contract

Hobbes thinks the state of nature is something we ought to avoid, at any cost except our own self-preservation (this being our "right of nature," as we saw above). But what sort of "ought" is this? There are two basic ways of interpreting Hobbes here. It might be a counsel of prudence: avoid the state of nature, if you're concerned to avoid violent death. In this case Hobbes's advice only applies to us (i) if we agree that violent death is what we should fear most and should therefore avoid; and (ii) if we agree with Hobbes that only an unaccountable sovereign stands between human beings and the state of nature. This line of thought fits well with an egoistic reading of Hobbes, but we'll see that it faces serious problems.

The other way of interpreting Hobbes is not without problems either. This takes Hobbes to be saying that we ought, morally speaking, to avoid the state of nature. We have a duty to do what we can to avoid this situation arising, and a duty to end it, if at all possible. Hobbes often makes his view clear, that we have such moral obligations. But then two difficult questions arise: Why these obligations? And why are they obligatory?

Hobbes frames the issues in terms of an older vocabulary, using the idea of natural law that many ancient and medieval philosophers had relied on. Like them, he thinks that human reason can discern some eternal principles to govern our conduct. These principles are independent of (though also complementary to) whatever moral instruction we might get from God or religion. In other words, they are laws given by nature rather than revealed by God. But Hobbes makes radical changes to the content of these so-called laws of nature. In particular, he doesn't think that natural law provides any scope whatsoever to criticize or disobey the actual laws made by a government. He thus disagrees with those Protestants who thought that religious conscience might sanction disobedience of "immoral" laws, and with Catholics who thought that the commandments of the Pope have primacy over those of national political authorities.

Although he sets out nineteen laws of nature, it is the first two that are politically crucial. A third, that stresses the important of keeping to contracts we have entered into, is important in Hobbes's moral justifications of obedience to the sovereign. (The remaining sixteen can be quite simply encapsulated in the formula, "do as you would be done by." While the details are important for scholars of Hobbes, they do not affect the overall theory and will be ignored here.) The first law reads as follows:

> Every man ought to endeavor peace, as far as he has hope of obtaining it, and when he cannot obtain it, that he may seek and use all helps and advantages of war. (Leviathan, xiv.4)

This repeats the points we have already seen about our "right of nature," so long as peace does not appear to be a realistic prospect. The second law of nature is more complicated:

> That a man be willing, when others are so too, as far-forth as for peace and defense of himself he shall think it necessary, to lay down this right to all things, and be contented with so much liberty against other men, as he would allow other men against himself. (Leviathan, xiv.5)

What Hobbes tries to tackle here is the transition from the state of nature to civil society. But how he does this is misleading and has generated much confusion and disagreement. The way that Hobbes describes this second law of nature makes it look as if we should all put down our weapons, give up (much of) our "right of nature," and jointly authorize a sovereign who will tell us what is permitted and punish us if we don't obey. But the problem is obvious. If the state of nature is anything like as bad as Hobbes has argued, then there's just no way people could ever make an agreement like this or put it into practice.

At the end of Leviathan, Hobbes seems to concede this point, saying "there is scarce a commonwealth in the world whose beginnings can in conscience be justified" ("Review and Conclusion," 8). That is: governments have invariably been foisted upon people by force and fraud, not by collective agreement. But Hobbes means to defend every existing government that is powerful enough to secure peace among its subjects-not just a mythical government that's been created by a peaceful contract out of a state of nature. His basic claim is that we should behave as if we had voluntarily entered into such a contract with everyone else in our society-everyone else, that is, except the sovereign authority.

In Hobbes's myth of the social contract, everyone except the person or group who will wield sovereign power lays down their "right to all things." They agree to limit drastically their right of nature, retaining only a right to defend their lives in case of immediate threat. (How limited this right of nature becomes in civil society has caused much dispute, because deciding what is an immediate threat is a question of judgment. It certainly permits us to fight back if the sovereign tries to kill us. But what if the sovereign conscripts us as soldiers? What if the sovereign looks weak and we doubt whether he can continue to secure peace...?) The sovereign, however, retains his (or her, or their) right of nature, which we have seen is effectively a right to all things-to decide what everyone else should do, to decide the rules of property, to judge disputes and so on.

Hobbes concedes that there are moral limits on what sovereigns should do (God might call a sovereign to account). However, since in any case of dispute the sovereign is the only rightful judge-on this earth, that is-those moral limits make no practical difference. In every moral and political matter, the decisive question for Hobbes is always: who is to judge? As we have seen, in the state of nature, each of us is judge in our own cause, part of the reason why Hobbes thinks it is inevitably a state of war. Once civil society exists, the only rightful judge is the sovereign.

Why Should We Obey the Sovereign?

If we had all made a voluntary contract, a mutual promise, then it might seem half-way plausible to think we have an obligation to obey the sovereign (although even this requires the claim that promising is a moral value that overrides all others). If we have been conquered or, more fortunately, have simply been born into a society with an established political authority, this seems quite improbable. Hobbes has to make three steps here, all of which have seemed weak to many of his readers. First of all, he insists that promises made under threat of violence are nonetheless freely made, and just as binding as any others. Second, he has to put great weight on the moral value of promise keeping, which hardly fits with the absence of duties in the state of nature. Third, he has to give a story of how those of us born and raised in a political society have made some sort of implied promise to each other to obey, or at least, he has to show that we are bound (either morally or out of self-interest) to behave as if we had made such a promise. In the first place, Hobbes draws on his mechanistic picture of the world, to suggest that threats of force do not deprive us of liberty. Liberty, he says, is freedom of motion, and I am free to move whichever way I wish, unless I am literally enchained. If I yield to threats of violence, that is my choice, for physically I could have done otherwise. If I obey the sovereign for fear of punishment or in fear of the state of nature, then that is equally my choice. Such obedience then comes, for Hobbes, to constitute a promise that I will continue to obey.

Second, promises carry a huge moral weight for Hobbes, as they do in all social contract theories. The question, however, is why we should think they are so important. Why should my (coerced) promise oblige me, given the wrong you committed in threatening me and demanding my valuables? Hobbes has no good answer to this question. His theory suggests that (in the state of nature) you could do me no wrong, as the right of nature dictates that we all have a right to all things. Likewise, promises do not oblige in the state of nature, inasmuch as they go against our right of nature. In civil society, the sovereign's laws dictate what is right and wrong; if your threat was wrongful, then my promise will not bind me. But as the sovereign is outside of the original contract, he sets the terms for everyone else: so his threats create obligations.

As this suggests, Hobbesian promises are strangely fragile. Implausibly binding so long as a sovereign exists to adjudicate and enforce them, they lose all power should things revert to a state of nature. Relatedly, they seem to contain not one jot of loyalty. To be logically consistent, Hobbes needs to be politically implausible. Now there are passages where Hobbes sacrifices consistency for plausibility, arguing we have a duty to fight for our (former) sovereign even in the midst of civil war. Nonetheless the logic of his theory suggests that, as soon as government starts to weaken and disorder sets in, our duty of obedience lapses. That is, when the sovereign power needs our support, because it is no longer able to coerce us, there is no effective judge or enforcer of covenants, so that such promises no longer override our right of nature. This turns common sense on its head. Surely a powerful government can afford to be challenged, for instance by civil disobedience or conscientious objection? But when civil conflict and the state of nature threaten, in other words when government is failing, then we might reasonably think that political unity is as morally important as Hobbes always suggests. A similar question of loyalty also comes up when the sovereign power has been usurped-when Cromwell has supplanted the King, when a foreign invader has ousted our government. Right from the start, Hobbes's critics saw that his theory makes turncoats into moral heroes: our allegiance belongs to whoever happens to be holding the gun(s). Perversely, the only crime the makers of a coup can commit is to fail.

Why does this problem come about? To overcome the fact that his contract is a fiction, Hobbes is driven to construct a "sort of" promise out of the fact of our subjugation to whatever political authority exists. He stays wedded to the idea that obedience can only find a moral basis in a "voluntary" promise, because only this seems to justify the almost unlimited obedience and renunciation of individual judgment he's determined to prove. It is no surprise that Hobbes's arguments creak at every point: nothing could bear the weight of justifying such an overriding duty. All the difficulties in finding a reliable moral obligation to obey might tempt us back to the idea that Hobbes is some sort of egoist. However, the difficulties with this tack are even greater. There are two sorts of egoism commentators have attributed to Hobbes: psychological and ethical. The first theory says that human beings always act egoistically, the second that they ought to act egoistically. Either view might support this simple idea: we should obey the sovereign, because his political authority is what keeps us from the evils of the natural condition. But the basic problem with such egoistic interpretations, from the point of view of Hobbes's system of politics, is shown when we think about cases where selfishness seems to conflict with the commands of the sovereign-for example, where illegal conduct will benefit us or keep us from danger.

For a psychologically egoist agent, such behaviour will be irresistible; for an ethically egoist agent, it will be morally obligatory. Now, providing the sovereign is sufficiently powerful and well-informed, he can prevent many such cases arising by threatening and enforcing punishments of those who disobey. Effective threats of punishment mean that obedience is in our self-interest. But such threats will not be effective when we think our disobedience can go undetected. After Orwell's 1984 we can imagine a state that is so powerful that no reasonable person would ever think disobedience could pay. But for Hobbes, such a powerful sovereign was not even conceivable: he would have had to assume that there'd be many situations where people could reasonably hope to "get away with it." (Likewise, under non-totalitarian, liberal politics, there are many situations where illegal behaviour is very unlikely to be detected or punished.) So, still thinking of egoistic agents, the more people do get away with it, the more reason others have to think they can do the same. Thus the problem of disobedience threatens to "snowball," undermining the sovereign and plunging selfish agents back into the chaos of the state of nature.

In other words, sovereignty as Hobbes imagined it, and liberal political authority as we know it, can only function where people feel some additional motivation apart from pure self-interest. Moreover, there is strong evidence that Hobbes was well aware of this. Part of Hobbes's interest in religion (a topic that occupies half of Leviathan) lies in its power to shape human conduct. Sometimes this does seem to work through self-interest, as in crude threats of damnation and hell-fire. But Hobbes's main interest lies in the educative power of religion, and indeed of political authority. Religious practices, the doctrines taught in the universities (!), the beliefs and habits inculcated by the institutions of government and society: how these can encourage and secure respect for law and authority seem to be even more important to Hobbes's political solutions than his theoretical social contract or shaky appeals to simple self-interest.

What are we to conclude, then, given the difficulties in finding a reliable moral or selfish justification for obedience? In the end, for Hobbes, everything rides on the value of peace. Hobbes wants to say both that civil order is in our "enlightened" self-interest, and that it is of overwhelming moral value. Life is never going to be perfect for us, and life under the sovereign is the best we can do. Recognizing this aspect of everyone's self interest should lead us to recognize the moral value of supporting whatever authority we happen to live under. For Hobbes, this moral value is so great-and the alternatives so stark-that it should override every threat to our self-interest except the imminent danger of death. The million-dollar question is then: is a life of obedience to the sovereign really the best human beings can hope for?

Life Under the Sovereign

Hobbes has definite ideas about the proper nature, scope and exercise of sovereignty. Much that he says is cogent, and much of it can reduce the worries we might have about living under this drastically authoritarian sounding regime. Many commentators have stressed, for example, the importance Hobbes places upon the rule of law. His claim that much of our freedom, in civil society, "depends on the silence of the laws" is often quoted (Leviathan, xxi.18). In addition, Hobbes makes many points that are obviously aimed at contemporary debates about the rights of King and Parliament-especially about the sovereign's rights as regards taxation and the seizure of property, and about the proper relation between religion and politics. Some of these points continue to be relevant, others are obviously anachronistic: evidently Hobbes could not have imagined the modern state, with its vast bureaucracies, massive welfare provision and complicated interfaces with society. Nor could he have foreseen how incredibly powerful the state might become, meaning that "sovereigns" such as Hitler or Stalin might starve, brutalize and kill their subjects, to such an extent that the state of nature looks clearly preferable.

However, the problem with all of Hobbes's notions about sovereignty is that-on his account-it is not Hobbes the philosopher, nor we the citizens, who decide what counts as the proper nature, scope or exercise of sovereignty. He faces a systematic problem: justifying any limits or constraints on the sovereign involves making judgments about moral or practical requirements. But one of his greatest insights, still little recognized by many moral philosophers, is that any right or entitlement is only practically meaningful when combined with a concrete judgment as to what it dictates in some given case. Hobbes's own failure, however understandable, to foresee the growth of government and its powers only supports this thought: that the proper nature, scope or exercise of sovereignty is a matter of complex judgment. Alone among the people who comprise Hobbes's commonwealth, it is the sovereign who judges what form he should appear in, how far he should reach into the lives of his subjects, and how he should exercise his powers.

It should be added that the one part of his system that Hobbes concedes not to be proven with certainty is just this question: who or what should constitute the sovereign power. It was natural for Hobbes to think of a King, or indeed a Queen. But he was certainly very familiar with ancient forms of government, including aristocracy (government by an elite) and democracy (government by the citizens, who formed a relatively small group within the total population). Hobbes was also aware that an assembly such as Parliament could constitute a sovereign body. All have advantages and disadvantages, he argues. But the unity that comes about from having a single person at the apex, together with fixed rules of succession that pre-empt dispute about who this person should be, makes monarchy Hobbes's preferred option.

In fact, if we want to crack open Hobbes's sovereign, to be able to lay down concrete ideas about its nature and limits, we must begin with the question of judgment. For Hobbes, dividing capacities to judge between different bodies is tantamount to letting the state of nature straight back in. "For what is it to divide the power of a commonwealth, but to dissolve it; for powers divided mutually destroy each other." Beyond the example of England in the 1640s, Hobbes hardly bothers to argue the point, although it is crucial to his entire theory. Always in his mind is the Civil War that arose when Parliament claimed the right to judge rules of taxation, and thereby prevented the King from ruling and making war as he saw fit, and when churches and religious sects claimed prerogatives that went against the King's decisions.

Especially given modern experiences of the division of powers, however, it's easy to see that these examples are extreme and atypical. We might recall the American constitution, where powers of legislation, execution and case-by-case judgment are separated (to Congress, President and the judiciary respectively) and counter-balance one another. Each of these bodies is responsible for judging different questions. There are often, of course, boundary disputes, as to whether legislative, executive or judicial powers should apply to a given issue, and no one body is empowered to settle this crucial question of judgment. Equally obviously, however, such disputes have not led to a state of nature (well, at least if we think of the US after the Civil War).

For Hobbes it is simply axiomatic that disputation as to who should judge important social and political issues spells the end of the commonwealth. For us, it is equally obvious that only a few extreme forms of dispute have this very dangerous power. Dividing the powers that are important to government need not leave a society more open to those dangerous conflicts. Indeed, many would now argue that political compromises which provide different groups and bodies with independent space to judge certain social or political issues can be crucial for preventing disputes from escalating into violent conflict or civil war.

Far less is Hobbes's whole philosophy to be put down to the fear of civil tumult and the desire to think out a theory of government adequate to its restraint. Leviathan is a work of great and enduring importance just because it is not a mere political pamphlet. It owes life and colour to the time at which it was written; but another force also contributed to its making-a conception of larger scope, which gives it the unity of a philosophical masterpiece. This underlying conception and all the author's most striking ideas are to be found in the treatise completed in 1640-when political troubles were obviously at hand, but, as yet, no personal danger threatened. In logic and lucidity, this earlier treatise is not surpassed by the later work, though it fails to give the same constant impression of reality. It is a text-book such as philosophers have sometimes written for statesmen, to instruct them in the principles of their craft; and it did not entirely escape the usual fate of such efforts. Before Hobbes set about writing it, the fundamental idea of a philosophy had taken root in his mind; and this idea he owed to the new mechanical theory, and, in particular, to Galileo's teaching. Motion, he came to think, was the one reality; all other things are but "fancies, the offspring of our brains." He did not now, or, indeed, afterwards, work out a mechanical theory of the physical universe, as Descartes, for instance, was doing. But he had a bolder-if an impossible-project. Descartes restricted mechanism to the extended world, maintained the independence of mental existence and held the latter to be of all things most certain.

Hobbes did not thus limit the applications of his new idea. He thought he could pass from external motions to "the internal motions of men," and, thence, to sovereignty and justice. This is his own account, and it agrees with what we know otherwise. Neither the mechanical theory, nor the psychology, is an afterthought introduced to bolster up a foregone political conclusion. They have their roots too deep in Hobbes's mind. It is true, the desired transitions could not logically be made, and Hobbes found out the difficulty later. But, when civil disturbance forced his hand and led to the elaboration of his ethical and political doctrine, this doctrine was found to be in harmony with the idea from which his view of the universe started. The external and mechanical character of the political theory is an indication of its unreality, but it bears witness, also, to the unity of conception that dominates the whole philosophy.

All things, according to Hobbes, "have but one universal cause, which is motion." But, for him, as for other writers of his day, "motion" is not a merely abstract conception; it includes movement of masses or of particles. From geometry, which treats of abstract motion, he thus passes, without a break, to physics, and, thence, to moral philosophy; for the "motions of the mind" have physical causes. And, by this synthetical method, proceeding from principles, we "come to the causes and necessity of constituting commonwealths." This method he always kept in view, and it gives unity to his theory. But he never carried out the impossible task of applying it in detail. He admits that there is another and an easier way:

For the causes of the motions of the mind are known, not only by ratiocination, but also by the experience of every man that takes the pains to observe those motions within himself.

If he "will but examine his own mind," he will find that the appetites of men and the passions of their minds are such that, unless they be restrained by some power, they will always be making war upon one another. By adopting this method, Hobbes thinks he can appeal to each man's experience to confirm the truth of his doctrine.

Leviathan is divided into four parts, which treat, respectively of Man, of a Commonwealth, of a Christian Commonwealth and of the Kingdom of Darkness. Man comes first, for he is both the matter and the artificer of the Leviathan; and, at the outset, he is considered alone, as an individual thing played upon by external bodies; "for there is no conception in a man's mind which hath not at first, totally or by parts, been begotten upon the organs of sense." Diverse external motions produce diverse motions in us; and, in reality, there is nothing else; "but their appearance to us is fancy," though this name is commonly restricted to "decaying sense." The thoughts thus raised succeed one another in an order sometimes controlled by a "passionate thought," sometimes not. By the most noble and profitable invention of speech, names have been given to thoughts, whereby society and science have been made possible, and also absurdity: for words are wise men's counters, they do but reckon by them; but they are the money of fools.

Reason is but reckoning; addition and subtraction are its processes, logic is "computation." So far, man is regarded as if he were a thinking being only. But he is also active. The internal motions set up by the action of objects upon the senses become reactions upon the external world; and these reactions are all of the nature of tendencies towards that which "helps the vital motion," that is, ministers to the preservation of the individual, or tendencies away from things of an opposite nature. Thus, we have appetite or desire for certain things, and these we are said to love, and we call them good. In a similar way, we have aversion from certain other things, which we hate and call evil. Pleasure is "the appearance or sense of good"; displeasure, "the appearance or sense of evil." Starting from these definitions, Hobbes proceeds to describe the whole emotional and active nature of man as a consistent scheme of selfishness. The following characteristic summary comes from Elements of Law:

The comparison of the life of man to a race, though it holdeth not in every point, yet it holdeth so well for this our purpose, that we may thereby both see and remember almost all the passions before mentioned. But this race we must suppose to have no other goal, nor other garland, but being foremost; and in it: To endeavour, is appetite. To be remiss, is sensuality. To consider them behind, is glory. To consider them before, humility. To lose ground with looking back, vain glory. To be holden, hatred. To turn back, repentance. To be in breath, hope. To be weary, despair. To endeavour to overtake the next, emulation. To supplant or overthrow, envy. To resolve to break through a stop foreseen, courage. To break through a sudden stop, anger. To break through with ease, magnanimity. To lose ground by little hindrances, pusillanimity. To fall on the sudden, is disposition to weep. To see another fall, disposition to laugh. To see one out-gone whom we would not, is pity. To see one out-go we would not, is indignation. To hold fast by another, is to love. To carry him on that so holdeth, is charity. To hurt one's-self for haste, is shame. Continually to be out-gone, is misery. Continually to out-go the next before, is felicity and to forsake the course, is to die.

Theory of Human Nature and of Sovereignty

Out of this contention of selfish units, Hobbes, in some way, has to derive morality and the social order. Yet, in the state of nature there are no rules for the race of life-not even the rule of the strongest, for Hobbes thinks that there is little difference between men's faculties, and, at any rate, "the weakest has strength enough to kill the strongest." Thus, for gain, for safety and for reputation (which is a sign of power), each man desires whatever may preserve or enrich his own life, and, indeed, by nature, "every man has a right to everything, even to one another's body." Thus, the natural state of man is a state of war, in which "every man is enemy to every man." In this condition, as he points out, there is no place for industry, or knowledge, or arts, or society, but only "continual fear and danger of violent death; and the life of man solitary, poor, nasty, brutish, and short." Nor, in this state, is there any difference of right and wrong, mine and thine; "force and fraud are in war the two cardinal virtues."

Hobbes betrays some hesitation in speaking of the historical reality of this state of universal war. But the point, perhaps, is not fundamental. What is essential is the view of human nature as so constituted as to make every man his neighbour's enemy. The view was not entirely new; he was not the first satirist of the "golden age." His originality lies in the consistency of his picture of its anarchy, and in the amazing skill with which he makes the very misery of this state lead on to social order: the freedom of anarchy yields at once and forever to the fetters of power. The transition is effected by the social contract-an instrument familiar to medieval philosophers and jurists. So long as the state of nature endures, life is insecure and wretched. Man cannot improve this state, but he can get out of it; therefore, the fundamental law of nature is to seek peace and follow it; and, from this, emerges the second law, that, for the sake of peace, a man should be willing to lay down his right to all things, when other men are, also, willing to do so.

From these two are derived all the laws of nature of the moralists. The laws of nature are immutable and eternal, says Hobbes, and, in so saying, conforms to the traditional view-but with one great difference. Hooker, who followed the older theory, had said that the laws of nature "bind men absolutely, even as they are men, although they have never any settled fellowship, never any solemn agreement amongst themselves." But Hobbes holds that their authority, for any man, is not absolute; it is strictly conditional on other men being willing to obey them; and this requires an agreement of wills-a contract. Contracts, again, require a power to enforce them: "covenants of mutual trust where there is a fear of not performance on either part are invalid"; and the only way to obtain such a common power is for all men to give up their rights to one man, or one assembly of men, and to acknowledge his acts as their own "in those things which concern the common peace and safety." This man, or assembly, will thus bear the "person" of the whole multitude. They have contracted with one another to be his subjects. But the sovereign himself is under no contract: he has rights but no duties. From this, it follows, logically, that sovereignty cannot be limited, divided, or forfeited. The conduct of the commonwealth in peace and war, and the rights of subjects against one another, are decided by the sovereign. He is sole legislator, supreme ruler and supreme judge. And this holds, whether the sovereignty lies in one man or in an assembly. Hobbes always maintained the superiority of monarchy to other forms of government; but he never thought that this superiority was capable of the demonstrative proof that he claimed for his general theory. There is a story that, before leaving Paris, Hobbes told Edward Hyde (afterwards earl of Clarendon) that he was publishing Leviathan because he "had a mind to go home." If he was serious in making the remark reported by Clarendon, he must have been referring to the "Review and Conclusion," with which the work closes, and in which he speaks of the time at which submission to a conqueror may lawfully be made. The book in no way modifies his earlier views on the merits of monarchy.

A man cannot serve two masters: "mixed government" is no government; nor can the spiritual power be independent of the temporal. The doctrines "that every private man is judge of good and evil actions," and "that whatsoever a man does against his conscience is a sin," are seditious and repugnant to civil society. By living in a commonwealth, a man takes the law for his conscience. These positions may seem to complete the political theory, and few readers now care to pursue the matter further. But

Hobbes's commonwealth professes to be a Christian commonwealth. He must show the place which religion occupies in it, and also expose the errors which have led to nations being overshadowed by the spiritual power. His theory is Erastianism pushed to its extremest limits. The inner life—the true home of religion for the religious man—shrinks to a point; while its external expression in doctrine and observance is described as part of the order that depends on the will of the sovereign.

Hobbes can cite Scripture for his purpose; he anticipates some of the results of modern Biblical criticism; and he has theories about God, the Trinity, the atonement and the last judgment-all of them in harmony with his general principles. His doctrine of God is, in modern phrase, agnostic. The attributes we ascribe to Him only signify our desire to honour Him: "we understand nothing of what he is, but only that he is." In this, Hobbes follows the doctrine of negative attributes, worked out by some medieval theologians. But his doctrine of the Trinity is, surely, original. It is in substance this: that God who is always one and the same was the person represented by Moses, the person represented by his Son incarnate, and the person represented by the apostles. Again, the kingdom of God is a real kingdom, instituted by covenant or contract: which contract was made by Moses, broken by the election of Saul to the kingship, restored by Christ and proclaimed by the apostles. But the kingdom of Christ "is not of this world"; it is of the world to come after the general resurrection; "therefore neither can his ministers (unless they be kings) require obedience in his name." There are two things specially opposed to this theory. On the one hand, there is the enthusiasm which results from the claim either to personal illumination by the spirit of God or to private interpretation of Scripture. On the other hand, there is the claim to dominion on the part of the organised spiritual power. Both claims were rampant in Hobbes's day, and he seeks to undermine them both by criticism. There is no argument, he says, by which a man can be convinced that God has spoken immediately to some other man, "who (being a man) may err, and (which is more) may lie."

And, as regards Scripture, it is for sovereigns as the sole legislators to say which books are canonical, and, therefore, to them, also, must belong the authority for their interpretation. Of all the abuses that constitute what Hobbes calls the Kingdom of Darkness, the greatest arise from the erroneous tenet "that the present church now militant on earth is the kingdom of God." Through this error, not only the Roman, but, also, the presbyterian, clergy have been the authors of darkness in religion, and encroached upon the civil power. The Roman church alone has been thorough in its work. The pope, in claiming dominion over all Christendom, has forsaken the true kingdom of God, and he has built up his power out of the ruins of heathen Rome. For "the papacy is no other than the ghost of the deceased Roman empire, sitting crowned upon the grave thereof." Taken as a whole, Hobbes's Leviathan has two characteristics which stamp it with the mark of genius. In the first place, it is a work of great imaginative power, which shows how the whole fabric of human life and society is built up out of simple elements. And, in the second place, it is distinguished by a remarkable logical consecutiveness, so that there are very few places in which any lack of coherence can be detected in the thought. It is true that the social order, as Hobbes presents it, produces an impression of artificiality; but this is hardly an objection, for it was his deliberate aim to show the artifice by which it had been constructed and the danger which lay in any interference with the mechanism.

It is true, also, that the state of nature and the social contract are fictions passed off as facts; but, even to this objection, an answer might be made from within the bounds of his theory. It is in his premises, not in his reasoning, that the error lies. If human nature were as selfish and anarchical as he represents it, then morality and the political order could arise and flourish only by its restraint, and the alternative would be, as he describes it, between complete insecurity and absolute power. But, if his view of man be mistaken, then the whole fabric of his thought crumbles. When we recognise that the individual is neither real nor intelligible apart from his social origin and traditions, and that the social factor influences his thought and motives, the opposition between self and others becomes less fundamental, the abrupt alternatives of Hobbism lose their validity and it is possible to regard morality and the state as expressing the ideal and sphere of human activity, and not as simply the chains by which man's unruly passions are kept in check.

The Critics of Hobbes

John Bramhall, bishop of Derry, and, afterwards, archbishop of Armagh, was one of the most vigorous and persistent of Hobbes's critics. His first work was in defence of the royal power (1643). Afterwards he engaged in a discussion of the question of free-will with Hobbes when they were both in France. When the controversy was renewed and became public, he wrote *A Defence of the True Liberty of Human Actions from Antecedent and Extrinsicall Necessity* (1655). Hobbes replied, and Bramhall followed, in 1658, with Castigations of Mr. Hobbes, to which there was an appendix called "The Catching of Leviathan the Great Whale." In this appendix, more famous than the rest of the treatise, he attacked the whole religious and political theory of Hobbes, and gave rise to the complaint of the latter that the bishop.

> hath put together diverse sentences picked out of my Leviathan, which stand there plainly and firmly proved, and sets them down without their proofs, and without the order of their dependance one upon another; and calls them atheism, blasphemy, impiety, subversion of religion, and by other names of that kind.

Two younger polemical writers may be mentioned along with Bramhall. Thomas Tenison, a future archbishop of Canterbury, was one of the young churchmen militant who must needs try their arms "in thundering upon Hobbes's steel-cap." *In The Creed of Mr. Hobbes* examined (1670), he selected a number of Hobbes's confident assertions and set them together so as to show their mutual inconsistencies. In two dialogues, published in 1672 and 1673, John Eachard, afterwards master of St. Catharine's hall, Cambridge, adopted a similar method, and showed no little wit and learning in his criticism.

These writers are the most notable of a number of early critics of Hobbes who made no independent contributions of their own to philosophy. And their criticism dealt with results rather than with principles. A satisfactory criticism of Hobbes has to penetrate to the principles of the mechanical philosophy which he adopted, and to the view of human nature which he set forth in conformity with those principles. Criticism of this more fundamental kind was attempted by certain of the Cambridge Platonists, 5 especially by Cudworth and More;and they were fitted for the task by their sympathetic study of the spiritual philosophy of Plato in the ancient world and of Descartes in their own day-two thinkers for whom Hobbes had no appreciation.

Major Political Writings

Hobbes wrote several versions of his political philosophy, including *The Elements of Law, Natural and Politic* (also under the titles *Human Nature* and *De Corpore Politico*) published in 1650, De Cive (1642) published in English as Philosophical Rudiments Concerning Government and Society in 1651, the English Leviathan published in 1651, and its Latin revision in 1668. Others of his works are also important in understanding his political philosophy, especially his history of the English Civil War, *Behemoth* (published 1679), *De Corpore* (1655), *De Homine* (1658), *Dialogue Between a Philosopher and a Student of the Common Laws of England* (1681), and *The Questions Concerning Liberty, Necessity, and Chance* (1656). All of Hobbes's major writings are collected in The English Works of Thomas Hobbes, edited by Sir William Molesworth (11 volumes, London 1839-45), and Thomae Hobbes' *Opera Philosophica Quae Latina Scripsit Omnia,* also edited by Molesworth (5 volumes; London, 1839-45). Readers new to Hobbes should begin with Leviathan, being sure to read Parts Three and Four, as well as the more familiar and often excerpted Parts One and Two. There are many fine overviews of Hobbes's normative philosophy, some of which are listed in the following selected bibliography of secondary works.

The Philosophical Project

Hobbes sought to discover rational principles for the construction of a civil polity that would not be subject to destruction from within. Having lived through the period of political disintegration culminating in the English Civil War, he came to the view that the burdens of even the most oppressive government are "scarce sensible, in respect of the miseries, and horrible calamities, that accompany a Civill Warre". Because virtually any government would be better than a civil war, and, according to Hobbes's analysis, all but absolute governments are systematically prone to dissolution into civil war, people ought to submit themselves to an absolute political authority. Continued stability will require that they also refrain from the sorts of actions that might undermine such a regime. In particular, Hobbes aimed to demonstrate the reciprocal relationship between political obedience and peace.

The State of Nature

To establish these conclusions, Hobbes invites us to consider what life would be like in a state of nature, that is, a condition without government. Perhaps we would imagine that people might fare best in such a state, where each decides for himself how to act, and is judge, jury and executioner in his own case whenever disputes arise—and that at any rate, this state is the appropriate baseline against which to judge the justifiability of political arrangements. Hobbes terms this situation "the condition of mere nature", a state of perfectly private judgment, in which there is no agency with recognized authority to arbitrate disputes and effective power to enforce its decisions.

Hobbes's near descendant, John Locke, insisted in his Second Treatise of Government that the state of nature was indeed to be preferred to subjection to the arbitrary power of an absolute sovereign. But Hobbes famously argued that such a "dissolute condition of masterlesse men, without subjection to Lawes, and a coercive Power to tye their hands from rapine, and revenge" would make impossible all of the basic security upon which comfortable, sociable, civilized life depends.

There would be "no place for industry, because the fruit thereof is uncertain; and consequently no culture of the earth; no navigation, nor use of the commodities that may be imported by Sea; no commodious Building; no Instruments of moving and removing such things as require much force; no Knowledge of the face of the Earth; no account of Time; no Arts; no Letters; and which is worst of all, continual fear, and danger of violent death; And the life of man, solitary, poor, nasty, brutish, and short."

If this is the state of nature, men have strong reasons to avoid it, which can be done only by submitting to some mutually recognized public authority, for "so long a man is in the condition of mere nature, (which is a condition of war,) as private appetite is the measure of good and evil."

Although many readers have criticized Hobbes's state of nature as unduly pessimistic, he constructs it from a number of individually plausible empirical and normative assumptions. He assumes that people are sufficiently similar in their mental and physical attributes that no one is invulnerable nor can expect to be able to dominate the others.

Hobbes assumes that people generally "shun death", and that the desire to preserve their own lives is very strong in most people. While people have local affections, their benevolence is limited, and they have a tendency to partiality. Concerned that others should agree with their own high opinions of themselves, people are sensitive to slights. They make evaluative judgments, but often use seemingly impersonal terms like 'good' and 'bad' to stand for their own personal preferences.

They are curious about the causes of events, and anxious about their futures; according to Hobbes, these characteristics incline people to adopt religious beliefs, although the content of those beliefs will differ depending upon the sort of religious education one has happened to receive. With respect to normative assumptions, Hobbes ascribes to each person in the state of nature a liberty right to preserve herself, which he terms "the right of nature". This is the right to do whatever one sincerely judges needful for one's preservation; yet because it is at least possible that virtually anything might be judged necessary for one's preservation, this theoretically limited right of nature becomes in practice an unlimited right to potentially anything, or, as Hobbes puts it, a right "to all things". Hobbes further assumes as a principle of practical rationality, that people should adopt what they see to be the necessary means to their most important ends.

The State of Nature is a State of War

Taken together, these plausible descriptive and normative assumptions yield a state of nature potentially fraught with divisive struggle. The right of each to all things invites serious conflict, especially if there is competition for resources, as there will surely be over at least scarce goods such as the most desirable lands, spouses, etc.

People will quite naturally fear that others may (citing the right of nature) invade them, and may rationally plan to strike first as an anticipatory defense. Moreover, that minority of prideful or "vain-glorious" persons who take pleasure in exercising power over others will naturally elicit preemptive defensive responses from others. Conflict will be further fueled by disagreement in religious views, in moral judgments, and over matters as mundane as what goods one actually needs, and what respect one properly merits.

Hobbes imagines a state of nature in which each person is free to decide for himself what he needs, what he's owed, what's respectful, right, pious, prudent, and also free to decide all of these questions for the behaviour of everyone else as well, and to act on his judgments as he thinks best, enforcing his views where he can. In this situation where there is no common authority to resolve these many and serious disputes, we can easily imagine with Hobbes that the state of nature would become a "state of war", even worse, a war of "all against all".

Further Questions about the State of Nature

In response to the natural question whether humanity ever was generally in any such state of nature, Hobbes notes that all sovereigns are in this state with respect to one another. He opined that many now civilized peoples were formerly in that state, and some few peoples—the savages of 17th C. America, for instance—were still to his day in the state of nature. Most significantly, Hobbes asserts that the state of nature will be easily recognized by those whose formerly peaceful states have collapsed into civil war. While the state of nature's condition of perfectly private judgment is an abstraction, something resembling it too closely for comfort remains a perpetually present possibility, to be feared, and avoided. Do the other assumptions of Hobbes's philosophy license the existence of this imagined state of isolated individuals pursuing their private judgments?

Probably not, since, as feminist critics among others have noted, children are by Hobbes's theory assumed to have undertaken an obligation of obedience to their parents in exchange for nurturing, and so the primitive units in the state of nature will include families ordered by internal obligations, as well as individuals.

The bonds of affection, sexual affinity, and friendship--as well as of clan membership and shared religious belief--may further decrease the accuracy of any purely individualistic model of the state of nature. This concession need not impugn Hobbes's analysis of conflict in the state of nature, since it may turn out that competition, diffidence and glory-seeking are disastrous sources of conflicts among small groups just as much as they are among individuals. Still, commentators seeking to answer the question how precisely we should understand Hobbes's state of nature are investigating the degree to which Hobbes imagines that to be a condition of interaction among isolated individuals.

Another important open question is that of what, exactly, it is about human beings that makes it the case (supposing Hobbes is right) that our communal life is prone to disaster when we are left to interact according only to our own individual judgments. Perhaps, while people do wish to act for their own best long-term interest, they are shortsighted, and so indulge their current interests without properly considering the effects of their current behaviour on their long-term interest. This would be a type of failure of rationality. Alternative, it may be that people in the state of nature are fully rational, but are trapped in a situation that makes it individually rational for each to act in a way that is sub-optimal for all, perhaps finding themselves in the familiar 'prisoner's dilemma' of game theory. Or once again, it may be that Hobbes's state of nature would be peaceful but for the presence of persons (just a few, or perhaps all, to some degree) whose passions overrule their calmer judgments; who are prideful, spiteful, partial, envious, jealous, and in other ways prone to behave in ways that lead to war. Such an account would understand irrational human passions to be the source of conflict. Which, if any, of these accounts adequately answers to Hobbes's text is a matter of continuing debate among Hobbes scholars.

Absolutism

Although Hobbes offered some mild pragmatic grounds for preferring monarchy to other forms of government, his main concern was to argue that effective government—whatever its form—must have absolute authority. Its powers must be neither divided nor limited. The powers of legislation, adjudication, enforcement, taxation, war-making (and the less familiar right of control of normative doctrine) are connected in such a way that a loss of one may thwart effective exercise of the rest; for example, legislation without interpretation and enforcement will not serve to regulate conduct.

Only a government that possesses all of what Hobbes terms the "essential rights of sovereignty" can be reliably effective, since where partial sets of these rights are held by different bodies that disagree in their judgments as to what is to be done, paralysis of effective government, or degeneration into a civil war to settle their dispute, may occur. Similarly, to impose limitation on the authority of the government is to invite irresoluble disputes over whether it has overstepped those limits. If each person is to decide for herself whether the government should be obeyed, factional disagreement—and war to settle the issue, or at least paralysis of effective government—are quite possible.

To refer resolution of the question to some further authority, itself also limited and so open to challenge for overstepping its bounds, would be to initiate an infinite regress of non-authoritative 'authorities' (where the buck never stops). To refer it to a further authority itself unlimited, would be just to relocate the seat of absolute sovereignty, a position entirely consistent with Hobbes's insistence on absolutism. To avoid the horrible prospect of governmental collapse and return to the state of nature, people should treat their sovereign as having absolute authority.

The Limits of Political Obligation

While Hobbes insists that we should regard our governments as having absolute authority, he reserves to subjects the liberty of disobeying those of their government's commands that would require them to sacrifice their lives or honour, at least when the commonwealth's survival does not depend on their doing so. This exception has understandably intrigued those who study Hobbes. His ascription of apparently inalienable rights what he calls the "true liberties of subjects"—seems incompatible with his defense of absolute sovereignty. Moreover, if the sovereign's failure to provide adequate protection to subjects extinguishes their obligation to obey, and if it is left to each subject to judge for herself the adequacy of that protection, it seems that people have never really exited the fearsome state of nature.

Religion and Social Instability

The last crucial aspect of Hobbes's political philosophy is his treatment of religion. Hobbes progressively expands his discussion of Christian religion in each revision of his political philosophy, until it comes in Leviathan to comprise roughly half the book. There is no settled consensus on how Hobbes understands the significance of religion within his political theory. Some commentators have argued that Hobbes is trying to demonstrate to his readers the compatibility of his political theory with core Christian commitments, since it may seem that Christians' religious duties forbid their affording the sort of absolute obedience to their governors which Hobbes's theory requires of them. Others have doubted the sincerity of his professed Christianity, arguing that by the use of irony or other subtle rhetorical devices, Hobbes sought to undermine his readers' religious beliefs. Howsoever his intentions are properly understood, Hobbes's obvious concern with the power of religious belief is a fact that interpreters of his political philosophy must seek to explain.

Conclusion

What happens, then, if we do not follow Hobbes in his arguments that judgment must, by necessity or by social contract or both, be the sole province of the sovereign? If we are optimists about the power of human judgment, and about the extent of moral consensus among human beings, we have a straightforward route to the concerns of modern liberalism. Our attention will not be on the question of social and political order, rather on how to maximize liberty, how to define social justice, how to draw the limits of government power, and how to realize democratic ideals.

We will probably interpret Hobbes as a psychological egoist, and think that the problems of political order that obsessed him were the product of an unrealistic view of human nature, or unfortunate historical circumstances, or both. If we are less optimistic about human judgment in morals and politics, however, we should not doubt that Hobbes's problems remain our problems.

But hindsight shows grave limitations to his solutions. Theoretically, Hobbes fails to prove that we have an almost unlimited obligation to obey the sovereign. His arguments that sovereignty-the power to judge moral and political matters, and enforce those judgments-cannot be divided are not only weak; they are simply refuted by the (relatively) successful distribution of powers in modern liberal societies. Not least, the horrific crimes of twentieth century dictatorships show beyond doubt that judgment about right and wrong cannot be a question only for our political leaders.

If Hobbes's problems are real and his solutions only partly convincing, where will we go? It might reasonably be thought that this is the central question of modern political thought. We will have no doubt that peaceful coexistence is one of the greatest goods of human life, something worth many inconveniences, sacrifices and compromises.

We will see that there is moral force behind the laws and requirements of the state, simply because human beings do indeed need authority and systems of enforcement if they are to cooperate peacefully. But we can hardly accept that, because human judgment is weak and faulty, that there can be only one judge of these matters-precisely because that judge might turn out to be very faulty indeed. Our concern will be how we can effectively divide power between government and people, while still ensuring that important questions of moral and political judgment are peacefully adjudicated. We will be concerned with the standards and institutions that provide for compromise between many different and conflicting judgments. And all the time, we will remember Hobbes's reminder that human life is never without inconvenience and troubles, that we must live with a certain amount of bad, to prevent the worst: fear of violence, and violent death.

5

John Locke

John Locke (August 29, 1632 – October 28, 1704) was an English philosopher. Locke is considered the first of the British Empiricists, but is equally important to social contract theory. His ideas had enormous influence on the development of epistemology and political philosophy, and he is widely regarded as one of the most influential Enlightenment thinkers, classical republicans, and contributors to liberal theory. His writings influenced Voltaire and Rousseau, many Scottish Enlightenment thinkers, as well as the American revolutionaries. This influence is reflected in the American Declaration of Independence.

Locke's theory of mind is often cited as the origin for modern conceptions of identity and "the self", figuring prominently in the later works of philosophers such as David Hume, Jean-Jacques Rousseau and Immanuel Kant. Locke was the first philosopher to define the self through a continuity of "consciousness." He also postulated that the mind was a "blank slate" or "tabula rasa"; that is, contrary to Cartesian or Christian philosophy, Locke maintained that people are born without innate ideas.

Life

Locke's father, who was also named John Locke, was a country lawyer and clerk to the Justices of the Peace in Chew Magna, who had served as a captain of cavalry for the Parliamentarian forces during the early part of the English Civil War. His mother, Agnes Keene, was a tanner's daughter and reputed to be very beautiful. Both parents were Puritans. Locke was born on August 29, 1632, in a small thatched cottage by the church in Wrington, Somerset, about twelve miles from Bristol. He was baptised the same day. Soon after Locke's birth, the family moved to the market town of Pensford, about seven miles south of Bristol, where Locke grew up in a rural Tudor house in Belluton.

In 1647, Locke was sent to the prestigious Westminster School in London under the sponsorship of Alexander Popham, a member of Parliament and former commander of the younger Locke's father. After completing his studies there, he was admitted to Christ Church, Oxford. The dean of the college at the time was John Owen, vice-chancellor of the university. Although a capable student, Locke was irritated by the undergraduate curriculum of the time. He found the works of modern philosophers, such as Rene Descartes, more interesting than the classical material taught at the university. Through his friend Richard Lower, whom he knew from the Westminster School, Locke was introduced to medicine and the experimental philosophy being pursued at other universities and in the English Royal Society, of which he eventually became a member.

Locke was awarded a bachelor's degree in 1656 and a master's degree in 1658. He obtained a bachelor of medicine in 1674, having studied medicine extensively during his time at Oxford and worked with such noted scientists and thinkers as Robert Boyle, Thomas Willis, Robert Hooke and Richard Lower. In 1666, he met Lord Anthony Ashley Cooper, 1st Earl of Shaftesbury, who had come to Oxford seeking treatment for a liver infection. Cooper was impressed with Locke and persuaded him to become part of his retinue.

Locke had been looking for a career and in 1667 moved into Shaftesbury's home at Exeter House in London, to serve as Lord Ashley's personal physician. In London, Locke resumed his medical studies under the tutelage of Thomas Sydenham. Sydenham had a major effect on Locke's natural philosophical thinking — an *effect that would become evident in the An Essay Concerning Human Understanding.*

Locke's medical knowledge was put to the test when Shaftesbury's liver infection became life-threatening. Locke coordinated the advice of several physicians and was probably instrumental in persuading Shaftesbury to undergo an operation (then life-threatening itself) to remove the cyst. Shaftesbury survived and prospered, crediting Locke with saving his life.

It was in Shaftesbury's household, during 1671, that the meeting took place, described in the Epistle to the reader of the Essay, which was the genesis of what would later become Essay. Two extant Drafts still survive from this period. It was also during this time that Locke served as Secretary of the Board of Trade and Plantations and Secretary to the Lords and Proprietors of the Carolinas, helping to shape his ideas on international trade and economics.

Shaftesbury, as a founder of the Whig movement, exerted great influence on Locke's political ideas. Locke became involved in politics when Shaftesbury became Lord Chancellor in 1672. Following Shaftesbury's fall from favour in 1675, Locke spent some time travelling across France. He returned to England in 1679 when Shaftesbury's political fortunes took a brief positive turn. Around this time, most likely at Shaftesbury's prompting, Locke composed the bulk of the *Two Treatises of Government*. Locke wrote the Treatises to defend the Glorious Revolution of 1688, but also to counter the absolutist political philosophy of Sir Robert Filmer and Thomas Hobbes. Though Locke was associated with the influential Whigs, his ideas about natural rights and government are today considered quite revolutionary for that period in English history. However, Locke fled to the Netherlands, Holland, in 1683, under strong suspicion of involvement in the Rye House Plot (though there is little evidence to suggest that he was directly involved in the scheme). In the Netherlands Locke had time to return to his writing, spending a great deal of time re-working the Essay and composing the Letter on Toleration. Locke did not return home until after the Glorious Revolution. Locke accompanied William of Orange's wife back to England in 1688. The bulk of Locke's publishing took place after his arrival back *in England – his aforementioned Essay Concerning Human Understanding*, the *Two Treatises of Civil Government* and *A Letter* Concerning Toleration all appearing in quick succession upon his return from exile.

Locke's close friend Lady Masham invited him to join her at the Mashams' country house in Essex. Although his time there was marked by variable health from asthma attacks, he nevertheless became an intellectual hero of the Whigs. During this period he discussed matters with such figures as John Dryden and Isaac Newton.

He died in October 28, 1704 due to declining health, and is buried in the churchyard of the village of High Laver, east of Harlow in Essex, where he had lived in the household of Sir Francis Masham since 1691. Locke never married nor had children.

Events that happened during Locke's lifetime include the English Restoration, the Great Plague of London and the Great Fire of London. He did not quite see the Act of Union of 1707, though the thrones of England and Scotland were held by the same monarch throughout his lifetime. Constitutional monarchy and parliamentary democracy were in their infancy during Locke's time.

The Law of Nature

Perhaps the most central concept in Locke's political philosophy is his theory of natural law and natural rights. The natural law concept existed long before Locke as a way of expressing the idea that there were certain moral truths that applied to all people, regardless of the particular place where they lived or the agreements they had made. The most important early contrast was between laws that were by nature, and thus generally applicable, and those that were conventional and operated only in those places where the particular convention had been established. This distinction is sometimes formulated as the difference between natural law and positive law.

Natural law is also distinct from divine law in that the latter, in the Christian tradition, normally referred to those laws that God had directly revealed through prophets and other inspired writers. Natural law can be discovered by reason alone and applies to all people, while divine law can be discovered only through God's special revelation and applies only to those to whom it is revealed and who God specifically indicates are to be bound. Thus some seventeenth-century commentators, Locke included, held that not all of the 10 commandments, much less the rest of the Old Testament law, were binding on all people. The 10 commandments begin "Hear O Israel" and thus are only binding on the people to whom they were addressed (Works 6:37). As we will see below, even though Locke thought natural law could be known apart from special revelation, he saw no contradiction in God playing a part in the argument, so long as the relevant aspects of God's character could be discovered by reason alone.

In Locke's theory, divine law and natural law are consistent and can overlap in content, but they are not coextensive. Thus there is no problem for Locke if the Bible commands a moral code that is stricter than the one that can be derived from natural law, but there is a real problem if the Bible teaches what is contrary to natural law. In practice, Locke avoided this problem because consistency with natural law was one of the criteria he used when deciding the proper interpretation of Biblical passages.

In the century before Locke, the language of natural rights also gained prominence through the writings of such thinkers as Grotius, Hobbes, and Puffendorf. Whereas natural law emphasized duties, natural rights normally emphasized privileges or claims to which an individual was entitled. There is considerable disagreement as to how these factors are to be understood in relation to each other in Locke's theory. Leo Strauss, and many of his followers, take rights to be paramount, going so far as to portray Locke's position as essentially similar to that of Hobbes. They point out that Locke defended a hedonist theory of human motivation (Essay 2.20) and claim that he must agree with Hobbes about the essentially self-interested nature of human beings. Locke, they claim, only recognizes natural law obligations in those situations where our own preservation is not in conflict, further emphasizing that our right to preserve ourselves trumps any duties we may have.

On the other end of the spectrum, more scholars have adopted the view of Dunn, Tully, and Ashcraft that it is natural law, not natural rights, that is primary. They hold that when Locke emphasized the right to life, liberty, and property he was primarily making a point about the duties we have toward other people: duties not to kill, enslave, or steal. Most scholars also argue that Locke recognized a general duty to assist with the preservation of mankind, including a duty of charity to those who have no other way to procure their subsistence. These scholars regard duties as primary in Locke because rights exist to insure that we are able to fulfill our duties. Simmons takes a position similar to the latter group, but claims that rights are not just the flip side of duties in Locke, nor merely a means to performing our duties. Instead, rights and duties are equally fundamental because Locke believes in a "robust zone of indifference" in which rights protect our ability to make choices. While these choices cannot violate natural law, they are not a mere means to fulfilling natural law either.

Another point of contestation has to do with the extent to which Locke thought natural law could, in fact, be known by reason. Both Strauss and Peter Laslett, though very different in their interpretations of Locke generally, see Locke's theory of natural law as filled with contradictions. In the Essay Concerning Human Understanding, Locke defends a theory of moral knowledge that negates the possibility of innate ideas (Essay Book 1) and claims that morality is capable of demonstration in the same way that Mathematics is. Yet nowhere in any of his works does Locke make a full deduction of natural law from first premises. More than that, Locke at times seems to appeal to innate ideas in the Second Treatise, and in The Reasonableness of Christianity he admits that no one has ever worked out all of natural law from reason alone. Strauss infers from this that the contradictions exist to show the attentive reader that Locke does not really believe in natural law at all. Laslett, more conservatively, simply says that Locke the philosopher and Locke the political writer should be kept very separate.

To understand Locke's position on the ground of natural law it must be situated within a larger debate in natural law theory that predates Locke, the so-called "voluntarism-intellectualism," or "voluntarist-rationalist" debate. At its simplest, the voluntarist declares that right and wrong are determined by God's will and that we are obliged to obey the will of God simply because it is the will of God. Unless these positions are maintained, the voluntarist argues, God becomes superfluous to morality since both the content and the binding force of morality can be explained without reference to God. The intellectualist replies that this understanding makes morality arbitrary and fails to explain why we have an obligation to obey God. With respect to the grounds and content of natural law, Locke is not completely clear. On the one hand, there are many instances where he makes statements that sound voluntarist to the effect that law requires a law giver with authority. Locke also repeatedly insists in the Essays on the Law of Nature that created beings have an obligation to obey their creator. On the other hand there are statements that seem to imply an external moral standard to which God must conform.

Locke clearly wants to avoid the implication that the content of natural law is arbitrary. Several solutions have been proposed. One solution suggested by Herzog makes Locke an intellectualist by grounding our obligation to obey God on a prior duty of gratitude that exists independent of God. A second option, suggested by Simmons, is simply to take Locke as a voluntarist since that is where the preponderance of his statements point. A third option, suggested by Tuckness (and implied by Grant), is to treat the question of voluntarism as having two different parts, grounds and content. On this view, Locke was indeed a voluntarist with respect to the question "why should we obey the law of nature?" Locke thought that reason, apart from the will of a superior, could only be advisory. With respect to content, divine reason and human reason must be sufficiently analogous that human beings can reason about what God likely wills. Locke takes it for granted that since God created us with reason in order to follow God's will, human reason and divine reason are sufficiently similar that natural law will not seem arbitrary to us.

Those interested in the contemporary relevance of Locke's political theory must confront its theological aspects. Straussians make Locke's theory relevant by claiming that the theological dimensions of his thought are primarily rhetorical; they are "cover" to keep him from being persecuted by the religious authorities of his day. Others, such as Dunn, take Locke to be of only limited relevance to contemporary politics precisely because so many of his arguments depend on religious assumptions that are no longer widely shared. More recently a number of authors, such as Simmons and Vernon, have tried to separate the foundations of Locke's argument from other aspects of it. Simmons, for example, argues that Locke's thought is over-determined, containing both religious and secular arguments. He claims that for Locke the fundamental law of nature is that "as much as possible mankind is to be preserved." At times, he claims, Locke presents this principle in rule-consequentialist terms: it is the principle we use to determine the more specific rights and duties that all have. At other times, Locke hints at a more Kantian justification that emphasizes the impropriety of treating our equals as if they were mere means to our ends. Waldron, in his most recent work on Locke, explores the opposite claim: that Locke's theology actually provides a more solid basis for his premise of political equality than do contemporary secular approaches that tend to simply assert equality. With respect to the specific content of natural law, Locke never provides a comprehensive statement of what it requires. In the Two Treatises, Locke frequently states that the fundamental law of nature is that as much as possible mankind is to be preserved. Simmons argues that in Two Treatises 2.6 Locke presents (1) a duty to preserve one's self, (2) a duty to preserve others when self-preservation does not conflict, (3) a duty not to take away the life of another, and (4) a duty not to act in a way that "tends to destroy" others. Libertarian interpreters of Locke tend to downplay duties of type 1 and 2. Locke presents a more extensive list in his earlier, and unpublished in his lifetime, Essays on the Law of Nature. Interestingly, Locke here includes praise and honour of the deity as required by natural law as well as what we might call good character qualities.

State of Nature

Locke's concept of the state of nature has been interpreted by commentators in a variety of ways. At first glance it seems quite simple. Locke writes "want [lack] of a common judge, with authority, puts all persons in a state of nature" and again, "Men living according to reason, without a common superior on earth, to judge between them, is properly the state of nature." Many commentators have taken this as Locke's definition, concluding that the state of nature exists wherever there is no legitimate political authority able to judge disputes and where people live according to the law of reason. On this account the state of nature is distinct from political society, where a legitimate government exists, and from a state of war where men fail to abide by the law of reason.

Simmons presents an important challenge to this view. Simmons points out that the above statement is worded as a sufficient rather than necessary condition. Two individuals might be able, in the state of nature, to authorize a third to settle disputes between them without leaving the state of nature, since the third party would not have, for example, the power to legislate for the public good. Simmons also claims that other interpretations often fail to account for the fact that there are some people who live in states with legitimate governments who are nonetheless in the state of nature: visiting aliens, children below the age of majority, and those with a "defect" of reason. He claims that the state of nature is a relational concept describing a particular set of moral relations that exist between particular people, rather than a description of a particular geographical territory. The state of nature is just the way of describing the moral rights and responsibilities that exist between people who have not consented to the adjudication of their disputes by the same legitimate government. The groups just mentioned either have not or cannot give consent, so they remain in the state of nature. Thus A may be in the state of nature with respect to B, but not with C.

Simmons' account stands in sharp contrast to that of Strauss. According to Strauss, Locke presents the state of nature as a factual description of what the earliest society is like, an account that when read closely reveals Locke's departure from Christian teachings. State of nature theories, he and his followers argue, are contrary to the Biblical account in Genesis and evidence that Locke's teaching is similar to that of Hobbes. As noted above, on the Straussian account Locke's apparently Christian statements are only a façade designed to conceal his essentially anti-Christian views. According to Simmons, since the state of nature is a moral account, it is compatible with a wide variety of social accounts without contradiction. If we know only that a group of people are in a state of nature, we know only the rights and responsibilities they have toward one another; we know nothing about whether they are rich or poor, peaceful or warlike. A complementary interpretation is made by John Dunn with respect to the relationship between Locke's state of nature and his Christian beliefs. Dunn claimed that Locke's state of nature is less an exercise in historical anthropology than a theological reflection on the condition of man. On Dunn's interpretation, Locke's state of nature thinking is an expression of his theological position, that man exists in a world created by God for God's purposes but that governments are created by men in order to further those purposes.

Locke's theory of the state of nature will thus be tied closely to his theory of natural law, since the latter defines the rights of persons and their status as free and equal persons. The stronger the grounds for accepting Locke's characterization of people as free, equal, and independent, the more helpful the state of nature becomes as a device for representing people. Still, it is important to remember that none of these interpretations claims that Locke's state of nature is only a thought experiment, in the way Kant and Rawls are normally thought to use the concept. Locke did not respond to the argument "where have there ever been people in such a state" by saying it did not matter since it was only a thought experiment. Instead, he argued that there are and have been people in the state of nature. (Two Treatises 2.14) It seems important to him that at least some governments have actually been formed in the way he suggests. How much it matters whether they have been or not will be discussed below under the topic of consent, since the central question is whether a good government can be legitimate even if it does not have the actual consent of the people who live under it; hypothetical contract and actual contract theories will tend to answer this question differently.

Consent, Political Obligation, and the Ends of Government

The most direct reading of Locke's political philosophy finds the concept of consent playing a central role. His analysis begins with individuals in a state of nature where they are not subject to a common legitimate authority with the power to legislate or adjudicate disputes. From this natural state of freedom and independence, Locke stresses individual consent as the mechanism by which political societies are created and individuals join those societies. While there are of course some general obligations and rights that all people have from the law of nature, special obligations come about only when we voluntarily undertake them. Locke clearly states that one can only become a full member of society by an act of express consent. The literature on Locke's theory of consent tends to focus on how Locke does or does not successfully answer the following objection: few people have actually consented to their governments so no, or almost no, governments are actually legitimate. This conclusion is problematic since it is clearly contrary to Locke's intention.

Locke's most obvious solution to this problem is his doctrine of tacit consent. Simply by walking along the highways of a country a person gives tacit consent to the government and agrees to obey it while living in its territory. This, Locke thinks, explains why resident aliens have an obligation to obey the laws of the state where they reside, though only while they live there. Inheriting property creates an even stronger bond, since the original owner of the property permanently put the property under the jurisdiction of the commonwealth. Children, when they accept the property of their parents, consent to the jurisdiction of the commonwealth over that property. There is debate over whether the inheritance of property should be regarded as tacit or express consent. On one interpretation, by accepting the property, Locke thinks a person becomes a full member of society, which implies that he must regard this as an act of express consent. Grant suggests that Locke's ideal would have been an explicit mechanism of society whereupon adults would give express consent and this would be a precondition of inheriting property. On the other interpretation, Locke recognized that people inheriting property did not in the process of doing so make any explicit declaration about their political obligation.

However this debate is resolved, there will be in any current or previously existing society many people who have never given express consent, and thus some version of tacit consent seems needed to explain how governments could still be legitimate. Simmons finds it difficult to see how merely walking on a street or inheriting land can be thought of as an example of a "deliberate, voluntary alienating of rights." It is one thing, he argues, for a person to consent by actions rather than words; it is quite another to claim a person has consented without being aware that they have done so. To require a person to leave behind all of their property and emigrate in order to avoid giving tacit consent is to create a situation where continued residence is not a free and voluntary choice. Simmons' approach is to agree with Locke that real consent is necessary for political obligation but disagree about whether most people in fact have given that kind of consent. Simmons claims that Locke's arguments push toward "philosophical anarchism," the position that most people do not have a moral obligation to obey the government, even though Locke himself would not have made this claim.

Hannah Pitkin takes a very different approach. She claims that the logic of Locke's argument makes consent far less important in practice than it might appear. Tacit consent is indeed a watering down of the concept of consent, but Locke can do this because the basic content of what governments are to be like is set by natural law and not by consent. If consent were truly foundational in Locke's scheme, we would discover the legitimate powers of any given government by finding out what contract the original founders signed. Pitkin, however, thinks that for Locke the form and powers of government are determined by natural law. What really matters, therefore, is not previous acts of consent but the quality of the present government, whether it corresponds to what natural law requires. Locke does not think, for example, that walking the streets or inheriting property in a tyrannical regime means we have consented to that regime. It is thus the quality of the government, not acts of actual consent, that determine whether a government is legitimate. Simmons objects to this interpretation, saying that it fails to account for the many places where Locke does indeed say a person acquires political obligations only by his own consent.

John Dunn takes a still different approach. He claims that it is anachronistic to read into Locke a modern conception of what counts as "consent." While modern theories do insist that consent is truly consent only if it is deliberate and voluntary, Locke's concept of consent was far more broad. For Locke, it was enough that people be "not unwilling." Voluntary acquiescence, on Dunn's interpretation, is all that is needed. As evidence Dunn can point to the fact that many of the instances of consent Locke uses, such as "consenting" to the use of money, make more sense on this broad interpretation. Simmons objects that this ignores the instances where Locke does talk about consent as a deliberate choice and that, in any case, it would only make Locke consistent at the price of making him unconvincing.

A related question has to do with the extent of our obligation once consent has been given. The interpretive school influenced by Strauss emphasizes the primacy of preservation. Since the duties of natural law apply only when our preservation is not threatened, then our obligations cease in cases where our preservation is directly threatened. This has important implications if we consider a solider who is being sent on a mission where death is extremely likely. Grant points out that Locke believes a solider who deserts from such a mission is justly sentenced to death. Grant takes Locke to be claiming not only that desertion laws are legitimate in the sense that they can be blamelessly enforced (something Hobbes would grant) but that they also imply a moral obligation on the part of the soldier to give up his life for the common good (something Hobbes would deny). According to Grant, Locke thinks that our acts of consent can in fact extend to cases where living up to our commitments will risk our lives.

The decision to enter political society is a permanent one for precisely this reason: the society will have to be defended and if people can revoke their consent to help protect it when attacked, the act of consent made when entering political society would be pointless since the political community would fail at the very point where it is most needed. People make a calculated decision when they enter society, and the risk of dying in combat is part of that calculation. Grant also thinks Locke recognizes a duty based on reciprocity since others risk their lives as well. Most of these approaches focus on Locke's doctrine of consent as a solution to the problem of political obligation. A different approach asks what role consent plays in determining, here and now, the legitimate ends that governments can pursue. One part of this debate is captured by the debate between Seliger and Kendall, the former viewing Locke as a constitutionalist and the latter viewing him as giving almost untrammeled power to majorities. On the former interpretation, a constitution is created by the consent of the people as part of the creation of the commonwealth. On the latter interpretation, the people create a legislature which rules by majority vote. A third view, advanced by Tuckness, holds that Locke was flexible at this point and gave people considerable flexibility in constitutional drafting.

A second part of the debate focuses on ends rather than institutions. Locke states in the *Two Treatises* that the power of the Government is limited to the public good. It is a power that hath "no other end but preservation" and therefore cannot justify killing, enslaving, or plundering the citizens.

Libertarians like Nozick read this as stating that governments exist only to protect people from infringements on their rights. An alternate interpretation, advanced in different ways by Tuckness, draws attention to the fact that in the following sentences the formulation of natural law that Locke focuses on is a positive one, that "as much as possible" mankind is to be preserved. On this second reading, government is limited to fulfilling the purposes of natural law, but these include positive goals as well as negative rights. On this view, the power to promote the common good extends to actions designed to increase population, improve the military, strengthen the economy and infrastructure, and so on, provided these steps are indirectly useful to the goal of preserving the society. This would explain why Locke, in the Letter, describes government promotion of "arms, riches, and multitude of citizens" as the proper remedy for the danger of foreign attack.

Toleration

In Locke's *Letter Concerning Toleration,* he develops several lines of arguments that are intended to establish the proper spheres for religion and politics. His central claims are that government should not use force to try to bring people to the true religion and that religious societies are voluntary organizations that have no right to use coercive power over their own members or those outside their group. One recurring line of argument that Locke uses is explicitly religious. Locke argues that neither the example of Jesus nor the teaching of the New Testament gives any indication that force is a proper way to bring people to salvation. He also frequently points out what he takes to be clear evidence of hypocrisy, namely that those who are so quick to persecute others for small differences in worship or doctrine are relatively unconcerned with much more obvious moral sins that pose an even greater threat to their eternal state.

In addition to these and similar religious arguments, Locke gives three reasons that are more philosophical in nature for barring governments from using force to encourage people to adopt religious beliefs. First, he argues that the care of men's souls has not been committed to the magistrate by either God or the consent of men. This argument resonates with the structure of argument used so often in the Two Treatises to establish the natural freedom and equality of mankind. There is no command in the Bible telling magistrates to bring people to the true faith and people could not consent to such a goal for government because it is not possible for people, at will, to believe what the magistrate tells them to believe. Their beliefs are a function of what they think is true, not what they will. Locke's second argument is that since the power of the government is only force, while true religion consists of genuine inward persuasion of the mind, force is incapable of bringing people to the true religion. Locke's third argument is that even if the magistrate could change people's minds, a situation where everyone accepted the magistrate's religion would not bring more people to the true religion. Many of the magistrates of the world believe religions that are false.

Locke's contemporary, Jonas Proast, responded by saying that Locke's three arguments really amount to just two, that true faith cannot be forced and that we have no more reason to think that we are right than anyone else has. Proast argued that force can be helpful in bringing people to the truth "indirectly, and at a distance." His idea was that although force cannot directly bring about a change of mind or heart, it can cause people to consider arguments that they would otherwise ignore or prevent them from hearing or reading things that would lead them astray. If force is indirectly useful in bringing people to the true faith, then Locke has not provided a persuasive argument. As for Locke's argument about the harm of a magistrate whose religion is false using force to promote it, Proast claimed that this was irrelevant since there is a morally relevant difference between affirming that the magistrate may promote the religion he thinks true and affirming that he may promote the religion that actually is true. Proast thought that unless one was a complete skeptic, one must believe that the reasons for one's own position are objectively better than those for other positions.

Jeremy Waldron (1993), in an influential article, restated the substance of Proast's objection for a contemporary audience. He argued that, leaving aside Locke's Christian arguments, his main position was that it was instrumentally irrational, from the perspective of the persecutor, to use force in matters of religion because force acts only on the will and belief is not something that we change at will. Waldron pointed out that this argument blocks only one particular reason for persecution, not all reasons. Thus it would not stop someone who used religious persecution for some end other than religious conversion, such as preserving the peace. Even in cases where persecution does have a religious goal, Waldron agrees with Proast that force may be indirectly effective in changing people's beliefs. Much of the current discussion about Locke's contribution to contemporary political philosophy in the area of toleration centers on whether Locke has a good reply to these objections from Proast and Waldron.

Some contemporary commentators try to rescue Locke's argument by redefining the religious goal that the magistrate is presumed to seek. Susan Mendus, for example, notes that successful brainwashing might cause a person to sincerely utter a set of beliefs, but that those beliefs might still not count as genuine. Beliefs induced by coercion might be similarly problematic. Paul Bou Habib argues that what Locke is really after is sincere inquiry and that Locke thinks inquiry undertaken only because of duress is necessarily insincere. These approaches thus try to save Locke's argument by showing that force really is incapable of bringing about the desired religious goal.

Other commentators focus on Locke's first argument about proper authority, and particularly on the idea that authorization must be by consent. David Wootton argues that even if force occasionally works at changing a person's belief, it does not work often enough to make it rational for persons to consent to the government exercising that power. A person who has good reason to think he will not change his beliefs even when persecuted has good reason to prevent the persecution scenario from ever happening. Richard Vernon argues that we want not only to hold right beliefs, but also to hold them for the right reasons. Since the balance of reasons rather than the balance of force should determine our beliefs, we would not consent to a system in which irrelevant reasons for belief might influence us.

Other commentators focus on the third argument, that the magistrate might be wrong. Here the question is whether Locke's argument is question begging or not. The two most promising lines of argument are the following. Wootton argues that there are very good reasons, from the standpoint of a given individual, for thinking that governments will be wrong about which religion is true. Governments are motivated by the quest for power, not truth, and are unlikely to be good guides in religious matters. Since there are so many different religions held by rulers, if only one is true then likely my own ruler's views are not true. Wootton thus takes Locke to be showing that it is irrational, from the perspective of the individual, to consent to government promotion of religion.

A different interpretation of the third argument is presented by Tuckness. He argues that the likelihood that the magistrate may be wrong generates a principle of toleration based on what is rational from the perspective of a legislator, not the perspective of an individual citizen. Drawing on Locke's later writings on toleration, he argues that Locke's theory of natural law assumes that God, as author of natural law, takes into account the fallibility of those magistrates who will carry out the commands of natural law.

If "use force to promote the true religion" were a command of natural law addressed to all magistrates, it would not promote the true religion in practice because so many magistrates wrongly believe that their religion is the true one. Tuckness claims that in Locke's later writings on toleration he moved away from arguments based on what it is instrumentally rational for an individual to consent to. Instead, he emphasized testing proposed principles based on whether they would still fulfill their goal if universally applied by fallible human beings.

Much of Locke's work is characterized by opposition to authoritarianism. This opposition is both on the level of the individual person and on the level of institutions such as government and church. For the individual, Locke wants each of us to use reason to search after truth rather than simply accept the opinion of authorities or be subject to superstition. He wants us to proportion assent to propositions to the evidence for them. On the level of institutions it becomes important to distinguish the legitimate from the illegitimate functions of institutions and to make the corresponding distinction for the uses of force by these institutions. The positive side of Locke's anti-authoritarianism is that he believes that using reason to try to grasp the truth, and determining the legitimate functions of institutions will optimize human flourishing for the individual and society both in respect to its material and spiritual welfare. This in turn, amounts to following natural law and the fulfillment of the divine purpose for humanity. Locke's monumental An Essay Concerning Human Understanding concerns itself with determining the limits of human understanding in respect to God, the self, natural kinds and artifacts, as well as a variety of different kinds of ideas. It thus tells us in some detail what one can legitimately claim to know and what one cannot. Locke also wrote a variety of important political, religious and educational works including the Two Treatises of Government, the Letters Concerning Toleration, The Reasonableness of Christianity and Some Thoughts Concerning Education.

Two Treatises of Government

The introduction of the work was written latter than the main text, and gave people the impression that the book was written in 1688 to justify the Glorious Revolution. We now know that the Two Treatises of Government were written during the Exclusion crisis and were probably intended to justify the general armed rising which the Country Party leaders were planning. It was a truly revolutionary work. Supposing that the Two Treatises may have been intended to explain and defend the revolutionary plot against Charles II and his brother, how does it do this?

The First Treatise of Government is a polemical work aimed at refuting the patriarchal version of the Divine Right of Kings doctrine put forth by Sir Robert Filmer. Locke singles out Filmer's contention that men are not "naturally free" as the key issue, for that is the "ground" or premise on which Filmer erects his argument for the claim that all "legitimate" government is "absolute monarchy."-kings being descended from the first man, Adam. Early in the First Treatise Locke denies that either scripture or reason supports Filmer's premise or arguments. In what follows, Locke minutely examines key Biblical passages.

The Second Treatise of Government provides Locke's positive theory of government-he explicitly says that he must do this "lest men fall into the dangerous belief that all government in the world is merely the product of force and violence." Locke's account involves several devices which were common in seventeenth and eighteenth century political philosophy-natural rights theory and the social contract. Natural rights are those rights which we are supposed to have as human beings before ever government comes into being. We might suppose, that like other animals, we have a natural right to struggle for our survival. Locke will argue that we have a right to the means to survive. When Locke comes to explain how government comes into being, he uses the idea that people agree that their condition in the state of nature is unsatisfactory, and so agree to transfer some of their rights to a central government, while retaining others. This is the theory of the social contract. There are many versions of natural rights theory and the social contract in seventeenth and eighteenth century European political philosophy, some conservative and some radical. Locke's version belongs on the radical side of the spectrum. These radical natural right theories influenced the ideologies of the American and French revolutions.

The Second Treatise of Government

Here is the subject matter of the various chapters of the Second Treatise:

- Chapter 1 Book I: the definition of Political power
- Chapter II-VII: the bases of government, states of nature, war, slavery, the nature of property
- Chapters VIII-XIV: the nature of political power and legitimate civil government

- Chapter XV: recapitulates the fundamental distinctions between paternal, political and despotic power.
- Chapter XVI-XVIII: elaborates the nature of illegitimate civil government. It specifies three forms of such illegitimacy: 1. an unjust foreign conquest, 2. internal usurpation of political rule and 3. tyrannical extension of power by those who were originally legitimately in power.
- Chapter XIX: gives the conditions under which legitimate revolution may occur.

Figuring out what the proper or legitimate role of civil government is would be a difficult task indeed if one were to examine the vast complexity of existing civil governments. How should one proceed? One strategy is to consider what life is like in the absence of civil government. Presumably this is a simpler state, one which may be easier to understand. Then one might see what role civil government ought to play. This is the strategy which Locke pursues, following Hobbes and others. So, in the first chapter of the Second Treatise Locke defines political power. Political power, then, I take to be a right of making laws with penalties of death, and consequently all less penalties, for the regulating and preserving of property, and of employing the force of the community, in the execution of such laws, and in the defence of the common-wealth from foreign injury; and all this only for the public good. In the second chapter of The Second Treatise Locke describes the state in which there is no government with real political power. This is the state of nature. It is sometimes assumed that the state of nature is a state in which there is no government at all. This is only partially true. It is possible to have in the state of nature either no government, illegitimate government, or legitimate government with less than full political power.

If we consider the state of nature before there was government, it is a state of political equality in which there is no natural superior or inferior. From this equality flows the obligation to mutual love and the duties that people owe one another, and the great maxims of justice and charity. Was there ever such a state? There has been considerable debate about this. Still, it is plain that both Hobbes and Locke would answer this question affirmatively. Whenever people have not agreed to establish a common political authority, they remain in the state of nature. It's like saying that people are in the state of being naturally single until they are married. Locke clearly thinks one can find the state of nature in his time at least in the inland vacant parts of America and in the relations between different peoples. Perhaps the historical development of states also went though the stages of a state of nature. An alternative possibility is that the state of nature is not a real historical state, but rather a theoretical construct, intended to help determine the proper function of government. If one rejects the historicity of states of nature, one may still find them a useful analytical device. For Locke, it is very likely both.

The Social Contract Theory

Just as natural rights and natural law theory had a florescence in the 17th and 18th century, so did the social contract theory. Why is Locke a social contract theorist? Is it merely that this was one prevailing way of thinking about government at the time which Locke blindly adopted? I think the answer is that there is something about Locke's project which pushes him strongly in the direction of the social contract. One might hold that governments were originally instituted by force, and that no agreement was involved. Were Locke to adopt this view, he would be forced to go back on many of the things which are at the heart of his project in the Second Treatise. Remember that The Second Treatise provides Locke's positive theory of government, and that he explicitly says that he must do this "lest men fall into the dangerous belief that "all government in the world is merely the product of force and violence."

So, while Locke might admit that some governments come about through force or violence, he would be destroying the most central and vital distinction, that between legitimate and illegitimate civil government, if he admitted that legitimate civil government can come about in this way. So, for Locke, legitimate civil government is instituted by the explicit consent of those governed. (See the section on Consent, Political Obligation, and the Ends of Government in the entry on Locke's Political Philosophy.) Those who make this agreement transfer to the civil government their right of executing the law of nature and judging their own case. These are the powers which they give to the central government, and this is what makes the justice system of civil governments a legitimate function of such governments. Ruth Grant has persuasively argued that the establishment of civil government is in effect a two step process. Universal consent is necessary to form a political community. Consent to join a community once given is binding and cannot be withdrawn. This makes political communities stable. Grant writes: "Having established that the membership in a community entails the obligation to abide by the will of the community, the question remains: Who rules?" The answer to this question is determined by majority rule. The point is that universal consent is necessary to establish a political community, majority consent to answer the question who is to rule such a community. Universal consent and majority consent are thus different in kind, not just in degree. Grant writes:

> Locke's argument for the right of the majority is the theoretical ground for the distinction between duty to society and duty to government, the distinction that permits an argument for resistance without anarchy. When the designated government dissolves, men remain obligated to society acting through majority rule.

It is entirely possible for the majority to confer the rule of the community on a king and his heirs, or a group of oligarchs or on a democratic assembly. Thus, the social contract is not inextricably linked to democracy. Still, a government of any kind must perform the legitimate function of a civil government.

The Function of Civil Government

Locke is now in a position to explain the function of a legitimate civil government and distinguish it from illegitimate civil government. The aim of such a legitimate civil government is to preserve, so far as possible, the rights to life, liberty, health and property of its citizens, and to prosecute and punish those of its citizens who violate the rights of others others and to pursue the public good even where this may conflict with the rights of individuals. In doing this it provides something unavailable in the state of nature, an impartial judge to determine the severity of the crime, and to set a punishment proportionate to the crime. This is one of the main reasons why civil society is an improvement on the state of nature. An illegitimate civil government will fail to protect the rights to life, liberty, health and property of its subjects, and in the worst cases, such an illegitimate government will claim to be able to violate the rights of its subjects, that is it will claim to have despotic power over its subjects. Since Locke is arguing against the position of Sir Robert Filmer who held that patriarchal power and political power are the same, and that in effect these amount to despotic power, Locke is at pains to distinguish these three forms of power, and to show that they are not equivalent.

Thus at the beginning of Chapter XV Of Paternal, Political and Despotic power considered together he writes: "THOUGH I have had occasion to speak of these before, yet the great mistakes of late about government, having as I suppose arisen from confounding these distinct powers one with another, it may not be amiss, to consider them together." Chapters VI and VII give Locke's account of paternal and political power respectively. Paternal power is limited. It lasts only through the minority of children, and has other limitations. Political power, derived as it is from the transfer of the power of individuals to enforce the law of nature, has with it the right to kill in the interest of preserving the rights of the citizens or otherwise supporting the public good. Despotic power, by contrast, implies the right to take the life, liberty, health and at least some of the property of any person subject to such a power.

Rebellion and Regicide

At the end of the *Second Treatise* we learn about the nature of illegitimate civil governments and the conditions under which rebellion and regicide are legitimate and appropriate. As noted above, scholars now hold that the book was written during the Exclusion crisis, and may have been written to justify a general insurrection and the assassination of the king of England and his brother. The argument for legitimate revolution follows from making the distinction between legitimate and illegitimate civil government. A legitimate civil government seeks to preserve the life, health, liberty and property of its subjects, insofar as this is compatible with the public good. Because it does this it deserves obedience. An illegitimate civil government seeks to systematically violate the natural rights of its subjects. It seeks to make them illegitimate slaves. Because an illegitimate civil government does this, it puts itself in a state of nature and a state of war with its subjects. The magistrate or king of such a state violates the law of nature and so makes himself into a dangerous beast of prey who operates on the principle that might makes right, or that the strongest carries it. In such circumstances, rebellion is legitimate as is the killing of such a dangerous beast of prey. Thus Locke justifies rebellion and regicide (regarded by many during this period as the most heinous of crimes) under certain circumstances. Presumably this was the justification that was going to be offered for the killing of the King of England and his brother had the Rye House Plot succeeded.

The Political Philosophy of John Locke

John Locke (1632-1704) presents an intriguing figure in the history of political philosophy whose brilliance of exposition and breadth of scholarly activity remains profoundly influential.

Locke proposed a radical conception of political philosophy deduced from the principle of self-ownership and the corollary right to own property, which in turn is based on his famous claim that a man earns ownership over a resource when he mixes his labour with it. Government, he argued, should be limited to securing the life and property of its citizens, and is only necessary because in an ideal, anarchic state of nature, various problems arise that would make life more insecure than under the protection of a minimal state. Locke is also renown for his writings on toleration in which he espoused the right to freedom of conscience and religion (except when religion was deemed intolerant!), and for his cogent criticism of hereditary monarchy and patriarchalism. After his death, his mature political philosophy leant support to the British Whig party and its principles, to the Age of Enlightenment, and to the development of the separation of the State and Church in the American Constitution as well as to the rise of human rights theories in the Twentieth Century. However, a closer study of any philosopher reveals aspects and depths that introductory caricatures (including this one) cannot portray, and while such articles seemingly present a completed sketch of all that can ever be known of a great thinker, it must always be remembered that a great thinker is rarely captured in a few pages or paragraphs by a lesser one, or one that approaches him with particular philosophical interest or bias: the reader, once contented with the glosses provided here, should always return to and scrutinise Locke in the original-just as an academic exposition of Beethoven's Eroica symphony will always be a sallow reflection of the actual music.

This article summarises the general drift of Locke's political thinking, leaving the other IEP article on Locke to examine his general philosophy and his theory of knowledge. The article touches on his biography as it relates to the development of his political thought, and it also provides an analysis of some of the issues that his philosophy raises-especially with regards to the Two Treatises of Government. Locke is rightly famous for his Treatises, yet during his life he repudiated his authorship, although he subtly recommended them as essential reading in letters and thoughts on reading for gentlemen. The Treatises swiftly became a classic in political philosophy, and its popularity has remained undiminished since his time: the 'John Locke academic industry' is vibrant and broad with an academic journal (John Locke Studies) and books regularly coming out dealing with his philosophy. After the English civil war, politics was dominated by the question of the "norman yoke" (i.e. the status quo), and what civil institutions should be like. Locke was a contemporary of many levellers, who fought for universal franchise and, to varying degrees, for the levelling of property rights and distribution, from those who called for universal rights to property, to radicals who claimed for the abolition of private property and the instigation of communal living. Opponents (largely conservative) to the levellers charged them with undermining the institution of property itself, and framed the debate in terms of property and its relation to the state. At the same time, the English were one of many nations exploring the Americas, and trying to claim rights to the land there in the footsteps of the puritans. Locke was one such property owner, and so his project can be understood both as an attack on the conservative elements of the contemporary debate, and as a defense of property as a socially necessary institution. In stating the case for property, the levellers and their sympathisers made reference to the state of nature, and used theological arguments to suggest both that property is just and that the conservative landlords' use of land was fundamentally unjust.

Locke's writing was also a reaction against Sir Robert Filmer, and to a lesser extent Thomas Hobbes and other monarchists, who claimed a divine absolute right to power on the behalf of the monarchy. As Laslett has pointed out, Filmer's treatise Patriacha traced the lineage of kings back to Adam in the bible, and blamed Adam's fall from Eden on his attempting to exercise his personal liberty against the wishes of an absolute God. So one could say that Locke was forced to provide a theological basis for his arguments, irrespective of his own beliefs (though it seems more than likely that Locke did believe in the theological basis anyway).

God, and the Law of Nature

Locke's logical foundation and ultimate justification is God, who, according to Locke's interpretation of the Bible, gave mankind collectively the earth, and whom all men are obliged to obey. His method is the application of reason, to find the institutions and social/political norms that will best promote the survival of all men. Since God created us, we are all God's property. To Locke, this means that our first responsibility is self-preservation, since to allow ourselves to come to harm would be failing to uphold our obligation to God. We must also not damage others, nor allow them to come to harm else it conflicts with our self-preservation, since that is also damaging God's property.

Stewardship of the earth and of other men is therefore implied, although our first duty is always to ourselves, and our duty to others only holds us insofar as they must exist. Locke's implicit logic here is that with property we care only that it continues to exist, which is an odd assumption, since one could easily extend Locke's basis for stewardship to say that God would want his possessions kept in good condition, and that we therefore have a further responsibility to ensure all people enjoy a certain level of prosperity and happiness.

Locke begins with the state of nature, by which he means the state of affairs prior to the formation of a political state, and where there are no requirements of positive law, only our duties to God. In the state of nature, Locke asserts, we also have the divine right to exercise our gift of reason to decide upon and impose morality. We therefore have the right to punish wrongdoers to return them and God's property as a whole from an immoral to a moral state of affairs, and to prevent further similarly immoral acts. In this, Locke allows the right to punishment to go beyond the right to self-preservation, to include the preservation of a particular social order throughout a political community, rather like Hobbes.

But though he allows for the right of punishment, Locke says that it must be decided upon by an impartial authority, such that the right to self-preservation is respected, and to impose morality isotropically throughout society, without problems of self-interest biasing decisions. Also, if we were to allow arbitrary power, we wouldn't be able to perform our duty to God; we would neutralise the problem of others threatening our right to self-preservation, but in doing so submit the right to an absolute dictator. So Locke suggests that any state of affairs more dangerous than the state of nature is immoral. In other words, to perform our duties to God, we must ensure that political institutions make life less dangerous, and more conducive to the preservation of all human lives, than the state of nature. The only way to guarantee this is therefore to have a contractual handover of authority to a government, one to which all would consent, and which violates nobody's natural rights.

The End of Locke's Life (1689-1704)

After his return from exile, Locke published *An Essay Concerning Human Understanding* and *The Two Treatises of Government*. In addition, Popple's translation of Locke's A Letter Concerning Toleration was also published. It is worth noting that the *Two Treatises* and the *Letter Concerning Toleration* were published anonymously. Locke took up residence in the country at Oates in Essex, the home of Sir Francis and Lady Masham (Damaris Cudworth). Locke had met Damaris Cudworth in 1682 and became involved intellectually and romantically with her. She was the daughter of Ralph Cudworth, the Cambridge Platonist, and a philosopher in her own right. After Locke went into exile in Holland in 1683, she married Sir Francis Masham. Locke and Lady Masham remained good friends and intellectual companions to the end of Locke's life. During the remaining years of his life Locke oversaw four more editions of the Essay and engaged in controversies over the Essay most notably in a series of published letters with Edward Stillingfleet, Bishop of Worcester. In a similar way, Locke defended the Letter Concerning Toleration against a series of attacks. He wrote *The Reasonableness of Christianity* and *Some Thoughts on Education* during this period as well.

Nor was Locke finished with public affairs. In 1696 the Board of Trade was revived. Locke played an important part in its revival and served as the most influential member on it until 1700. The Board of Trade was, in Peter Laslett's phrase "... the body which administered the United States before the American revolution." (Laslett in Yolton 1990 p. 127) The board was, in fact, concerned with a wide range of issues, from the Irish wool trade and the suppression of piracy, to the governance of the colonies and the treatment of the poor in England. During these last eight years of his life, Locke was asthmatic, and he suffered so much from it that he could only bear the smoke of London during the four warmer months of the year. Locke plainly engaged in the activities of the Board out of a strong sense of patriotic duty. After his retirement from the Board of Trade in 1700, Locke remained in retirement at Oates until his death on Sunday 28 October 1704.

Locke has an atomic or perhaps more accurately a corpuscular theory of ideas. There is, that is to say, an analogy between the way atoms or corpuscles combine into complexes to form physical objects and the way ideas combine. Ideas are either simple or complex. We cannot create simple ideas, we can only get them from experience. In this respect the mind is passive. Once the mind has a store of simple ideas, it can combine them into complex ideas of a variety of kinds. In this respect the mind is active. Thus, Locke subscribes to a version of the empiricist axiom that there is nothing in the intellect that was not previously in the senses- where the senses are broadened to include reflection. Book III deals with the nature of language, its connections with ideas and its role in knowledge. Book IV, the culmination of the previous reflections, explains the nature and limits of knowledge, probability, and the relation of reason and faith. Let us now consider the Essay in some detail.

6

Jean-Jacques Rousseau

Jean-Jacques Rousseau, (June 28, 1712 – July 2, 1778) was a major philosopher, literary figure, and composer of the Enlightenment whose political philosophy influenced the French Revolution and the development of liberal, conservative and socialist theory. With his *Confessions*, *Reveries of a Solitary Walker* and other writings, he invented modern autobiography and encouraged a new focus on the building of subjectivity that bore fruit in the work of thinkers as diverse as Hegel and Freud. His novel *Julie, ou la nouvelle Heloïse* was one of the best-selling fictional works of the eighteenth century and was important to the development of romanticism. Rousseau made important contributions to music as a theorist and a composer. He was buried in Paris Pantheon in 1794.

Biography

Rousseau was born in Geneva (an associated member of the Old Confederation, known today as the Helvetian Confederation or Switzerland) and throughout his life described himself as a citizen of Geneva. Nine days after his birth, his mother Suzanne Bernard Rousseau, died of birth complications. To avoid imprisonment, his father Isaac, a failed watchmaker, abandoned him in 1722. His childhood education consisted solely of reading Plutarch's *Lives* and Calvinist sermons. He often read in a public garden – which he later described as the most serene part of growing up.

According to Rousseau's account in Book I of the *Confessions*, his experience of corporal punishment at the hands of the pastor's sister was important in the formation of his sexuality. So important in fact that he admits in a description of his masochism of deliberately being disobedient in order to provoke punishment. Like most submissive sexual fetishists, he was also an exhibitionist. He prowled the backstreets of Turin, and exposed himself to unsuspecting women. Of this he admitted enjoying a "foolish pleasure" of displaying himself before their eyes.

After several years of apprenticeship to a notary and then an engraver, Rousseau left Geneva at age 16 on March 14, 1728. He then met a French Catholic baroness named Françoise-Louise de Warens. She was thirteen years older and later became his lover. Rousseau's sex life was largely unsatisfying due to suffering from a birth defect called hypospadias. The Baroness provided Rousseau the education of a nobleman by sending him to Catholic school. Apart from studying Aristotle, Rousseau also became familiar with Latin and the dramatic arts.

In order to present the Academie des Sciences with a new system of numbered musical notation, he moved to Paris in 1742. His system is based on a single line displaying numbers representing intervals between notes and dots and commas indicating rhythmic values. The system was intended to be compatible with typography. Believing the system was impractical and unoriginal, the Academy rejected it. However, in some parts of the world, a version of the system remains in use.

He was secretary to the French ambassador in Venice from 1743 to 1744, whose republican government Rousseau often referred to in his later political work. After eleven months in this position, he was dismissed and fled to Paris to avoid prosecution by the Venetian Senate. There he befriended and lived with Therese Levasseur, a semi-literate seamstress who, according to Rousseau, bore him five children, though this number may not be accurate. Soon after birth, the children were deposited at an orphanage. As the mortality rate for orphanage children was very high, most of them likely perished. When Rousseau became known as a theorist of education and child-rearing, his abandonment of his children was used by enemies, including Voltaire, to attack him. In his defense, Rousseau explained he would have been a poor father and that the children would have a better life at the foundling home. While in Paris, he became friends with French philosopher Diderot and beginning with some articles on music in 1749, he contributed several articles to the latter's *Encyclopedie*. His most noted work was an article on political economy written in 1755. Soon after, his friendship with Diderot and the Encyclopedists became strained. Diderot later described Rousseau as being,"deceitful, vain as Satan, ungrateful, cruel, hypocritical, and full of malice."

In 1749, as Rousseau was walking to visit Diderot in a Vincennes prison, he read an essay competition entry sponsored by the Academie de Dijon, named the *Mercure de France*. The work asked whether the development of the arts and sciences had been morally beneficial. Rousseau said this question caused him to immediately perceive the principle of the natural goodness of humanity on which all his later philosophical works were based. He answered the competition question in the negative, in his 1750 "Discourse on the Arts and Sciences", which won him first prize and gained him significant fame.

He continued his interest in music and his opera Le Devin du Village was performed for King Louis XV in 1752. The same year, the visit of a troupe of Italian musicians to Paris, and their performance of Giovanni Battista Pergolesi's La Serva Padrona, prompted the Querelle des Bouffons, which pitted protagonists of French music against supporters of the Italian style. Rousseau was an enthusiastic supporter of the Italians against Jean-Philippe Rameau and others, making an important contribution with his *Letter on French Music.*

Rousseau returned to Geneva where he reconverted to Calvinism and regained his official Genevan citizenship in 1754. In 1755, Rousseau completed his second major work, the *Discourse on the origin and basis of inequality among men* (the Discourse on Inequality). This caused him to gradually become estranged from his former friends such as Diderot and Grimm and from benefactors such as Madame d'Epinay. He pursued an important but unconsummated romantic attachment with Sophie d'Houdetot. Following his break with the Encyclopedists, he enjoyed the support and patronage of one of the wealthiest nobles in France, Duc de Luxembourg.

In 1761, Rousseau published the successful romantic novel *Julie, ou la nouvelle Heloïse* (*The New Heloise*). In 1762, he published two major books, *Du Contrat Social, Principes du droit politique* (in English, literally *Of the Social Contract, Principles of Political Right*) in April and then *Emile, or On Education* in May. The books criticized religion and were banned in France and Geneva. Rousseau was forced to flee arrest and made stops in Bern and Motiers in Switzerland, where he enjoyed the protection of Frederick, the Great of Prussia and his local representative, Lord Keith. While in Motiers, Rousseau wrote the Constitutional Project for Corsica (*Project de Constitution pour la Corse*).

His house in Motiers was stoned on the night of September 6, 1765 – he took refuge with the philosopher David Hume in Great Britain. Isolated at Wootton on the borders of Derbyshire and Staffordshire, Rousseau suffered a serious decline in his mental health and began to experience paranoid fantasies about plots against him involving Hume and others. Rousseau's letter to Hume, in which he articulates the perceived misconduct, sparked an exchange which was published in and received with great interest in contemporary Paris.

While he was not allowed to return to France before 1770, Rousseau returned under the name "Renou," in 1767. In 1768 he went through a legally invalid marriage to Therese, and in 1770 he returned to Paris. As a condition of his return, he was not allowed to publish any books, but after completing his *Confessions*, Rousseau began private readings in 1771. At the request of Madame d'Epinay the police ordered him to stop, and the *Confessions* was only partially published in 1782, four years after his death. All his subsequent works were only to appear posthumously.

In 1772, he was invited to present recommendations for a new constitution for the Polish-Lithuanian Commonwealth, resulting in the *Considerations on the Government of Poland*, which was to be his last major political work. In 1776 he completed *Dialogues: Rousseau Judge of Jean-Jacques* and began work on the *Reveries of the Solitary Walker*. In order to support himself, he returned to copying music. Rousseau's final years were largely spent in deliberate withdrawal, however he did respond favourably to an approach from the composer Gluck, whom he met in 1774. One of Rousseau's last pieces of writing was a critical yet enthusiastic analysis of Gluck's opera Alceste. While taking a morning walk on the estate of the Marquis de Giradin at Ermenonville (28 miles northeast of Paris), Rousseau suffered a hemorrhage and died on July 2, 1778.

Rousseau was initially buried on the Ile des Peupliers. His remains were moved to the Pantheon in Paris in 1794, sixteen years after his death and located directly across from those of his contemporary Voltaire. The tomb was designed to resemble a rustic temple, to recall Rousseau's theories of nature. In 1834, the Genevan government reluctantly erected a statue in his honour on the tiny Ile Rousseau in Lake Geneva. In 2002, the Espace Rousseau was established at 40 Grand-Rue, Geneva, Rousseau's birthplace.

Philosophy

Theory of Natural Man

Rousseau saw a fundamental divide between society and human nature. Rousseau believed that man was good when in the state of nature (the state of all other animals, and the condition humankind was in before the creation of civilization and society), but is corrupted by society. This idea has often led to attributing the idea of the noble savage to Rousseau, an expression first used by John Dryden in *The Conquest of Granada* (1672). Rousseau, however, never used the expression himself and it does not adequately render his idea of the natural goodness of humanity. Rousseau's idea of natural goodness is complex and easy to misunderstand. Contrary to what might be suggested by a casual reading, the idea does not imply that humans in the state of nature act morally; in fact, terms such as 'justice' or 'wickedness' are simply inapplicable to pre-political society as Rousseau understands it. Humans there may act with all of the ferocity of an animal. They are good because they are self-sufficient and thus not subject to the vices of political society. He viewed society as artificial and held that the development of society, especially the growth of social interdependence, has been inimical to the well-being of human beings.

In Rousseau's philosophy, society's negative influence on men centres on its transformation of *amour de soi*, a positive self-love, into *amour-propre*, or pride. *Amour de soi* represents the instinctive human desire for self-preservation, combined with the human power of reason. In contrast, *amour-propre* is artificial and forces man to compare himself to others, thus creating unwarranted fear and allowing men to take pleasure in the pain or weakness of others. Rousseau was not the first to make this distinction; it had been invoked by, among others, Vauvenargues.

In "Discourse on the Arts and Sciences" Rousseau argued that the arts and sciences had not been beneficial to humankind because they were not human needs, but rather a result of pride and vanity. Moreover, the opportunities they created for idleness and luxury contributed to the corruption of man. He proposed that the progress of knowledge had made governments more powerful and had crushed individual liberty. He concluded that material progress had actually undermined the possibility of true friendship by replacing it with jealousy, fear and suspicion.

His subsequent *Discourse on Inequality* tracked the progress and degeneration of mankind from a primitive state of nature to modern society. He suggested that the earliest human beings were solitary and differentiated from animals by their capacity for free will and their perfectibility. He also argued that these primitive humans were possessed of a basic drive to care for themselves and a natural disposition to compassion or pity.

As humans were forced to associate together more closely by the pressure of population growth, they underwent a psychological transformation and came to value the good opinion of others as an essential component of their own well-being. Rousseau associated this new self-awareness with a golden age of human flourishing. However, the development of agriculture, metallurgy, private property, and the division of labour led to humans becoming increasingly dependent on one another, and led to inequality. The resulting state of conflict led Rousseau to suggest that the first state was invented as a kind of social contract made at the suggestion of the rich and powerful. This original contract was deeply flawed as the wealthiest and most powerful members of society tricked the general population, and thus instituted inequality as a fundamental feature of human society. Rousseau's own conception of the social contract can be understood as an alternative to this *fraudulent form of association. At the end of the Discourse on*

Inequality, Rousseau explains how the desire to have value in the eyes of others, which originated in the golden age, comes to undermine personal integrity and authenticity in a society marked by interdependence, hierarchy, and inequality.

Political Theory

"The Social Contract"

Perhaps Rousseau's most important work is *The Social Contract,* which outlines the basis for a legitimate political order within a framework of classical republicanism. Published in 1762, it became one of the most influential works of political philosophy in the Western tradition. It developed some of the ideas mentioned in an earlier work, the article *Economie Politique,* featured in Diderot's *Encyclopedie.* The treatise begins with the dramatic opening lines, "Man is born free, and everywhere he is in chains. One man thinks himself the master of others, but remains more of a slave than they." Rousseau claimed that the state of nature was a primitive condition without law or morality, which human beings left for the benefits and necessity of cooperation.

As society developed, division of labour and private property required the human race to adopt institutions of law. In the degenerate phase of society, man is prone to be in frequent competition with his fellow men while at the same time becoming increasingly dependent on them. This double pressure threatens both his survival and his freedom. According to Rousseau, by joining together into civil society through the social contract and abandoning their claims of natural right, individuals can both preserve themselves and remain free. This is because submission to the authority of the general will of the people as a whole guarantees individuals against being subordinated to the wills of others and also ensures that they obey themselves because they are, collectively, the authors of the law.

While Rousseau argues that sovereignty should be in the hands of the people, he also makes a sharp distinction between sovereignty and government. The government is charged with implementing and enforcing the general will and is composed of a smaller group of citizens, known as magistrates. Rousseau was bitterly opposed to the idea that the people should exercise sovereignty via a representative assembly. Rather, they should make the laws directly. It was argued that this would prevent Rousseau's ideal state from being realized in a large society, such as France was at the time. Much of the subsequent controversy about Rousseau's work has hinged on disagreements concerning his claims that citizens constrained to obey the general will are thereby rendered free.

Education

Rousseau set out his views on education in *Emile,* a semi-fictitious work detailing the growth of a young boy of that name, presided over by Rousseau himself. He brings him up in the countryside, where, he believes, humans are most naturally suited, rather than in a city, where we only learn bad habits, both physical and intellectual. The aim of education, Rousseau says, is to learn how to live righteously. This is accomplished by following a guardian who can guide his pupil through various contrived learning experiences.

The growth of a child is divided into three sections, first to the age of about 12, when calculating and complex thinking is not possible, and children, according to his deepest conviction, live like animals. Second, from 12 to about 16, when reason starts to develop, and finally from the age of 16 onwards, when the child develops into an adult. During this stage, the young adult should learn a skill, such as carpentry. This trade is offered because it requires creativity and thought, but would not compromise one's morals. It is at this age that Emile finds a young woman to complement him. The book is based on Rousseau's ideals of healthy living. The boy must work out how to follow his social instincts and be protected from the vices of urban individualism and self-consciousness.

Rousseau's account of the education of Emile is, however, not an account of education of a gender-neutral "child." The education he proposes for Sophie, the young woman Emile is destined to marry, is importantly different to that of Emile. Sophie (as a representative of ideal womanhood) is educated to be governed (by her husband) while Emile (as a representative of the ideal man) is educated to be self-governing.

This is not an accidental feature of Rousseau's educational and political philosophy; it is essential to his account of the distinction between private, personal relations and the public world of political relations. The private sphere as Rousseau imagines it depends on the (naturalized) subordination of women in order for both it and the public political sphere (upon which it depends) to function as Rousseau imagines it could and should.

The education proposed in *Emile* has been criticized for being impractical, and the topic itself (the education of children) has led the text to be ignored by many studying Rousseau's more "political" works. However, of particular interest to anyone interested in Rousseau's intentions in Emile is a letter he wrote to his friend Cramer on October 13, 1764. In the letter, Rousseau answers the criticism of impracticability: "You say quite correctly that it is impossible to produce an Emile. But I cannot believe that you take the book that carries this name for a true treatise on education. It is rather a philosophical work on this principle advanced by the author in other writings that *man is naturally good*".

Religion

Rousseau was most controversial in his own time for his views on religion. His view that man is good by nature conflicts with the doctrine of original sin and his theology of nature expounded by the Savoyard Vicar in *Emile* led to the condemnation of the book *in both Calvinist Geneva and Catholic Paris. In the Social Contract* he claims that true followers of Jesus would not make good citizens. This was one of the reasons for the book's condemnation in Geneva. Rousseau attempted to defend himself against critics of his religious views in his Letter to Christophe de Beaumont, the Archbishop of Paris.

Legacy

At the time of the French Revolution, Rousseau's ideas were influential. Writers such as Benjamin Constant and Hegel sought to blame the excesses of the Revolution's Reign of Terror on Rousseau, but since popular sovereignty was exercised through representatives rather than directly, it cannot be said the Revolution was an implementation of Rousseau's ideas. The Declaration of the

Rights of Man, a result of the Revolution, has its philosophical foundation in the assumption that humans are born with inherent and inalienable rights, a notion Rousseau rejects.

Rousseau's ideas about education have profoundly influenced modern educational theory. In *Emile* he differentiates between healthy and "useless" crippled children. Only a healthy child can be the rewarding object of any educational work. John Darling's 1994 book *Child-Centred Education and its Critics* argues that the history of modern educational theory is a series of footnotes to Rousseau.

In his main writings, Rousseau identifies nature with the primitive state of savage man. Later he took nature to mean the spontaneity of the process by which man builds his egocentric, instinct based character and his little world. Nature thus signifies interiority and integrity, as opposed to that imprisonment and enslavement which society imposes in the name of progressive emancipation from cold-hearted brutality.

Hence, to go back to nature means to restore to man the forces of this natural process, to place him outside every oppressing bond of society and the prejudices of civilization. It is this idea that made his thought particularly important in Romanticism, though Rousseau himself is sometimes regarded as a figure of The Enlightenment. Despite some similarities in thought, there is little evidence that Rousseau had an impact on Thomas Jefferson and, indeed, he seems to have had little impact on 18th century political thought in the United States, which was dominated by Republicanism and Liberalism. However he did have some influence on several later Transcendentalists such as theologian William Ellery Channing and philosopher Henry David Thoreau.

The Discourses

Discourse on the Origin of Inequality

The Second Discourse, like the first, was a response to a question put forth by the academy of Dijon: "What is the origin of inequality among men; and is it authorized by the natural law?" Rousseau's response to this question, the Discourse on the Origin of Inequality, is significantly different from the *First Discourse* for several reasons. First, in terms of the academy's response, the *Second Discourse* was not nearly as well received. It exceeded the desired length, it was four times the length of the first, and made very bold philosophical claims; unlike the *First Discourse*, it did not win the prize.

However, as Rousseau was now a well-known and respected author, he was able to have it published independently. Secondly, if the *First Discourse* is indicative of Rousseau as a "counter-Enlightenment" thinker, the Second Discourse, by contrast, can rightly be considered to be representative of Enlightenment thought. This is primarily because Rousseau, like Hobbes, attacks the classical notion of human beings as naturally social. Finally, in terms of its influence, the *Second Discourse* is now much more widely read, and is more representative of Rousseau's general philosophical outlook. In the Confessions, Rousseau writes that he himself sees the Second Discourse as far superior to the first.

The Discourse on the Origin of Inequality is divided into four main parts: a dedication to the Republic of Geneva, a short preface, a first part, and a second part. The scope of Rousseau's project is not significantly different from that of Hobbes in the Leviathan or Locke in the Second Treatise on Government. Like them, Rousseau understands society to be an invention, and he attempts to explain the nature of human beings by stripping them of all of the accidental qualities brought about by socialization. Thus, understanding human nature amounts to understanding what humans are like in a pure state of nature. This is in stark contrast to the classical view, most notably that of Aristotle, which claims that the state of civil society is the natural human state.

Like Hobbes and Locke, however, it is doubtful that Rousseau meant his readers to understand the pure state of nature that he describes in the Second Discourse as a literal historical account. In its opening, he says that it must be denied that men were ever in the pure state of nature, citing revelation as a source which tells us that God directly endowed the first man with understanding (a capacity that he will later say is completely undeveloped in natural man). However, it seems in other parts of the Second Discourse that Rousseau is positing an actual historical account. Some of the stages in the progression from nature to civil society, Rousseau will argue, are empirically observable in so-called primitive tribes. And so the precise historicity with which one ought to regard Rousseau's state of nature is the matter of some debate.

Part one is Rousseau's description of human beings in the pure state of nature, uncorrupted by civilization and the socialization process. And although this way of examining human nature is consistent with other modern thinkers, Rousseau's picture of "man in his natural state," is radically different. Hobbes describes each human in the state of nature as being in a constant state of war against all others; hence life in the state of nature is solitary, poor, nasty, brutish, and short. But Rousseau argues that previous accounts such as Hobbes' have all failed to actually depict humans in the true state of nature. Instead, they have taken civilized human beings and simply removed laws, government, and technology. For humans to be in a constant state of war with one another, they would need to have complex thought processes involving notions of property, calculations about the future, immediate recognition of all other humans as potential threats, and possibly even minimal language skills. These faculties, according to Rousseau, are not natural, but rather, they develop historically. In contrast to Hobbes, Rousseau describes natural man as isolated, timid, peaceful, mute, and without the foresight to worry about what the future will bring.

Purely natural human beings are fundamentally different from the egoistic Hobbesian view in another sense as well. Rousseau acknowledges that self-preservation is one principle of motivation for human actions, but unlike Hobbes, it is not the only principle. If it were, Rousseau claims that humans would be nothing more than monsters. Therefore, Rousseau concludes that self-preservation, or more generally self-interest, is only one of two principles of the human soul. The second principle is pity; it is "an innate repugnance to see his fellow suffer." It may seem that Rousseau's depiction of natural human beings is one that makes them no different from other animals. However, Rousseau says that unlike all other creatures, humans are free agents. They have reason, although in the state of nature it is not yet developed. But it is this faculty that makes the long transition from the state of nature to the state of civilized society possible. He claims that if one examines any other species over the course of a thousand years, they will not have advanced significantly. Humans can develop when circumstances arise that trigger the use of reason. Rousseau's praise of humans in the state of nature is perhaps one of the most misunderstood ideas in his philosophy. Although the human being is naturally good and the "noble savage" is free from the vices that plague humans in civil society, Rousseau is not simply saying that humans in nature are good and humans in civil society are bad. Furthermore, he is not advocating a return to the state of nature, though some commentators, even his contemporaries such as Voltaire, have attributed such a view to him. Human beings in the state of nature are amoral creatures, neither virtuous nor vicious. After humans leave the state of nature, they can enjoy a higher form of goodness, moral goodness, which Rousseau articulates most explicitly in the Social Contract.

Having described the pure state of nature in the first part of the *Second Discourse,* Rousseau's task in the second part is to explain the complex series of historical events that moved humans from this state to the state of present day civil society. Although they are not stated explicitly, Rousseau sees this development as occurring in a series of stages. From the pure state of nature, humans begin to organize into temporary groups for the purposes of specific tasks like hunting an animal. Very basic language in the form of grunts and gestures comes to be used in these groups. However, the groups last only as long as the task takes to be completed, and then they dissolve as quickly as they came together.

The next stage involves more permanent social relationships including the traditional family, from which arises conjugal and paternal love. Basic conceptions of property and feelings of pride and competition develop in this stage as well. However, at this stage they are not developed to the point that they cause the pain and inequality that they do in present day society. If humans could have remained in this state, they would have been happy for the most part, primarily because the various tasks that they engaged in could all be done by each individual.

The next stage in the historical development occurs when the arts of agriculture and metallurgy are discovered. Because these tasks required a division of labour, some people were better suited to certain types of physical labour, others to making tools, and still others to governing and organizing workers. Soon, there become distinct social classes and strict notions of property, creating conflict and ultimately a state of war not unlike the one that Hobbes describes. Those who have the most to lose call on the others to come together under a social contract for the protection of all. But Rousseau claims that the contract is specious, and that it was no more than a way for those in power to keep their power by convincing those with less that it was in their interest to accept the situation. And so, Rousseau says, "All ran to meet their chains thinking they secured their freedom, for although they had enough reason to feel the advantages of political establishment, they did not have enough experience to foresee its dangers." *The Discourse on the Origin of Inequality* remains one of Rousseau's most famous works, and lays the foundation for much of his political thought as it is expressed in the Discourse on Political Economy and Social Contract. Ultimately, the work is based on the idea that by nature, humans are essentially peaceful, content, and equal. It is the socialization process that has produced inequality, competition, and the egoistic mentality.

Discourse on Political Economy

The Discourse on Political Economy originally appeared in Diderot and d'Alembert's Encyclopedia. In terms of its content the work seems to be, in many ways, a precursor to the Social Contract, which would appear in 1762. And whereas the Discourse on the Sciences and Arts and the Discourse on the Origin of Inequality look back on history and condemn what Rousseau sees as the lack of morality and justice in his own present day society, this work is much more constructive. That is, the Discourse on Political Economy explains what he takes to be a legitimate political regime.

The work is perhaps most significant because it is here that Rousseau introduces the concept of the "general will," a major aspect of his political thought which is further developed in the Social Contract. There is debate among scholars about how exactly one ought to interpret this concept, but essentially, one can understand the general will in terms of an analogy. A political society is like a human body. A body is a unified entity though it has various parts that have particular functions. And just as the body has a will that looks after the well-being of the whole, a political state also has a will which looks to its general well-being. The major conflict in political philosophy occurs when the general will is at odds with one or more of the individual wills of its citizens.

With the conflict between the general and individual wills in mind, Rousseau articulates three maxims which supply the basis for a politically virtuous state: (1) Follow the general will in every action; (2) Ensure that every particular will is in accordance with the general will; and (3) Public needs must be satisfied. Citizens follow these maxims when there is a sense of equality among them, and when they develop a genuine respect for law. This again is in contrast to Hobbes, who says that laws are only followed when people fear punishment. That is, the state must make the penalty for breaking the law so severe that people do not see breaking the law to be of any advantage to them. Rousseau claims, instead, that when laws are in accordance with the general will, good citizens will respect and love both the state and their fellow citizens. Therefore, citizens will see the intrinsic value in the law, even in cases in which it may conflict with their individual wills.

The General Will

The concept of the general will, first introduced in the Discourse on Political Economy, is further developed in the Social Contract although it remains ambiguous and difficult to interpret. The most pressing difficulty that arises is in the tension that seems to exist between liberalism and communitarianism. On one hand, Rousseau argues that following the general will allows for individual diversity and freedom. But at the same time, the general will also encourages the well-being of the whole, and therefore can conflict with the particular interests of individuals. This tension has led some to claim that Rousseau's political thought is hopelessly inconsistent, although others have attempted to resolve the tension in order to find some type of middle ground between the two positions. Despite these difficulties, however, there are some aspects of the general will that Rousseau clearly articulates. First, the general will is directly tied to Sovereignty: but not Sovereignty merely in the sense of whomever holds power.

Simply having power, for Rousseau, is not sufficient for that power to be morally legitimate. True Sovereignty is directed always at the public good, and the general will, therefore, speaks always infallibly to the benefit of the people. Second, the object of the general will is always abstract, or for lack of a better term, general. It can set up rules, social classes, or even a monarchial government, but it can never specify the particular individuals who are subject to the rules, members of the classes, or the rulers in the government. This is in keeping with the idea that the general will speaks to the good of the society as a whole. It is not to be confused with the collection of individual wills which would put their own needs, or the needs of particular factions, above those of the general public. This leads to a related point. Rousseau argues that there is an important distinction to be made between the general will and the collection of individual wills: "There is often a great deal of difference between the will of all and the general will. The latter looks only to the common interest; the former considers private interest and is only a sum of private wills. But take away from these same wills the pluses and minuses that cancel each other out, and the remaining sum of the differences is the general will." (Social Contract, Vol. IV, p. 146). This point can be understood in an almost Rawlsian sense, namely that if the citizens were ignorant of the groups to which they would belong, they would inevitably make decisions that would be to the advantage of the society as a whole, and thus be in accordance with the general will.

Equality, Freedom, and Sovereignty

One problem that arises in Rousseau's political theory is that the Social Contract purports to be a legitimate state in one sense because it frees human beings from their chains. But if the state is to protect individual freedom, how can this be reconciled with the notion of the general will, which looks always to the welfare of the whole and not to the will of the individual? This criticism, although not unfounded, is also not devastating. To answer it, one must return to the concepts of Sovereignty and the general will. True Sovereignty, again, is not simply the will of those in power, but rather the general will. Sovereignty does have the proper authority override the particular will of an individual or even the collective will of a particular group of individuals. However, as the general will is infallible, it can only do so when intervening will be to the benefit of the society. To understand this, one must take note of Rousseau's emphasis on the equality and freedom of the citizens. Proper intervention on the part of the Sovereign is therefore best understood as that which secures the freedom and equality of citizens rather than that which limits them. Ultimately, the delicate balance between the supreme authority of the state and the rights of individual citizens is based on a social compact that protects society against factions and gross differences in wealth and privilege among its members.

Rousseau: Judge of Jean Jacques

The most distinctive feature of this late work, often referred to simply as the Dialogues, is that it is written in the form of three dialogues. The characters in the dialogues are "Rousseau" and an interlocutor identified simply as a "Frenchman." The subject of these characters' conversations is the author "Jean-Jacques," who is the actual historical Rousseau. This somewhat confusing arrangement serves the purpose of Rousseau judging his own career.

The character "Rousseau," therefore, represents Rousseau had he not written his collected works but instead had discovered them as if they were written by someone else. What would he think of this author, represented in the Dialogues as the character "Jean-Jacques?" This self-examination makes two major claims. First, like the Reveries, it makes clearly evident the fact that Rousseau felt victimized and betrayed, and shows perhaps even more so than the Reveries, Rousseau's growing paranoia. And second, the Dialogues represent one of the few places that Rousseau claims his work is systematic. He claims that there is a philosophical consistency that runs throughout his works. Whether one accepts that such a system is present in Rousseau's philosophy or not is a question that was not only debated during Rousseau's time, but is also continually discussed among contemporary scholars.

Historical and Philosophical Influence

It is difficult to overestimate Rousseau's influence, both in the Western philosophical tradition, and historically. Perhaps his greatest directly philosophical influence is on the ethical thought of Immanuel Kant. This may seem puzzling at first glance. For Kant, the moral law is based on rationality, whereas in Rousseau, there is a constant theme of nature and even the emotional faculty of pity described in the Second Discourse. This theme in Rousseau's thought is not to be ignored, and it would be a mistake to understand Rousseau's ethics merely as a precursor to Kant; certainly Rousseau is unique and significant in his own respect. But despite these differences, the influence on Kant is undeniable. The Profession of Faith of the Savoyard Vicar is one text in particular that illustrates this influence. The Vicar claims that the correct view of the universe is to see oneself not at the centre of things, but rather on the circumference, with all people realizing that we have a common centre. This same notion is expressed in the Rousseau's political theory, particularly in the concept of the general will. In Kant's ethics, one of the major themes is the claim that moral actions are those that can be universalized. Morality is something separate from individual happiness: a view that Rousseau undoubtedly expresses as well.

A second major influence is Rousseau's political thought. Not only is he one of the most important figures in the history of political philosophy, later influencing Karl Marx among others, but his works were also championed by the leaders of the French Revolution. And finally, his philosophy was largely instrumental in the late eighteenth century Romantic Naturalism movement in Europe thanks in large part to Julie or the New Heloise and the Reveries of the Solitary Walker.

Contemporary Rousseau scholarship continues to discuss many of the same issues that were debated in the eighteenth century. The tension in his political thought between individual liberty and totalitarianism continues to be an issue of controversy among scholars. Another aspect of Rousseau's philosophy that has proven to be influential is his view of the family, particularly as it pertains to the roles of men and women.

7

John Stuart Mill

John Stuart Mill (20 May 1806 – 8 May 1873), British philosopher, political economist, civil servant and Member of Parliament, was an influential liberal thinker of the 19th century. He was an exponent of utilitarianism, an ethical theory developed by Jeremy Bentham, although his conception of it was very different from Bentham's.

Biography

John Stuart Mill was born in the Pentonville area of London, the eldest son of the Scottish philosopher and historian James Mill. John Stuart was educated by his father, with the advice and assistance of Jeremy Bentham and Francis Place. He was given an extremely rigorous upbringing, and was deliberately shielded from association with children his own age other than his siblings. His father, a follower of Bentham and an adherent of associationism, had as his explicit aim to create a genius intellect that would carry on the cause of utilitarianism and its implementation after he and Bentham were dead.

Mill was a notably precocious child; at the age of three he was taught Greek. By the age of eight he had read Aesop's *Fables*, Xenophon's *Anabasis*, and the whole of Herodotus, and was acquainted with Lucian, Diogenes Laertius, Isocrates and six dialogues of Plato. He had also read a great deal of history in English and had been taught arithmetic.

At the age of eight he began learning Latin, Euclid, and algebra, and was appointed schoolmaster to the younger children of the family. His main reading was still history, but he went through all the Latin and Greek authors commonly read in the schools and universities at the time, such as Horace, Virgil, Ovid, Tacitus, Homer, Dionysus, Sophocles, Euripides, Aristophanes and Thucydides. By the age of ten he could read Plato and Demosthenes with ease. His father also thought that it was important for Mill to study and compose poetry. One of Mill's earliest poetry compositions was a continuation of the Iliad. In his spare time, he also enjoyed reading about natural sciences and popular novels, such as *Don Quixote* and *Robinson Crusoe*.

His father James Mill's *History of India* was published in 1818; immediately thereafter, about the age of twelve, Mill began a thorough study of the scholastic logic, at the same time reading Aristotle's logical treatises in the original language. In the following year he was introduced to political economy and studied Adam Smith and David Ricardo with his father - ultimately completing their classical economic view of factors of production. Mill's *comptes rendus* of his daily economy lessons helped his father in writing *Elements of Political Economy*, which became the leading textbook exposition of doctrinaire Ricardian economics. Ricardo, who was a close friend of his father, used to invite the young Mill to his house for a walk in order to talk about political economy.

In his *Autobiography*, Mill described his father's teaching methods:

> "Such a mode of instruction was excellently calculated to form a thinker; but it required to be worked by a thinker, as close and vigorous as my father. The path was a thorny one, even to him, and I am sure it was so to me, notwithstanding the strong interest I took in the subject. He was often, and much beyond reason, provoked by my failures in cases where success could not have been expected; but in the main his method was right, and it succeeded. I do not believe that any scientific teaching ever was more thorough, or better fitted for training the faculties, than the mode in which logic and political economy were taught to me by my father. Striving, even in an exaggerated degree, to call forth the activity of my faculties, by making me find out everything for myself, he gave his explanations not before, but after, I had felt

the full force of the difficulties; and not only gave me an accurate knowledge of these two great subjects, as far as they were then understood, but made me a thinker on both. I thought for myself almost from the first, and occasionally thought differently from him, though for a long time only on minor points, and making his opinion the ultimate standard. At a later period I even occasionally convinced him, and altered his opinion on some points of detail: which I state to his honour, not my own. It at once exemplifies his perfect candour, and the real worth of his method of teaching."

At the age of fourteen, Mill stayed for one year in France, with the family of Sir Samuel Bentham, brother of Jeremy Bentham. The mountain scenery he saw in France made the deepest impression on him, which led to a lifelong taste for mountain landscapes. The lively and friendly way of life of the French also left a deep impression on him.

In Montpellier, he attended the winter courses on chemistry, zoology, logic of the *Faculte des Sciences,* as well as taking a course of the higher mathematics with a private professor. While coming and going from France, he stayed in Paris for a few days in the house of the renowned economist Jean-Baptiste Say, who was a friend of Mill's father. There he met many leaders of the Liberal party, as well as other notable Parisiens, including Henri Saint-Simon.

A contemporary record of Mill's studies from eight to thirteen is published in Bain's sketch of his life. It suggests that his autobiography rather understates the amount of work done.

This intensive study however had injurious effects on Mill's mental health, and state of mind. At the age of twenty he suffered a nervous breakdown. As explained in chapter V of his *Autobiography,* this was caused by the great physical and mental arduousness of his studies which had suppressed any feelings he might have developed normally in childhood. Nevertheless, this depression eventually began to dissipate, as he began to find solace in the *Memoires* of Jean-François Marmontel and the poetry of William Wordsworth - his capacity for emotion resurfaced - Mill remarking that the "cloud gradually drew off".

Mill refused to study at Oxford University or Cambridge University, because he refused to take Anglican orders from the "white devil". Instead he followed his father to work for the British East India Company until 1858. In 1851, Mill married Harriet Taylor after 21 years of an intimate friendship. Taylor was married when they met, and their relationship was close but chaste during the years before her first husband died. Brilliant in her own right, Taylor was a significant influence on Mill's work and ideas during both friendship and marriage. His relationship with Harriet Taylor reinforced Mill's advocacy of women's rights. He cites her influence in his final revision of *On Liberty*, which was published shortly after her death, and she appears to be obliquely referenced in *The Subjection of Women*. Taylor died in 1858 after developing severe lung congestion, only seven years into her marriage to Mill. Between the years 1865-1868 Mill served as Lord Rector of the University of St. Andrews, where he gave an inaugural speech on the value of culture. During the same period, 1865-68, he was a Member of Parliament for City and Westminster, and was often associated with the Liberal Party. During his time as an MP, Mill advocated easing the burdens on Ireland, and became the first person in Parliament to call for women to be given the right to vote. Mill became a strong advocate of women's rights and such political and social reforms as proportional representation, labour unions, and farm cooperatives. In 1869, he argued for the right of women to vote. In *Considerations on Representative Government*, Mill called for various reforms of Parliament and voting, especially proportional representation, the Single Transferable Vote, and the extension of suffrage. He was godfather to Bertrand Russell. He died in Avignon, France in 1873, and is buried alongside his wife.

Significant Works

Mill wrote on a startling number of topics. All his major texts, however, play a role in defending his new philosophic radicalism and the intellectual, moral, political, and social agendas associated with it.

A System of Logic

Though Mill's biography reveals his openness to intellectual exploration, his most basic philosophical commitment-to naturalism-never seriously wavers. He is committed to the idea that our best methods of explaining the world are those employed by the natural sciences. Anything that we can know about human minds and wills comes from treating them as part of the causal order investigated by the sciences, rather than as special entities that lie outside it. By taking the methods of the natural sciences as the only route to knowledge about the world, Mill sees himself as rejecting the "German, or a priori view of human knowledge," (CW, I.233) or, as he also calls it, "intuitionism," which was espoused in different ways by Kant, Reid, and their followers in Britain (e.g. Whewell and Hamilton). Though there are many differences among intuitionist thinkers, one "grand doctrine" that Mill suggests they all affirm is the view that "the constitution of the mind is the key to the constitution of external nature-that the laws of the human intellect have a necessary correspondence with the objective laws of the universe, such that these may be inferred from those."

The intuitionist doctrine conceives of nature as being largely or wholly constituted by the mind rather than more or less imperfectly observed by it. One of the great dangers presented by this doctrine, from the perspective of Mill's a posteriori school, is that it supports the belief that one can know universal truths about the world through evidence (including intuitions or Kantian categories of the understanding) provided by the mind alone rather than by nature. If the mind constitutes the world that we experience, then we can understand the world by understanding the mind. It was this freedom from appeal to nature and the lack of independent (i.e. empirical) checks to the knowledge claims associated with it that Mill found so disturbing. For Mill, the problems with intuitionism extend far beyond the metaphysical and epistemological to the moral and political. As Mill says in his Autobiography when discussing his important treatise of 1843, *A System of Logic*:

The notion that truths external to the mind may be known by intuition or consciousness, independently of observation and experience, is, I am persuaded, in these times, the great intellectual support of false doctrines and bad institutions. By the aid of this theory, every inveterate belief and every intense feeling, of which the origin is not remembered, is enabled to dispense with the obligation of justifying itself by reason, and is erected into its own all-sufficient voucher and justification. There never was such an instrument devised for consecrating all deep-seated prejudices. And the chief strength of this false philosophy in morals, politics, and religion, lies in the appeal which it is accustomed to make to the evidence of mathematics and of the cognate branches of physical science. To expel it from these, is to drive it from its stronghold.

This charge against intuitionism, that it frees one from the obligation of justifying one's beliefs, has strong roots in philosophic radicalism. We find Bentham, in his 1789 *An Introduction to the Principles of Morals and Legislation*, attacking non-utilitarian moral systems for just this reason: "They consist all of them in so many contrivances for avoiding the obligation of appealing to any external standard, and for prevailing upon the reader to accept of the author's sentiment or opinion as a reason and that a sufficient one for itself." Mill thus saw his own commitment to the naturalism and empiricism of the "a posteriori school" of thought as part of a broader social and political agenda that advocated for reform and also undercut traditional foundations of conservatism.

Intuitionism, however, is often taken to be on much firmer ground than empiricism when it comes to accounting for our knowledge of mathematics and logic. This is especially true if one rejects the idea, found in people like Hobbes and Hume, that mathematical propositions like 2 + 3 = 5 are true merely because of the meaning of the constituents of the proposition, or, as Hume puts it, because of the proposition's "relations of ideas." Mill agrees with those (including Kant) who maintain that logical and mathematical truths are not merely linguistic-that they contain substantive, non-linguistic information. But this leaves Mill with the problem of accounting for the apparent necessity of such truths-a necessity which seems to rule out their origin in experience. To successfully attack intuitionism in "its stronghold," the System of Logic needs to provide alternative grounds for basic principles of logic and mathematics (e.g. the principle of non-contradiction). In particular, Mill needs to show how "that peculiar character of what are called necessary truths" may be explained from experience and association alone. The object of logic "is to ascertain how we come by that portion of our knowledge (much the greatest portion) which is not intuitive: and by what criterion we can, in matters not self-evident, distinguish between things proved and things not proved, between what is worthy and what is unworthy of belief." It should be noted that logic goes beyond formal logic for Mill and into the conditions of truth more generally.

Mill's argument that the principles of mathematics and logic are justified by appeal to experience depends upon his distinction between verbal and real propositions, that is, between propositions that do not convey new information to the person who understands the meaning of the proposition's terms and those propositions that do convey new information. The point of the distinction between verbal and real propositions is, first, to stress that all real propositions are a posteriori. Second, the distinction emphasizes that verbal propositions are empty of content; they tell us about language (i.e. what words mean) rather than about the world. In Kantian terms, Mill wants to deny the possibility of synthetic a priori propositions, while contending that we can still make sense of our knowledge of subjects like logic and mathematics.

This distinction between verbal and real propositions depends, in turn, upon Mill's analysis of the meaning of propositions, i.e. how the meanings of constituents of propositions determine the meaning of the whole. A proposition, in which something is affirmed or denied of something, is formed by putting together two "names" or terms (subject and predicate) and a copula. The subject is the name "denoting the person or thing which something is affirmed or denied of." The predicate is "the name denoting that which is affirmed or denied." The copula is "the sign denoting that there is an affirmation or denial," which thereby enables "the hearer or reader to distinguish a proposition from any other kind of discourse." In the proposition 'gold is yellow' for example, the copula 'is' shows that the quality yellow is being affirmed of the substance gold.

Mill divides names into general and singular names. All names, except proper names (e.g. Ringo, Buckley, etc) and names that signify an attribute only (e.g. whiteness, length), have a connotation and a denotation. That is, they both connote or imply some attribute(s) and denote or pick out individuals that fall under that description. The general name "man," for example, denotes Socrates, Picasso, Plutarch and an indefinite number of other individuals, and it does so because they all share some attribute(s) (e.g. rational animal, featherless biped, etc.) connoted by man. The name "white" denotes all white things and implies or connotes the attribute whiteness.

The word "whiteness," by contrast, denotes or signifies an attribute but does not connote an attribute. Instead, it operates like a proper name in that its meaning derives entirely from what it denotes. The meaning of a typical proposition is that the thing(s) denoted by the subject has the attribute(s) connoted by the predicate. In sentences like "Eleanor is tired" and "All men are mortal," though the subjects pick out their objects differently (through a proper name and through an attribute, respectively), Mill's basic story about the meaning of propositions holds.

Things become much more difficult with identity statements like "Hesperus is Phosphorus." In this case, we have two proper names that pick out the same object (the planet Venus). Under Mill's view, these proper names should have the same meaning because they denote the same object. But this appears untenable because the statement seems informative. It doesn't seem plausible that the proposition merely states that an object is identical with itself, which would be the proposition's meaning if Mill's views on the meaning of proper names were correct.

This discussion of the nature of names or terms enables us to understand Mill's treatment of verbal and real propositions. Verbal propositions assert something about the meaning of names rather than about matters of fact. This means that, "since names and their signification are entirely arbitrary, such propositions are not, strictly speaking, susceptible of truth or falsity, but only of conformity or disconformity to usage or convention." This kind of proposition simply "asserts of a thing under a particular name, only what is asserted of it in the fact of calling it by that name; and which, therefore, either gives no information, or gives it respecting the name, not the thing." As such, verbal propositions are empty of content and they are the only things we know a priori, independently of checking the correspondence of the proposition to the world.

Real propositions, in contrast, "predicate of a thing some fact not involved in the signification of the name by which the proposition speaks of it; some attribute not connoted by that name." Such propositions convey information that is not already included in the names or terms employed, and their truth or falsity depends on whether or not they correspond to relevant features of the world. Thus, "George is on the soccer team" predicates something of the subject George that is not included in its meaning (in this case, the denotation of the individual person) and its being true or not depends upon whether George is, in fact, on the team.

Mill's great contention in the System of Logic is that logic and mathematics contain real, rather than merely verbal, propositions. He claims, for example, that the law of contradiction (i.e. the same proposition cannot at the same time be false and true) and the law of excluded middle (i.e. either a proposition is true or it is false) are both real propositions. They are, like the axioms of geometry, experimental truths, not truths known a priori. They represent generalizations or inductions from observation-very well-justified inductions, to be sure, but inductions nonetheless. This leads Mill to say that the necessity typically ascribed to the truths of mathematics and logic by his intuitionist opponents is an illusion, thereby undermining intuitionist argumentative fortifications at their strongest point. A System of Logic thus represents the most thorough attempt to argue for empiricism in epistemology, logic, and mathematics before the twentieth century. Though revolutionary advances in logic and philosophy of language in the late nineteenth and early twentieth centuries have rendered many of Mill's technical points about semantics and logic obsolete, the basic philosophical vision that Mill defends is very much a live option.

There are some other topics covered in the System of Logic that are of interest. First is Mill's treatment of deduction (in the form of the syllogism). His discussion is driven by one basic concern: Why wouldn't a deduction simply tell us what we already know? How can it be informative? Mill discounts two common views about the syllogism, namely, that it is useless (because it tells us what we already know) and that it is the correct analysis of what the mind actually does when it discovers truths. To understand why Mill discounts these ways of thinking about deduction, we need to understand his views on inference.

The key point here is that all inference is from particular to particular. When we infer that the Duke of Wellington is mortal from "All men are mortal," what we are really doing is inferring the Duke's mortality from the mortality of the individual people with whose mortality we are familiar. What the mind does in making a deductive inference is not to move from a universal truth to a particular one. Rather, it moves from truths about a number of particulars to a smaller number (or one). The general statement that "All men are mortal" only allows us to more easily register what we know-it reflects neither the true inference being made nor the warrant or evidence we have for making the inference. Though general propositions are not necessary for reasoning, they are heuristically useful (as are the syllogisms that employ them). They aid us in memory and comprehension.

Mill's famous treatment of induction reveals the a posteriori grounds for belief. He focuses on four different methods of experimental inquiry that attempt to single out from the circumstances that precede or follow a phenomenon the ones that are linked to the phenomenon by an invariable law. That is, we test to see if a purported causal connection exists by observing the relevant phenomena under an assortment of situations. If we wish, for example, to know whether a virus causes a disease, how can we prove it? What counts as good evidence for such a belief? The four methods of induction or experimental inquiry-the methods of agreement, of difference, of residues, and of concomitant variation-provide answers to these questions by showing what we need to demonstrate in order to claim that a causal law holds. Can we show, using the method of difference, that when the virus is not present the disease is also absent? If so, then we have some grounds for believing that the virus causes the disease.

Another issue addressed in *A System of Logic* that is of abiding interest is Mill's handling of free will. Mill's commitment to naturalism includes treating the human will as a potential object of scientific study: "Our will causes our bodily actions in the same sense, and in no other, in which cold causes ice, or a spark causes an explosion of gunpowder. The volition, a state of our mind, is the antecedent; the motion of our limbs in conformity to the volition, is the consequent." The questions that readily arise are how, under this view, can one take the will to be free and how can we preserve responsibility and feelings of choice?

In his autobiography, Mill recounts his own youthful, melancholy acceptance of the doctrine of "Philosophical Necessity" (advocated by, among others, Robert Owen and his followers): "I felt as if I was scientifically proved to be the helpless slave of antecedent circumstances; as if my character and that of all others had been formed for us by agencies beyond our control, and was wholly out of our own power." But it is precisely the idea that our character is formed for us, not by us, that Mill thinks is a "grand error." We have the power to alter our own character. Though our own character is formed by circumstances, among those circumstances are our own desires. We cannot directly will our characters to be one way rather than another, but we can will actions that shape those characters.

Mill addresses an obvious objection: what leads us to will to change our character? Isn't that determined? Mill agrees. Our desire to change our character is determined largely by our experience of painful and pleasant consequences associated with our character. For Mill, however, the important point is that, even if we don't control the desire to change our character, we are still left with the feeling of moral freedom, which is the feeling of being able to modify our own character "if we wish." What Mill wants to save in the doctrine of free will is simply the feeling that we have "real power over the formation of our own character." If we have the desire to change our character, we find that we can. If we lack that desire it is "of no consequence what we think forms our character," because we don't care about altering it. For Mill, this is a thick enough notion of freedom to avoid fatalism.

One of the basic problems for this kind of naturalistic picture of human beings and wills is that it clashes with our first-person image of ourselves as reasoners and agents. As Kant understood, and as the later hermeneutic tradition emphasizes, we think of ourselves as autonomous followers of objectively given rules. It seems extremely difficult to provide a convincing naturalistic account of, for example, making a choice (without explaining away as illusory our first-person experience of making choices). The desire to treat the will as an object, like ice or gunpowder, open to natural scientific study falls within Mill's broader claim that the moral sciences, which include economics, history, and psychology among others, are fundamentally similar to the natural sciences.

Though we may have difficulty running experiments in the human realm, that realm and its objects are, in principle, just as open to the causal explanations we find in physics or biology. Perhaps the most interesting element of his analysis of the moral sciences is his commitment to what has been called "methodological individualism," or the view that social and political phenomena are explicable by appeal to the behaviour of individuals. In other words, social facts are reducible to facts about individuals: "The laws of the phenomena of society are, and can be, nothing but the laws of the actions and passions of human beings united together in the social state. Men, however, in a state of society, are still men; their actions and passions are obedient to the laws of individual human nature. Men are not, when brought together, converted into another kind of substance with different properties."

This position puts Mill in opposition to Auguste Comte, a founding figure in social theory (he coined the term "sociology") and an important influence on, and correspondent with, Mill. Comte takes sociology rather than psychology to be the most basic of human sciences and takes individuals and their conduct to be best understood through the lens of social analysis.

To put it simplistically, for Comte, the individual is an abstraction from the whole-its beliefs and conduct are determined by history and society. We understand the individual best, on this view, when we see the individual as an expression of its social institutions and setting.

This naturally leads to a kind of historicism. Though Mill recognized the important influences of social institutions and history on individuals, for him society is nevertheless only able to shape individuals through affecting their experiences-experiences structured by universal principles of human psychology that operate in all times and places.

An Examination

Mill's attacks on intuitionism continued throughout his life. One notable example is his 1865 *An Examination of Sir William Hamilton's Philosophy*, which revisits much of the same ground as A System of Logic in the guise of a thorough-going criticism of Hamilton, a thinker influenced by Reid and Kant whom Mill took as representing "the great fortress of the intuitional philosophy in this country." The rather hefty volume explores "some of the disputed questions in the domain of psychology and metaphysics."

Among the doctrines given most attention is that of the "relativity of knowledge," something to which Mill takes Hamilton as insufficiently committed. It is the idea that we have no access to "things-in-themselves" (thus, the relativity versus absoluteness of knowledge) and that we are limited to analyzing the phenomena of consciousness. Mill, who accepts this basic principle, counts himself as a Berkeleian phenomenalist and famously defines matter in the Examination as "a Permanent Possibility of Sensation," thinks that Hamilton accepts this doctrine in a confused manner. "He affirms without reservation, that certain attributes (extension, figures, etc.) are known to us as they really exist out of ourselves; and also that all our knowledge of them is relative to us. And these two assertions are only reconcileable, if relativity to us is understood in the altogether trivial sense, that we know them only so far as our faculties permit."

Hamilton therefore seems to want to have his cake and eat it too when it comes to knowledge of the external world. On the one hand, he wants to declare that we have access to things as they are, thereby aligning himself with Reid's project of avoiding the fall into (Humean) skepticism-a fall prompted by the Lockean "way of ideas." On the other hand, he wants to follow Kant in limiting our knowledge of things-in-themselves, thereby reigning in the pretensions of metaphysical speculation. Mill avoids this dilemma by rejecting Hamilton's position that we know things outside as they really are.

Psychological Writings

As noted in the discussion of *A System of Logic*, Mill's commitment to "methodological individualism" makes psychology the foundational moral science. Though he never wrote a work of his own on psychology, he edited and contributed notes to an 1869 re-issue of his father's 1829 work in psychology, *Analysis of the Phenomena of the Human Mind*, and reviewed the work of his friend and correspondent, Alexander Bain.

All three were proponents of the associationist school of psychology, whose roots go back to Hobbes and especially Locke and whose members included Gay, Hartley, and Priestly in the eighteenth century and the Mills, Bain, and Herbert Spencer in the nineteenth century. Mill distinguishes between the a posteriori and a priori schools of psychology. The former "resolves the whole contents of the mind into experience." The latter emphasizes that "in every act of thought, down to the most elementary, there is an ingredient which is not given to the mind, but contributed by the mind in virtue of its inherent powers." In the a priori or intuitionist school, experience "instead of being the source and prototype of our ideas, is itself a product of the mind's own forces working on the impressions we receive from without, and has always a mental as well as an external element."

The associationist version of a posteriori psychology has two basic doctrines: "first, that the more recondite phenomena of the mind are formed out of the more simple and elementary; and, secondly, that the mental law, by means of which this formation takes place, is the Law of Association." The associationist psychologists, then, would attempt to explain mental phenomena by showing them to be the ultimate product of simpler components of experience (e.g. colour, sound, smell, pleasure, pain) connected to each other through associations.

These associations take two basic forms: resemblance and contiguity in space and/or time. Thus, these psychologists attempt to explain our idea of an orange or our feelings of greed as the product of simpler ideas connected by association. Part of the impulse for this account of psychology is its apparent scientific character and beauty. Associationism attempts to explain a large variety of mental phenomena on the basis of experience plus very few mental laws of association. It therefore appeals to those who are particularly drawn to simplicity in their scientific theories.

Another attraction of associationist psychology, however, is its implications for views on moral education and social reform. If the contents of our minds, including beliefs and moral feelings, are products of experiences that we undergo connected according to very simple laws, then this raises the possibility that human beings are capable of being radically re-shaped-that our natures, rather than being fixed, are open to major alteration. In other words, if our minds are cobbled together by laws of association working on the materials of experience, then this suggests that if our experiences were to change, so would our minds. This doctrine tends to place much greater emphasis on social and political institutions like the family, the workplace, and the state, than does the doctrine that the nature of the mind offers strong resistance to being shaped by experience (i.e. that the mind molds experience rather than being molded by it). Associationism thereby fits nicely into an agenda of reform, because it suggests that many of the problems of individuals are explained by their situations (and the associations that these situations promote) rather than by some intrinsic feature of the mind. As Mill puts it in the Autobiography in discussing the conflict between the intuitionist and a posteriori schools:

The practical reformer has continually to demand that changes be made in things which are supported by powerful and widely spread feelings, or to question the apparent necessity and indefeasibleness of established facts; and it is often an indispensable part of his argument to show, how these powerful feelings had their origin, and how those facts came to seem necessary and indefeasible. There is therefore a natural hostility between him and a philosophy which discourages the explanation of feelings and moral facts by circumstances and association, and prefers to treat them as ultimate elements of human nature...I have long felt that the prevailing tendency to regard all the marked distinctions of human character as innate, and in the main indelible, and to ignore the irresistible proofs that by far the greater part of those differences, whether between individuals, races, or sexes, are such as not only might but naturally would be produced by differences in circumstances, is one of the chief hindrances to the rational treatment of great social questions, and one of the greatest stumbling blocks to human improvement.

Utilitarianism

Another manoeuvre in his battle with intuitionism came when Mill published Utilitarianism (1861) in installments in Fraser's Magazine (it was later brought out in book form in 1863). It offers a candidate for a first principle of morality, a principle that provides us with a criterion distinguishing right and wrong. The utilitarian candidate is the principle of utility, which holds that "actions are right in proportion as they tend to promote happiness; wrong as they tend to produce the reverse of happiness. By happiness is intended pleasure and the absence of pain; by unhappiness, pain and the privation of pleasure."

History of the Principle of Utility

By Mill's time, the principle of utility possessed a long history stretching back to the 1730's (with roots going further back to Hobbes, Locke, and even to Epicurus). In the eighteenth and early nineteenth centuries, it had been explicitly invoked by three British intellectual factions. Though all may have agreed that an action's consequences for the general happiness were to dictate its rightness or wrongness, the reasons behind the acceptance of that principle and the uses to which the principle was put varied greatly. The earliest supporters of the principle of utility were the religious utilitarians represented by, among others, John Gay, John Brown, Soame Jenyns, and, most famously, William Paley, whose 1785 *The Principles of Moral and Political Philosophy* was one of the most frequently re-printed and well read books of moral thought of the late eighteenth and early nineteenth centuries (to Mill's dismay, Bentham's utilitarianism was often conflated with Paley's). Religious utilitarianism was very popular among the educated classes and dominated in the universities until the 1830's. These thinkers were all deeply influenced by Locke's empiricism and psychological hedonism and often stood opposed to the competing moral doctrines of Shaftesbury, Hutcheson, Clarke, and Wollaston.

The religious utilitarians looked to the Christian God to address a basic problem, namely how to harmonize the interests of individuals, who are motivated by their own happiness, with the interests of the society as a whole. Once we understand that what we must do is what God wills (because of God's power of eternal sanction) and that God wills the happiness of his creatures, morality and our own self-interest will be seen to overlap. God guarantees that an individual's self-interest lies in virtue, in furthering the happiness of others. Without God and his sanctions of eternal punishment and reward, it would be hard to find motives that "are likely to be found sufficient to withhold men from the gratification of lust, revenge, envy, ambition, avarice." As we shall see in a moment, another possible motivation for caring about the general happiness-this one non-religious-is canvassed by Mill in Chapter Three of *Utilitarianism*. In contrast to religious utilitarianism, which had few aspirations to be a moral theory that revises ordinary moral attitudes, the two late-eighteenth century secular versions of utilitarianism grew out of various movements for reform. The principle of utility-and the correlated commitments to happiness as the only intrinsically desirable end and to the moral equivalency of the happiness of different individuals-was itself taken to be an instrument of reform. One version of secular utilitarianism was represented by William Godwin (husband of Mary Wollstonecraft and father of Mary Shelley), who achieved great notoriety with the publication of his *Political Justice* of 1793. Though his fame (or infamy) was relatively short-lived, Godwin's use of the principle of utility for the cause of radical political and social critique began the identification of utilitarianism with anti-religiosity and with dangerous democratic values.

The second version of secular utilitarianism, and the one that inspired Mill, arose from the work of Jeremy Bentham. Bentham, who was much more successful than Godwin at building a movement around his ideas, employed the principle of utility as a device of political, social, and legal criticism. It is important to note, however, that Bentham's interest in the principle of utility did not arise from concern about ethical theory as much as from concern about legislative and legal reform.

This history enables us to understand Mill's invocation of the principle of utility in its polemical context-Mill's support of that principle should not be taken as mere intellectual exercise. In the realm of politics, the principle of utility served to bludgeon opponents of reform. First and foremost, reform meant extension of the vote. But it also meant legal reform, including overhaul of the common law system and of legal institutions, and varieties of social reform, especially of institutions that tended to favour aristocratic and moneyed interests.

Though Bentham and Godwin intended it to have this function in the late eighteenth century, utilitarianism became influential only when tied with the political machinery of the Radical party, which had particular prominence on the English scene in the 1830's. In the realm of ethical debate, Mill took his opponents to be the "intuitionists" led by Sedgwick and Whewell, both Cambridge men. They were the contemporary representatives of an ethical tradition that understood its history as tied to Butler, Reid, Coleridge, and turn of the century German thought (especially that of Kant). Though intuitionists and members of Mill's a posteriori or "inductive" school recognize "to a great extent, the same moral laws," they differ "as to their evidence and the source from which they derive their authority. According to the one opinion, the principles of morals are evident a priori, requiring nothing to command assent except that the meaning of the terms be understood. According to the other doctrine, right and wrong, as well as truth and falsehood, are questions of observation and experience."

The chief danger represented by the proponents of intuitionism was not from the ethical content of their theories per se, which defended honesty, justice, benevolence, etc., but from the kinds of justifications offered for their precepts and the support such a view lent to the social and political status quo. As we saw in the discussion of the System of Logic and with reference to Mill's statements in his Autobiography, he takes intuitionism to be dangerous because it allegedly enables people to ratify their own prejudices as moral principles-in intuitionism, there is no "external standard" by which to adjudicate differing moral claims (for example, Mill understood Kant's categorical imperative as getting any moral force it possesses either from considerations of utility or from mere prejudice hidden by hand-waving). The principle of utility, alternatively, evaluates moral claims by appealing to the external standard of pain and pleasure. It presented each individual for moral consideration as someone capable of suffering and enjoyment.

Basic Argument

Mill's defense of the principle of utility in Utilitarianism includes five chapters. In the first, Mill sets out the problem, distinguishes between the intuitionist and "inductive" schools of morality, and also suggests limits to what we can expect from proofs of first principles of morality. He argues that "(q)uestions of ultimate ends are not amenable to direct proof." All that can be done is to present considerations "capable of determining the intellect either to give or withhold its assent to the doctrine; and this is equivalent to proof." Ultimately, he will want to prove in Chapter Four the basis for the principle of utility-that happiness is the only intrinsically desirable thing-by showing that we spontaneously accept it on reflection. It is rather easy to show that happiness is something we desire intrinsically, not for the sake of other things. What is hard is to show that it is the only thing we intrinsically desire or value. Mill agrees that we do not always value things like virtue as means or instruments to happiness. We do sometimes seem to value such things for their own sakes. Mill contends, however, that on reflection we will see that when we appear to value them for their own sakes we are actually valuing them as parts of happiness. That is, we value virtue, freedom, etc. as things that make us happy by their mere possession. This is all the proof we can give that happiness is our only ultimate end; it must rely on introspection and on careful and honest examination of our feelings and motives.

In Chapter Two, Mill corrects misconceptions about the principle of utility. One misconception is that utilitarianism, by endorsing the Epicurean view "that life has...no higher end than pleasure" is a "doctrine worthy only of swine." Mill counters that "the accusation supposes human beings to be capable of no pleasures except those of which swine are capable." He proffers a distinction (one not found in Bentham) between higher and lower pleasures, with higher pleasures including mental, aesthetic, and moral pleasures. When we are evaluating whether or not an action is good by evaluating the happiness that we can expect to be produced by it, he argues that higher pleasures should be taken to be in kind (rather than by degree) preferable to lower pleasures. This has led scholars to wonder whether Mill's utilitarianism differs significantly from Bentham's and whether Mill's distinction between higher and lower pleasures creates problems for our ability to know what will maximize aggregate happiness.

A second objection to the principle of utility is that "it is exacting too much to require that people shall always act from the inducement of promoting the general interest of society." Mill replies that this is to "confound the rule of action with the motive of it." Ethics is supposed to tell us what our duties are, "but no system of ethics requires that the sole motive of all we do shall be a feeling of duty; on the contrary, ninety-nine hundredths of all our actions are done from other motives, and rightly so done if the rule of duty does not condemn them."

To do the right thing, in other words, we do not need to be constantly motivated by concern for the general happiness. The large majority of actions intend the good of individuals (including ourselves) rather than the good of the world. Yet the world's good is made up of the good of the individuals that constitute it and unless we are in the position of, say, a legislator, we act properly by looking to private rather than to public good. Our attention to the public well-being usually needs to extend only so far as is required to know that we aren't violating the rights of others.

Chapter Three addresses the topic of motivation again by focusing on the following question: What is the source of our obligation to the principle of utility? What, in other words, motivates us to act in ways approved of by the principle of utility? With any moral theory, one must remember that 'ought implies can,' i.e. that if moral demands are to be legitimate, we must be the kind of beings that can meet those demands.

Mill defends the possibility of a strong utilitarian conscience (i.e. a strong feeling of obligation to the general happiness) by showing how such a feeling can develop out of the natural desire we have to be in unity with fellow creatures-a desire that enables us to care what happens to them and to perceive our own interests as linked with theirs. Though Chapter Two showed that we do not need to attend constantly to the general happiness, it is nevertheless a sign of moral progress when the happiness of others, including the happiness of those we don't know, becomes important to us.

Finally, Chapter Five shows how utilitarianism accounts for justice. In particular, Mill shows how utilitarianism can explain the special status we seem to grant to justice and to the violations of it. Justice is something we are especially keen to defend. Mill begins by marking off morality (the realm of duties) from expediency and worthiness by arguing that duties are those things we think people ought to be punished for not fulfilling. He then suggests that justice is demarcated from other areas of morality, because it includes those duties to which others have correlative rights, "Justice implies something which it is not only right to do, and wrong not to do, but which some individual person can claim from us as his moral right." Though no one has a right to my charity, even if I have a duty to be charitable, others have rights not to have me injure them or to have me repay what I have promised.

Critics of utilitarianism have placed special emphasis on its inability to provide a satisfactory account of rights. For Mill, to have a right is "to have something which society ought to defend me in the possession of. If the objector goes on to ask why it ought, I can give no other reason than general utility." But what if the general utility demands that we violate your rights? The intuition that something is wrong if your rights can be violated for the sake of the general good provoked the great challenge to utilitarian conceptions of justice, levelled with special force by twentieth century thinkers like John Rawls.

On Liberty

The topic of justice received further treatment at Mill's hands in his famous 1859 book *On Liberty*. This work is the one, along with A System of Logic, that Mill thought would have the most longevity. It concerns civil and social liberty or, to look at it from the contrary point of view, the nature and limits of the power that can legitimately be exercised by society over the individual. Mill begins by retelling the history of struggle between rulers and ruled and suggests that social rather than political tyranny is the greater danger for modern, commercial nations like Britain. This social "tyranny of the majority" (a phrase Mill takes from Tocqueville) arises from the enforcement of rules of conduct that are both arbitrary and strongly adhered to.

The practical principle that guides the majority "to their opinions on the regulation of human conduct, is the feeling in each person's mind that everybody should be required to act as he, and those with whom he sympathizes, would like them to act." Such a feeling is particularly dangerous because it is taken to be self-justifying and self-evident. There is a need, therefore, for a rationally grounded principle which governs a society's dealings with individuals. This "one very simple principle"-often called the "harm principle"-entails that:

> The sole end for which mankind are warranted, individually or collectively, in interfering with the liberty of action of any of their number, is self-protection. That the only purpose for which power can be rightfully exercised over any member of a civilized community, against his will, is to prevent harm to others. His own good, either physical or moral, is not a sufficient warrant. He cannot rightfully be compelled to do or forbear because it will be better for him to do so, because it will make him happier, because, in the opinion of others, to do so would be wise, or even right. These are good reasons for remonstrating with him, or reasoning with him, or persuading him, or entreating him, but not for compelling him, or visiting him with any evil in case he do otherwise. (OL, 51-2)

This anti-paternalistic principle identifies three basic regions of human liberty: the "inward domain of consciousness," liberty of tastes and pursuits (i.e. of framing our own life plan), and the freedom to unite with others. Mill, unlike other liberal theorists, makes no appeal to "abstract right" in order to justify the harm principle. The reason for accepting the freedom of individuals to act as they choose, so long as they cause minimal or no harm to others, is that it would promote "utility in the largest sense, grounded on the permanent interests of man as a progressive being." In other words, abiding by the harm principle is desirable because it promotes what Mill calls the "free development of individuality" or the development of our humanity.

Behind this rests the idea that humanity is capable of progress-that latent or underdeveloped abilities and virtues can be actualized under the right conditions. Human nature is not static. It is not merely re-expressed in generations and individuals. It is "not a machine to be built after a model, and set to do exactly the work prescribed for it, but a tree, which requires to grow and develop itself on all sides, according to the tendency of the inward forces which make it a living thing." Though human nature can be thought of as something living, it is also, like an English garden, something amenable to improvement through effort. "Among the works of man, which human life is rightly employed in perfecting and beautifying, the first in importance surely is man himself." The two conditions that promote development of our humanity are freedom and variety of situation, both of which the harm principle encourages.

A basic philosophical problem presented by the work is what counts as "harm to others." Where should we mark the boundary between conduct that is principally self-regarding versus conduct that involves others? Does drug-use cause harm to others sufficient to be prevented? Does prostitution? Pornography? Should polygamy be allowed? How about public nudity? Though these are difficult questions, Mill provides the reader with a principled way of deliberating about them.

Women and Other Social-political Writings

Many volumes of Mill's writings deal with topics of social and political concern. These include writings on specific political problems in India, America, Ireland, France, and England, on the nature of democracy (Considerations on Representative Government) and civilization, on slavery, on law and jurisprudence, on the workplace, and on the family and the status of women. The last subject was the topic of Mill's well-known *The Subjection of Women*, an important work in the history of feminism.

The radical nature of Mill's call for women's equality is often lost to us after over a century of protest and changing social attitudes. Yet the subordination of women to men when Mill was writing remains striking. Among other indicators of this subordination are the following:

(1) British women had fewer grounds for divorce than men until 1923;

(2) Husbands controlled their wives personal property (with

the occasional exception of land) until the Married Women's Property Acts of 1870 and 1882;

(3) Children were the husband's;

(4) Rape was impossible within a marriage; and

(5) Wives lacked crucial features of legal personhood, since the husband was taken as the representative of the family (thereby eliminating the need for women's suffrage). This gives some indication of how disturbing and/or ridiculous the idea of a marriage between equals could appear to Victorians.

The object of the essay was to show "(t)hat the principle which regulates the existing social relations between the two sexes—the legal subordination of one sex to the other-is wrong in itself, and now one of the chief hindrances to human improvement; and that it ought to be replaced by a principle of perfect equality, admitting no power or privilege on the one side, nor disability on the other." This shows how Mill appeals to both the patent injustice of contemporary familial arrangements and to the negative moral impact of those arrangements on the people within them.

In particular, he discusses the ways in which the subordination of women negatively affects not only the women, but also the men and children in the family. This subordination stunts the moral and intellectual development of women by restricting their field of activities, pushing them either into self-sacrifice or into selfishness and pettiness. Men, alternatively, either become brutal through their relationships with women or turn away from projects of self-improvement to pursue the social "consideration" that women desire. It is important to note that Mill's concern for the status of women dovetails with the rest of his thought-it is not a disconnected issue.

For example, his support for women's equality was buttressed by associationism, which claims that minds are created by associative laws operating on experience. This implies that if we change the experiences and upbringing of women, then their minds will change.

This enabled Mill to argue against those who tried to suggest that the subordination of women to men reflected a natural order that women were by nature incapable of equality with men. If many women were incapable of true friendship with noble men, says Mill, that is not a result of their natures, but of their faulty environments.

Principles of Political Economy

Another work that addresses issues of social and political concern is Mill's *Principles of Political Economy* of 1848. The book went through numerous editions and served as the dominant British textbook in economics until being displaced by Alfred Marshall's 1890 *Principles of Economics.*

Mill intended the work as both a survey of contemporary economic thought (highlighting the theories of David Ricardo, but also including some contributions of his own on topics like international trade) and as an exploration of applications of economic ideas to social concerns.

It was "not a book merely of abstract science, but also of application, and treated *Political Economy* not as a thing by itself, but as a fragment of a greater whole." These two interests nicely divide the text into the first three more technical books on production, distribution, and exchange and the last two books, which address the influences of societal progress and of government on economic activity (and vice versa). The technical work is largely obsolete. Mill's relating of economics and society, however, remains of great interest.

In particular, Mill shared concerns with others (e.g. Carlyle, Coleridge, Southey, etc.) about the moral impact of industrialization. Though many welcomed the material wealth produced by industrialization, there was a sense that those very cornerstones of British economic growth-the division of labour (including the increasing simplicity and repetitiveness of the work) and the growing size of factories and businesses-led to a spiritual and moral deadening. Coleridge expressed this in his contrast of mere "civilization" with "cultivation":

> The permanency of the nation...and its progressiveness and personal freedom...depend on a continuing and progressive civilization. But civilization is itself but a mixed good, if not far more a corrupting influence, the hectic of

> disease, not the bloom of health, and a nation so distinguished more fitly to be called a varnished than a polished people, where this civilization is not grounded in cultivation, in the harmonious development of those qualities and faculties that characterize our humanity. We must be men in order to be citizens. (Coleridge 1839, 46).

"Civilization" expresses central features of modernization, including industrialism, cosmopolitanism, and increasing material wealth. But, for Coleridge, civilization needed to be subordinated to cultivation of our humanity.

This concern for the moral impact of economic growth explains, among other things, his commitment to a brand of socialism. In an essay on the French historian Michelet, Mill praises the monastic associations of Italy and France after the reforms of St. Benedict: "Unlike the useless communities of contemplative ascetics in the East, they were diligent in tilling the earth and fabricating useful products; they knew and taught that temporal work may also be a spiritual exercise." It was the desire to transform temporal work into a spiritual and moral exercise that led Mill to favour socialist changes in the workplace.

In order to transform the workplace from a setting filled with antagonism into a "school of sympathy" that would enable workers to feel a part of something greater than themselves-thereby mitigating the rampant selfishness encouraged by industrial society-Mill recommends "industrial co-operatives." Mill thought that these co-operatives had the advantage over communes or other socialist institutions because they were able to compete against traditional firms (his complaint against many other socialists is that they undervalued competition as a morally useful stimulus to activity). These co-operatives can take two forms: a profit-sharing system in which worker pay is tied to the success of the business or a worker co-operative in which workers share ownership of capital. The latter was preferable because it turned all the workers into entrepreneurs, calling upon many of the faculties that mere labour for pay left to atrophy.

Though Mill contended that labourers were generally unfit for socialism given their current level of education and development, he thought that modern industrial societies should take small steps towards fostering co-operatives. Included among these steps was the institution of limited partnerships. Up to Mill's time, partners shared full liability for losses, including any personal property they owned-obviously a strong deterrent to the founding of worker co-operatives. Mill's recommendations for the economic organization of society, like his political and social policies, always paid careful attention to how institutions, laws, and practices impacted the intellectual, moral, and affective well-being of the individuals operating under or within them.

Essays on Religion

Mill's criticism of traditional religious doctrines and institutions and his promotion of the "Religion of Humanity," also depended largely on concerns about human cultivation and education. Though the Benthamite "philosophic radicals," including Mill, took Christianity to be a particularly pernicious superstition that fostered indifference or hostility to human happiness (the keystone of utilitarian morality), Mill also thought that religion could potentially serve important ethical needs by supplying us with "ideal conceptions grander and more beautiful than we see realized in the prose of human life." In so doing, religion elevates our feelings, cultivates sympathy with others, and imbues even our smallest activities with a sense of purpose.

The posthumously published three Essays on Religion (1874)-on "Nature," the "Utility of Religion," and "Theism"-criticized traditional religious views and formulated an alternative in the guise of the Religion of Humanity. Along with the criticism of religion's moral effects that he shared with the Benthamites, Mill was also critical of the intellectual laziness that permitted belief in an omnipotent and benevolent God. He felt, following his father, that the world as we find it could not possibly have come from such a God given the evils rampant in it; either his power is limited or he is not wholly benevolent.

Beyond attacking arguments concerning the essence of God, Mill undermines a variety of arguments for his existence including all a priori arguments. He concludes that the only legitimate proof of God is an a posteriori and probabilistic argument from the design of the universe-the traditional argument (stemming from

Aristotle) that complex features of the world, like the eye, are unlikely to have arisen by chance, hence there must be a designer.

Inspired by Comte, Mill finds an alternative to traditional religion in the *Religion of Humanity*, in which an idealized humanity becomes an object of reverence and the morally useful features of traditional religion are supposedly purified and accentuated.

Humanity becomes an inspiration by being placed imaginatively within the drama of human history, which has a destination or point, namely the victory of good over evil. As Mill puts it, history should be seen as "the unfolding of a great epic or dramatic action," which terminates "in the happiness or misery, the elevation or degradation, of the human race." It is "an unremitting conflict between good and evil powers, of which every act done by any of us, insignificant as we are, forms one of the incidents."

As we begin to see ourselves as participants in this Manichean drama, as fighting alongside people like Socrates, Newton, and Jesus to secure the ultimate victory of good over evil, we become capable of greater sympathy, moral feeling, and an ennobled sense of the meaning of our own lives. The Religion of Humanity thereby acts as an instrument of human cultivation.

Mill's intellect engaged with the world rather than fled from it. His was not an ivory tower philosophy, even when dealing with the most abstract of philosophical topics. His work is of enduring interest because it reflects how a fine mind struggled with and attempted to synthesize important intellectual and cultural movements.

He stands at the intersections of conflicts between enlightenment and romanticism, liberalism and conservatism, and historicism and rationalism. In each case, as someone interested in conversation rather than pronouncement, he makes sincere efforts to move beyond polemic into sustained and thoughtful analysis. That analysis produced challenging answers to problems that still remain. Whether or not one agrees with his answers, Mill serves as a model for thinking about human problems in a serious and civilized way.

Works

Theory of Liberty

Mill's *On Liberty* addresses the nature and limits of the power that can be legitimately exercised by society over the individual. One argument that Mill develops further than any previous philosopher is the harm principle. The harm principle holds that each individual has the right to act as he wants, so long as these actions do not harm others. If the action is self-regarding, that is, if it only directly affects the person undertaking the action, then society has no right to intervene, even if it feels the actor is harming himself. Mill excuses those who are "incapable of self-government" from this principle, such as young children or those living in "backward states of society". It is important to emphasize that Mill did not consider giving offense to constitute "harm"; an action could not be restricted because it violated the conventions or morals of a given society. The idea of 'offense' causing harm and thus being restricted was later developed by Joel Feinberg in his 'offense principle' essentially an extension of J.S.Mill's 'harm principle'.

On Liberty involves an impassioned defense of free speech. Mill argues that free discourse is a necessary condition for intellectual and social progress. We can never be sure, he contends, that a silenced opinion does not contain some element of the truth. He also argues that allowing people to air false opinions is productive for two reasons. First, individuals are more likely to abandon erroneous beliefs if they are engaged in an open exchange of ideas. Second, by forcing other individuals to re-examine and re-affirm their beliefs in the process of debate, these beliefs are kept from declining into mere dogma. It is not enough for Mill that one simply has an unexamined belief that happens to be true; one must understand why the belief in question is the true one.

Mill's states the harm principle in Chapter 1 of *On Liberty*:

> "The sole end for which mankind are warranted, individually or collectively, in interfering with the liberty of action of any of their number, is self-protection. That the only purpose for which power can be rightfully exercised over any member of a civilized community,

> against his will, is to prevent harm to others. His own good, either physical or moral, is not sufficient warrant. He cannot rightfully be compelled to do or forbear because it will be better for him to do so, because it will make him happier, because, in the opinion of others, to do so would be wise, or even right...The only part of the conduct of anyone, for which he is amenable to society, is that which concerns others. In the part which merely concerns himself, his independence is, of right, absolute. Over himself, over his own body and mind, the individual is sovereign."

Though this principle seems clear, there are a number of complications. For example, Mill explicitly states that "harms" may include acts of omission as well as acts of commission. Thus, failing to rescue a drowning child counts as a harmful act, as does failing to pay taxes, or failing to appear as a witness in court. All such harmful omissions may be regulated, according to Mill. By contrast, it does not count as harming someone if — without force or fraud — the affected individual consents to assume the risk: thus one may permissibly offer unsafe employment to others, provided there is no deception involved. (Mill does, however, recognize one limit to consent: society should not permit people to sell themselves into slavery). In these and other cases, it is important to keep in mind that the arguments in *On Liberty* are grounded on the principle of Utility, and not on appeals to natural rights. The question of what counts as a self-regarding action and what actions, whether of omission or commission, constitute harmful actions subject to regulation, continues to exercise interpreters of Mill.

Additionally, Mill demonstrated a deep appreciation for the military, noting in his essay "The Contest In America":

> "War is an ugly thing, but not the ugliest of things. The decayed and degraded state of moral and patriotic feeling which thinks that nothing is worth war is much worse. The person who has nothing for which he is willing to fight, nothing which is more important than his own personal safety, is a miserable creature and has no chance of being free unless made and kept so by the exertions of better men than himself."

This particular version of the quotation is often used as a condensed version by military doctrines in order to express the message simply. The original, wordier full quotation is:

> "But war, in a good cause, is not the greatest evil which a nation can suffer. War is an ugly thing, but not the ugliest of things: the decayed and degraded state of moral and patriotic feeling which thinks nothing is worth a war, is worse. When a people are used as mere human instruments for firing cannon or thrusting bayonets, in the service and for the selfish purposes of a master, such war degrades a people. A war to protect other human beings against tyrannical injustice – a war to give victory to their own ideas of right and good, and which is their own war, carried on for an honest purpose by their free choice – is often the means of their regeneration. A man who has nothing which he is willing to fight for, nothing which he cares more about than he does about his personal safety, is a miserable creature who has no chance of being free, unless made and kept so by the exertions of better men than himself. As long as justice and injustice have not terminated their ever-renewing fight for ascendancy in the affairs of mankind, human beings must be willing, when need is, to do battle for the one against the other."

Mill's View on Social Liberty and Tyranny of Majority

Mill believes that "the struggle between Liberty and Authority is the most conspicuous feature in the portions of history." For him, liberty in antiquity was a "contest... between subjects, or some classes of subjects, and the government". By liberty, he meant protection against the tyranny of the political rulers" and he calls it "social liberty." He introduces different tyrannies such as social tyranny, and the tyranny of the majority.

Social Liberty for Mill was to put limits on the ruler's power so that he would not be able to use his power on his own wishes and make every kind of decision which could harm society; in other words, people should have the right to a say in the government's decisions. He said that social liberty was "the nature and limits of the power which can be legitimately exercised by society over the individual". It was attempted in two ways: first, by obtaining recognition of certain immunities, called political liberties or rights; second, by establishment of a system of "constitutional checks". However, limiting the power of government is not enough. "Society can and does execute its own mandates: and if it issues wrong mandates instead of right, or any mandates at all in things with which it ought not to meddle, it practises a social tyranny more formidable than many kinds of political oppression, since, though not usually upheld by such extreme penalties, it leaves fewer means of escape, penetrating much more deeply into the details of life, and enslaving the soul itself."

"The rulers should be identified with the people; that their interest and will should be the interest and will of the nation. The nation did not need to be protected against its own will." By will of nation, he means the will of "the most active part of people and the majority."

"The people, consequently, may desire to oppress a part of their number; and precautions are as much needed against this, as against any other abuse of power." He calls this type of power the "tyranny of majority" when the majority oppresses the minority by their decisions which could be harmful and wrong sometimes. As he writes, that tyranny of majority "is still vulgarly, held in dread, chiefly as operating through the acts of the public authorities."

Religious View

John Stuart Mill's religious view, influenced by John Locke, is that man is free to do anything unless he harms others. Individuals are rational enough to make decisions about their good being and choose any religion they want to. Government should interfere when it is for the protection of society. Mill explains, "The sole end for which mankind are warranted, individually or collectively, in interfering with the liberty of action of any of their number, is self-protection. That the only purpose for which power can be rightfully exercised over any member of a civilized community, against his will, is to prevent harm to others. His own good, either physical or moral, is not sufficient warrant. He cannot rightfully be compelled to do or forbear because it will be better for him to do so, because it will make him happier, because, in the opinion of others, to do so would be wise, or even right...The only part of the conduct of anyone, for which he is amenable to society, is that which concerns others. In the part which merely concerns him, his independence is, of right, absolute. Over himself, over his own body and mind, the individual is sovereign."

Non Secular Governance and Atheism

Mill stated on many occasions that the idea of religion involving doctrine repulsed him as it imposes an unchallengable opinion from an infallible authority such as God. He says: "I choose, by preference the cases which are least favourable to me - In which the argument against freedom of opinion, both on truth and that of utility, is considered the strongest. Let the opinions impugned be the belief of God and in a future state, or any of the commonly received doctrines of morality... But I must be permitted to observe that it is not the feeling sure of a doctrine (be it what it may) which I call an assumption of infallibility. It is the undertaking to decide that question *for others,* without allowing them to hear what can be said on the contrary side. And I denounce and reprobate this pretension not the less if I put forth on the side of my most solemn convictions.

However positive anyone's persuasion may be, not only of the faculty but of the pernicious consequences, but (to adopt expressions which I altogether condemn) the immorality and impiety of opinion—yet if, in pursuance of that private judgement, though backed by the public judgement of his country or contemporaries, he prevents the opinion from being heard in its defence, he assumes infallibility. And so far from the assumption being less objectionable or less dangerous because the opinion is called immoral or impious, this is the case of all others in which is most fatal."

Human Rights and Slavery

In 1850, Mill sent an anonymous letter (which came to be known under the title "The Negro Question") — in rebuttal to Thomas Carlyle's anonymous letter — to Fraser's Magazine for

Town and Country. Carlyle had defended slavery on grounds of genetic inferiority and claimed that the West Indies development was due to British ingenuity alone and dismissed any notion that there was a debtedness to imported slaves for building the economy there. Mill's rebuttal and references to the ongoing debate in the U.S. at the time regarding slavery were emphatic and eloquent. An excerpt — one lengthy paragraph — which turns metaphorical (highlighted in boldface) regarding the pivotal role of nurture over nature (defying race-based genetic disparagements) — and in which "professed moral reformer" and "your contributor" both refer to Carlyle — illustrates Mill's passionate defense of human rights and abhorrence of slavery:

> "But the great ethical doctrine of the discourse, than which a doctrine more damnable, I should think, never was propounded by a professed moral reformer, is, that one kind of human beings are born servants to another kind. "You will have to be servants," he tells the negroes, "to those that are born wiser than you, that are born lords of you — servants to the whites, if they are (as what mortal can doubt that they are?) born wiser than you." I do not hold him to the absurd letter of his dictum; it belongs to the mannerism in which he is enthralled like a child in swaddling clothes. By "born wiser," I will suppose him to mean, born more capable of wisdom: a proposition which, he says, no mortal can doubt, but which, I will make bold to say, that a full moiety of all thinking persons, who have attended to the subject, either doubt or positively deny. Among the things for which your contributor professes entire disrespect, is the analytical examination of [p.468] human nature. It is by analytical examination that we have learned whatever we know of the laws of external nature; and if he had not disdained to apply the same mode of investigation to the laws of the formation of character, he would have escaped the vulgar error of imputing every difference which he finds among human beings to an original difference of nature. As well might it be said, that of two trees, sprung from the same stock one cannot be taller than another but from greater vigour in the original seedling. Is nothing to be attributed to soil,

nothing to climate, nothing to difference of exposure — has no storm swept over the one and not the other, no lightning scathed it, no beast browsed on it, no insects preyed on it, no passing stranger stript [sic] off its leaves or its bark? If the trees grew near together, may not the one which, by whatever accident, grew up first, have retarded the other's development by its shade? Human beings are subject to an infinitely greater variety of accidents and external influences than trees, and have infinitely more operation in impairing the growth of one another; since those who begin by being strongest, have almost always hitherto used their strength to keep the others weak. What the original differences are among human beings, I know no more than your contributor, and no less; it is one of the questions not yet satisfactorily answered in the natural history of the species. This, however, is well known — that spontaneous improvement, beyond a very low grade — improvement by internal development, without aid from other individuals or peoples — is one of the rarest phenomena in history; and whenever known to have occurred, was the result of an extraordinary combination of advantages; in addition doubtless to many accidents of which all trace is now lost. No argument against the capacity of negroes for improvement, could be drawn from their not being one of these rare exceptions. It is curious, withal, that the earliest known civilization was, we have the strongest reason to believe, a negro civilization. The original Egyptians are inferred, from the evidence of their sculptures, to have been a negro race: it was from negroes, therefore, that the Greeks learnt their first lessons in civilization; and to the records and traditions of these negroes did the Greek philosophers to the very end of their career resort (I do not say with much fruit) as a treasury of mysterious wisdom. But I again renounce all advantage from facts: were the whites born ever so superior in intelligence to the blacks, and competent by nature to instruct and advise them, it would not be the less monstrous to assert that they had therefore a right either

> to subdue them by force, or circumvent them by superior skill; to throw upon them the toils and hardships of life, reserving for themselves, under the misapplied name of work, its agreeable excitements."

Mill is also famous for being one of the earliest and strongest supporters of women's liberation. His book *The Subjection of Women* is one of the earliest written on this subject by a male author. He felt that the oppression of women was one of the few remaining relics from ancient times, a set of prejudices that severely impeded the progress of humanity.

Utilitarianism

The canonical statement of Mill's Utilitarianism can be found in *Utilitarianism.* This philosophy has a long tradition, although Mill's account is primarily influenced by Jeremy Bentham, and Mill's father James Mill. However his conception of utilitarianism was so different from Bentham's that some modern thinkers have argued that he demonstrated libertarian ideals, and that he was not as much a consequentialist as was Bentham, though he did not reject consequentialism as Kant did. Bentham's famous formulation of Utilitarianism is known as the "greatest happiness principle." It holds that one must always act so as to produce the greatest happiness for the greatest number of people (within reason). One of Mill's major contributions to Utilitarianism is his argument for the qualitative separation of pleasures. Bentham treats all forms of happiness as equal, whereas Mill argues that intellectual and moral pleasures are superior to more physical forms of pleasure. Mill distinguishes between "happiness" and "contentment," claiming that the former is of higher value than the latter, a belief wittily encapsulated in his statement that "It is better to be a human being dissatisfied than a pig satisfied; better to be Socrates dissatisfied than a fool satisfied. And if the fool, or the pig, are of a different opinion, it is because they only know their own side of the question."

Mill defines the difference between higher and lower forms of happiness on the principle that those who have experienced both tend to prefer one over the other. This is, perhaps, in direct opposition to Bentham's statement that "Pushpin is as good as an

Opera," that if a simple child's game like hopscotch causes more pleasure to more people than a night at the opera house, it is more imperative upon a society to devote more resources to propagating hopscotch than running opera houses. Mill's argument is that the 'simple pleasures' tend to be preferred by people who have no experience with high art, and are therefore not in a proper position to judge. For this reason, in his life Mill supported legislation that would have granted extra voting power to university graduates, on the grounds that they were in a better position to judge what would be best for society. It should be noted that, in this example, Mill did not intend to devalue uneducated people, and he certainly would have advocated sending the poor but talented to universities; rather, he believed that education, and not the intrinsic nature of the educated, is what qualified them to have more influence in government.

Mill furthermore dealt with one of the prime problems associated with utilitarianism, that of schadenfreude. Detractors of utilitarianism argued, among other objections, that if enough people hated another person sufficiently that simply reducing the happiness of the object of their hatred would cause them pleasure, it would be incumbent upon a utilitarian society to aid them in harming the individual. Mill argued that, in order to have such an attitude of malice, a citizen would have to value his own pleasure over that of another, and so society is in no way obligated to indulge him, and, to the contrary, is fully permitted to suppress his actions. The qualitative account of happiness Mill advocates thus sheds light on his account presented in *On Liberty*. As Mill suggests in that text, utility is to be conceived in relation to mankind "as a progressive being," which includes the development and exercise of our rational capacities as we strive to achieve a "higher mode of existence". Thus the rejection of censorship and paternalism is intended to provide the necessary social conditions for the achievement of knowledge and the greatest ability for the greatest number to develop and exercise their deliberative and rational capacities.

Economic Philosophy

Mill's early economic philosophy was one of free markets. However, he accepted interventions in the economy, such as a tax on alcohol, if there were sufficient utilitarian grounds. He also accepted the principle of legislative intervention for the purpose of animal welfare. Mill believed that "equality of taxation" meant "equality of sacrifice" and that progressive taxation penalized those who worked harder and saved more and was therefore "a mild form of robbery".

Mill's *Principles of Political Economy*, first published in 1848, was one of the most widely read of all books on economics in the period. As Adam Smith's *Wealth of Nations* had during an earlier period, Mill's *Principles* dominated economics teaching. (In the case of Oxford University it was the standard text until 1919. The text that replaced it was written by Cambridge's Alfred Marshall).

Later in life, Mill moved to favour more socialist-oriented politics. According to his *Autobiography*:

> "In short, I was a democrat, but not the least of a Socialist. We were now much less democrats than I had been, because so long as education continues to be so wretchedly imperfect, we dreaded the ignorance and especially the selfishness and brutality of the mass: but our ideal of ultimate improvement went far beyond Democracy, and would class us decidedly under the general designation of Socialists. While we repudiated with the greatest energy that tyranny of society over the individual which most Socialistic systems are supposed to involve, we yet looked forward to a time when society will no longer be divided into the idle and the industrious;"

8

Karl Marx

Karl Heinrich Marx (May 5, 1818 – March 14, 1883) was a 19th-century philosopher, political economist, sociologist, humanist, political theorist and revolutionary. Often called the father of communism, Marx was both a scholar and a political activist. He addressed a wide range of political as well as social issues, and is known for, amongst other things, his analysis of history. His approach is indicated by the opening line Chapter 1 of the *The Communist Manifesto* (1848): "The history of all hitherto existing society is the history of class struggles". Marx argued that capitalism, like previous socioeconomic systems, will produce internal tensions which will lead to its destruction. Just as capitalism replaced feudalism, capitalism itself will be displaced by communism, a classless society which emerges after a transitional period in which the state would be nothing else but the revolutionary dictatorship of the proletariat.

On the one hand, Marx argued for a systemic understanding of socioeconomic change. On this model, it is the structural contradictions within capitalism which necessitate its end, giving way to communism: "The development of Modern Industry, therefore, cuts from under its feet the very foundation on which the bourgeoisie produces and appropriates products. What the bourgeoisie therefore produces, above all, are its own grave-diggers. Its fall and the victory of the proletariat are equally inevitable." — (*The Communist Manifesto*)

On the other hand, Marx argued that socioeconomic change occurred through organized revolutionary action. On this model, capitalism will end through the organized actions of an international working class: "Communism is for us not a state of affairs which is to be established, an ideal to which reality [will] have to adjust itself. We call communism the real movement which abolishes the present state of things. The conditions of this movement result from the premises now in existence." (from The German Ideology)

While Marx was a relatively obscure figure in his own lifetime, his ideas began to exert a major influence on workers' movements shortly after his death. This influence was given added impetus by the victory of the Marxist Bolsheviks in the Russian October Revolution, and there are few parts of the world which were not significantly touched by Marxian ideas in the course of the twentieth century. The relation of Marx to "Marxism" is a point of controversy. Marxism remains influential and controversial in academic and political circles.

Biography

Karl Heinrich Marx was born the third of seven children of a Jewish family in Trier, in the Kingdom of Prussia's Province of the Lower Rhine. His father, Heinrich Marx (1777–1838), who had descended from a long line of rabbis, converted to Christianity, despite his many deistic tendencies and his admiration of such Enlightenment figures as Voltaire and Rousseau. Marx's father was actually born Herschel Mordechai, son of Levy Mordechai (1743-1804) and wife Eva Lwow (1753-1823), but when the Prussian authorities would not allow him to continue practicing Law as a Jew, he joined the official denomination of the Prussian state, Lutheranism, which accorded him advantages, as one of a small minority of Lutherans in a predominantly Roman Catholic region. His mother was Henriette *nee* Pressburg (1788–1863). His siblings were Sophie (d. 1883) (m. Wilhelm Robert Schmalhausen), Hermann (1819-1842), Henriette (1820-1856), Louise (1821-1893) (m. Johann Carel Juta), Emilie, Caroline (1824-1847) and Eduard (1834-1837). His mother was the grand-aunt of industrialists Gerard Philips and Anton Philips and a maternal descendant of the Barent-Cohen family through her parents Isaac Heijmans Presburg (Presburg, c. 1747 – Nijmegen, May 3, 1832) and wife Nanette Salomon Barent-Cohen (Amsterdam, c. 1764 – Nijmegen, April 7, 1833), the daughter of Salomon David Barent Cohen (d. 1807) and wife Sara Brandes, in turn the uncle and aunt by marriage of Nathan Mayer Rothschild's wife.

Education

Marx was educated at home until the age of thirteen. After graduating from the Trier Gymnasium, Marx enrolled in the University of Bonn in 1835 at the age of seventeen to study law, where he joined the Trier Tavern Club drinking society and at one point served as its president; his grades suffered as a result. Marx was interested in studying philosophy and literature, but his father would not allow it because he did not believe that his son would be able to comfortably support himself in the future as a scholar. The following year, his father forced him to transfer to the far more serious and academically oriented Friedrich-Wilhelms-Universitat in Berlin. During this period, Marx wrote many poems and essays concerning life, using the theological language acquired from his liberal, deistic father, such as "the Deity," but also absorbed the atheistic philosophy of the Young Hegelians who were prominent in Berlin at the time. Marx earned a doctorate in 1841 *with a thesis titled The Difference Between the Democritean and* Epicurean Philosophy of Nature, but he had to submit his dissertation to the University of Jena as he was warned that his reputation among the faculty as a Young Hegelian radical would lead to a poor reception in Berlin.

Marx and the Young Hegelians

The Left, or Young Hegelians, consisted of a group of philosophers and journalists circling around Ludwig Feuerbach and Bruno Bauer opposing their teacher Hegel. Despite their criticism of Hegel's metaphysical assumptions, they made use of Hegel's dialectical method, separated from its theological content, as a powerful weapon for the critique of established religion and politics. Some members of this circle drew an analogy between post-Aristotelian philosophy and post-Hegelian philosophy. One of them, Max Stirner, turned critically against both Feuerbach and *Bauer in his book "Der Einzige und sein Eigenthum" (1845, The* Ego and Its Own), calling these atheists "pious people" for their reification of abstract concepts. Marx, at that time a follower of Feuerbach, was deeply impressed by the work and abandoned

Feuerbachian materialism and accomplished what recent authors have denoted as an "epistemological break." He developed the basic concept of historical materialism against Stirner in his book "Die Deutsche Ideologie" (1846, The German Ideology), which he did not publish. Another link to the Young Hegelians was Moses Hess, with whom Marx eventually disagreed, yet to whom he owed many of his insights into the relationship between state, society and religion.

Marx in Paris and Brussels

Towards the end of October 1843, Marx arrived in Paris, France. There, on August 28, 1844, at the Cafe de la Regence on the Place du Palais he began the most important friendship of his life, and one of the most important in history – he met Friedrich Engels. Engels had come to Paris specifically to see Marx, whom he had met only briefly at the office of the *Rheinische Zeitung* in 1842. He came to show Marx what would turn out to be perhaps Engels' greatest work, *The Condition of the Working Class in England in 1844*. Paris at this time was the home and headquarters to armies of German, British, Polish, and Italian revolutionaries. Marx, for his part, had come to Paris to work with Arnold Ruge, another revolutionary from Germany, on the *Deutsch-Franzosische Jahrbucher*.

After the failure of the *Deutsch-Franzosische Jahrbucher*, Marx, living on the Rue Vaneau, wrote for the most radical of all German newspapers in Paris, indeed in Europe, the *Vorwarts*, established and run by the secret society called *League of the Just*. Marx's topics were generally on the Jewish question and Hegel. When not writing, Marx studied the history of the French Revolution and read Proudhon. He also spent considerable time studying a side of life he had never been acquainted with before – a large urban proletariat. "[Hitherto exposed mainly to university towns...] Marx's sudden espousal of the proletarian cause can be directly attributed (as can that of other early German communists such as Weitling) to his first hand contacts with socialist intellectuals [and books] in France."

He re-evaluated his relationship with the Young Hegelians, and as a reply to Bauer's atheism wrote *On the Jewish Question*. This essay was mostly a critique of current notions of civil and human rights and political emancipation, which also included several critical references to Judaism as well as Christianity from a standpoint of social emancipation. Engels, a committed communist, kindled Marx's interest in the situation of the working class and guided Marx's interest in economics. Marx became a communist and set down his views in a series of writings known as the Economic and Philosophical Manuscripts of 1844, which remained unpublished until the 1930s. In the Manuscripts, Marx outlined a humanist conception of communism, influenced by the philosophy of Ludwig Feuerbach and based on a contrast between the alienated nature of labour under capitalism and a communist society in which human beings freely developed their nature in cooperative production.

In January 1845, after *Vorwarts* expressed its hearty approval of the assassination attempt on Frederick William IV, King of Prussia, Marx, among many others, were ordered to leave Paris. He and Engels moved on to Brussels, Belgium.

Marx devoted himself to an intensive study of history and elaborated on his idea of historical materialism, particularly in a manuscript (published posthumously as *The German Ideology*), the basic thesis of which was that "the nature of individuals depends on the material conditions determining their production." Marx traced the history of the various modes of production and predicted the collapse of the present one—industrial capitalism—and its replacement by communism. This was the first major work of what scholars consider to be his later phase, abandoning the Feuerbach-influenced humanism of his earlier work.

Next, Marx wrote *The Poverty of Philosophy* (1847), a response to Pierre-Joseph Proudhon's The Philosophy of Poverty and a critique of French socialist thought. These works laid the foundation for Marx and Engels' most famous work, *The Communist Manifesto*, first published on February 21, 1848, as the manifesto of the Communist League, a small group of European communists who had come to be influenced by Marx and Engels.

Back in Paris and Failure of the Springtime of Peoples

Later that year, Europe experienced tremendous revolutionary upheaval. Marx, was arrested and expelled from Belgium; in the meantime a radical movement had seized power from King Louis-Philippe in France, and invited Marx to return to Paris, where he witnessed the revolutionary June Days Uprising first hand.

In Cologne and exiled from Germany Again

When this collapsed in 1849, Marx moved back to Cologne and started the *Neue Rheinische Zeitung* ("New Rhenish Newspaper"). During its existence he was put on trial twice, on February 7, 1849 because of a press misdemeanor, and on the 8th charged with incitement to armed rebellion. Both times he was acquitted. The paper was soon suppressed and Marx returned to Paris, but was forced out again. This time he sought refuge in London.

London

Marx moved to London in May 1849, where he was to remain for the rest of his life. He briefly worked as correspondent for the New York Tribune in 1851. In 1855, the Marx family suffered a blow with the death of their son, Edgar, from tuberculosis. Meanwhile, Marx's major work on political economy made slow progress. By 1857 he had produced a gigantic 800 page manuscript on capital, landed property, wage labour, the state, foreign trade and the world market. This work however was not published until 1941, under the title *Grundrisse*. In the early 1860s he worked on composing three large volumes, the *Theories of Surplus Value*, which discussed the theoreticians of political economy, particularly Adam Smith and David Ricardo. This work, that was published posthumously under the editorship of Karl Kautsky is often seen as the Fourth book of *Capital*, and constitutes one of the first comprehensive treatises on the history of economic thought. In 1867, well behind schedule, the first volume of *Capital* was published, a work which analyzed the capitalist process of production. Here, Marx elaborated his labour theory of value and his conception of surplus value and exploitation which he argued would ultimately lead to a falling rate of profit and the collapse of industrial capitalism. Volumes II and III remained mere manuscripts upon which Marx continued to work for the rest of his life and were published posthumously by Engels. In 1859, *Marx was able to publish Contribution to the Critique of Political*

Economy, his first serious economic work. In his journalistic work of this period, Marx championed the Union cause in the American Civil War.

One reason why Marx was so slow to publish *Capital* was that he was devoting his time and energy to the First International, to whose General Council he was elected at its inception in 1864. He was particularly active in preparing for the annual Congresses of the International and leading the struggle against the anarchist wing led by Mikhail Bakunin (1814–1876). Although Marx won this contest, the transfer of the seat of the General Council from London to New York in 1872, which Marx supported, led to the decline of the International.

The most important political event during the existence of the International was the *Paris Commune of 1871* when the citizens of Paris rebelled against their government and held the city for two months. On the bloody suppression of this rebellion, Marx wrote one of his most famous pamphlets, *The Civil War in France*, an enthusiastic defense of the Commune.

During the last decade of his life, Marx's health declined and he was incapable of the sustained effort that had characterized his previous work. He did manage to comment substantially on contemporary politics, particularly in Germany and Russia. In Germany, in his *Critique of the Gotha Programme*, he opposed the tendency of his followers Wilhelm Liebknecht (1826–1900) and August Bebel (1840–1913) to compromise with the state socialism of Ferdinand Lassalle in the interests of a united socialist party. In his correspondence with Vera Zasulich, Marx contemplated the possibility of Russia's bypassing the capitalist stage of development and building communism on the basis of the common ownership of land characteristic of the village *Mir*.

Family Life

Karl Marx was married to Jenny von Westphalen, the educated daughter of a Prussian baron. Karl Marx's engagement to her was kept secret at first, and for several years was opposed by both the Marxes and Westphalens. Despite the objections, the two were married on June 19, 1843 in Kreuznacher Pauluskirche, Bad Kreuznach.

During the first half of the 1850s the Marx family lived in poverty and constant fear of creditors in a three room flat on Dean Street in Soho, London. Marx and Jenny already had four children and three more were to follow. Of these only three survived to adulthood. Marx's major source of income at this time was Engels, who was drawing a steadily increasing income from the family business in Manchester. This was supplemented by weekly articles *written as a foreign correspondent for the New York Daily Tribune.* Inheritances from one of Jenny's uncles and her mother who died in 1856 allowed the family to move to somewhat more salubrious lodgings at 9 Grafton Terrace, Kentish Town a new suburb on the then-outskirts of London. Marx generally lived a hand-to-mouth existence, forever at the limits of his resources, although this did extend to some spending on relatively bourgeois luxuries, which he felt were necessities for his wife and children given their social status and the mores of the time.

There is a disputed and uncorroborated rumour that Marx was the father of Frederick Demuth, the son of Marx's housekeeper, Lenchen Demuth.

Marx's children by his wife were: Jenny Caroline (m. Longuet; 1844–1883); Jenny Laura (m. Lafargue; 1845–1911); Edgar (1847–1855); Henry Edward Guy ("Guido"; 1849–1850); Jenny Eveline Frances ("Franziska"; 1851–1852); Jenny Julia Eleanor (1855–1898); and one more who died before being named (July 1857).

Marx's Life and Works

Karl Marx was born in Trier, in the German Rhineland, in 1818. Although his family was Jewish they converted to Christianity so that his father could pursue his career as a lawyer in the face of Prussia's anti-Jewish laws. A precocious schoolchild, Marx studied law in Bonn and Berlin, and then wrote a PhD thesis in Philosophy, comparing the views of Democritus and Epicurus. On completion of his doctorate in 1841 Marx hoped for an academic job, but he had already fallen in with too radical a group of thinkers and there was no real hope. Turning to journalism Marx rapidly became involved in political and social issues, and soon found himself having to consider communist theory. Of his many early writings, four, in particular stand out. 'Contribution to a

Critique of Hegel's Philosophy of Right, Introduction', and 'On The Jewish Question', were both written in 1843 and published in the Deutsch-Französische Jahrbücher. The Economic and Philosophical Manuscripts, written in Paris 1844, and the 'Theses on Feuerbach' of 1845 remained unpublished in Marx's lifetime.

The German Ideology, co-written with Engels, in 1845, was also unpublished but this is where we see Marx beginning to develop his theory of history. The Communist Manifesto is perhaps Marx's most widely read work, even if it is not the best guide to his thought. This was again jointly written with Engels and published with a great sense of excitement in 1848 as Marx returned to Germany from exile to take part in the revolution of 1848. With the failure of the revolution Marx moved to London where he remained for the rest of his life. He now concentrated on the study of economics, producing, in 1859, his Contribution to a Critique of Political Economy. This is largely remembered for its Preface, in which Marx sketches out what he calls 'the guiding principles' of his thought, on which many interpretations of historical materialism are based. Marx's main economic work is, of course, Capital Volume 1, published in 1867, although Volume 3, edited by Engels, and published posthumously in 1894, contains much of interest. Finally the late pamphlet Critique of the Gotha Programme (1875), is an important source for Marx's reflections on the nature and organisation of communist society.

The works so far mentioned amount only to a small fragment of Marx's opus, which will eventually run to around 100 large volumes when his collected works are completed. However the items selected above form the most important core from the point of view of Marx's connection with philosophy, although other works, such as the 18th Brumaire of Louis Napoleon (1852) are often regarded as equally important in assessing Marx's analysis of concrete political events. In what follows I shall concentrate on those texts and issues which have been given the greatest attention within the philosophical literature.

The Early Writings

The intellectual climate within which the young Marx worked was dominated by the influence of Hegel, and the reaction to

Hegel by a group known as the young-Hegelians, who rejected what they regarded as the conservative implications of Hegel's work. The most significant of these thinkers was Ludwig Feuerbach, who attempted to transform Hegel's metaphysics, and, thereby, provided a critique of Hegel's doctrine of religion and the state. A large portion of the philosophical content of Marx's works written in the early 1840s is a record of his struggle to define his own position in reaction to that of Hegel and Feuerbach and those of the other Young-Hegelians.

'On the Jewish Question'

In this text Marx begins to make clear the distance between him and that of his radical liberal colleagues among the Young Hegelians; in particular Bruno Bauer. Bauer had recently written against Jewish emancipation, from an atheist perspective, arguing that the religion of both Jews and Christians was a barrier to emancipation. In responding to Bauer Marx makes one of the most enduring arguments from his early writings, by means of introducing a distinction between political emancipation-essentially the grant of liberal rights and liberties-and human emancipation. Marx's reply to Bauer is that political emancipation is perfectly compatible with the continued existence of religion, as the example of the United States demonstrates then. However, pushing matters deeper, in an argument reinvented by innumerable critics of liberalism, Marx argues that not only is political emancipation insufficient to bring about human emancipation, it is in some sense also a barrier.

Liberal rights and ideas of justice are premised on the idea that each of us needs protection from other human beings. Therefore liberal rights are designed to protect us from such perceived threats. Freedom on such a view, is freedom from interference. What this view overlooks is the possibility-for Marx, the fact-that real freedom is to be found positively in our relations with other people. It is to be found in human community, not in isolation. So insisting on a regime of rights encourages us to view each other in ways which undermine the possibility of the real freedom we may find in human emancipation. Now we should be clear that Marx does not oppose political emancipation, for he clearly sees that liberalism is a great improvement on the systems of prejudice and discrimination which existed in the Germany of his day. Nevertheless such politically emancipated liberalism must be transcended on the route to genuine human emancipation. Unfortunately Marx never tells us what human emancipation is, although it is clear that it is closely related to the idea of non-alienated labour which we will explore below:

Economic and Philosophical Manuscripts

The Economic and Philosophical Manuscripts cover a wide range of topics including much interesting material on private property and communism, and on money, as well as developing Marx's critique of Hegel. However, they are best known for their account of alienated labour. Here Marx famously depicts the worker under capitalism as suffering from four types of alienated labour. First, from the product, which as soon as it is created is taken away from its producer. Second, in productive activity (work) which is experienced as a torment. Third, from species-being, for humans produce blindly and not in accordance with their truly human powers. Finally from other human beings, where the relation of exchange replaces mutual need. That these categories overlap in some respects is not a surprise given Marx's remarkable methodological ambition in these writings. Essentially he attempts to apply a Hegelian deduction of categories to economics, trying to demonstrate that all the categories of bourgeois economics-wages, rent, exchange, profit etc-are ultimately derived from an analysis of the concept of alienation. Consequently each category of alienated labour is supposed to be deducible from the previous one.

However, Marx gets no further than deducing categories of alienated labour from each other. Quite possibly in the course of writing he came to understand that a different methodology is required for approaching economic issues. Nevertheless we are left with a very rich text on the nature of alienated labour. The idea of non-alienation has to be inferred from the negative, with the assistance of one short passage at the end of the text 'On James Mill' in which non-alienated labour is briefly described in terms which emphasise both the immediate producer's enjoyment of production as a confirmation of his or her powers, and also the idea that production is to meet the needs of others, thus confirming for both parties our human essence as mutual dependence. Both sides of our species essence are revealed here: our individual human powers and our membership in the human community.

It is important to understand that for Marx alienation is not merely a matter of subjective feeling, or confusion. The bridge between Marx's early analysis of alienation and his later social theory is the idea that the alienated individual is 'a plaything of alien forces', albeit alien forces which are themselves a product of human action. In our daily lives we take decisions that have unintended consequences, which then combine to create large-scale social forces which may have an utterly unpredicted effect. In Marx's view the institutions of capitalism-themselves the consequences of human behaviour-come back to structure our future behaviour, determining the possibilities of our action. For example, for as long as a capitalist intends to stay in business he must exploit his workers to the legal limit. Whether wracked by guilt or not the capitalist must act as a ruthless exploiter. Similarly the worker must take the best job on offer; there is simply no other sane option. But by doing this we reinforce the very structures that oppress us. The urge to transcend this condition, and to take collective control of our destiny-whatever that would mean in practice-is one of the motivating and sustaining elements of Marx's attraction to communism.

Theses on Feuerbach

The Theses on Feuerbach contain one of Marx's most memorable remarks 'the philosophers have only interpreted the world, the point is to change it'. However the eleven theses as a whole provide, in the compass of a couple of pages, a remarkable digest of Marx's reaction to the philosophy of his day. Several of these have been touched on already (for example the discussions of religion in theses 4, 6 and 7, and revolution in thesis 3) so here I will concentrate only on the first, most overtly philosophy, thesis. In the first thesis Marx states his objections to 'all hitherto existing' materialism and idealism. Materialism is complimented for understanding the physical reality of the world, but is criticised for ignoring the active role of the human subject in creating the world we perceive. Idealism, at least as developed by Hegel, understands the active nature of the human subject, but confines it to thought or contemplation: the world is created through the categories we impose upon it. Marx combines the insights of both traditions to propose a view in which human beings do indeed create-or at least transform-the world they find themselves in, but this transformation happens not in thought but through actual material activity; not through the imposition of sublime concepts but through the sweat of their brow, with picks and shovels. This historical version of materialism, which transcends and thus rejects all existing philosophical thought, is the foundation of Marx's later theory of history. As Marx puts it in the 1844 Manuscripts, 'Industry is the real historical relationship of nature ... to man'. This thought, derived from reflection on the history of philosophy, sets the agenda for all Marx's future work.

Theory of History

Marx did not set out his theory of history in great detail. Accordingly it has to be constructed from a variety of texts, both those where he attempts to apply a theoretical analysis to past and future historical events, and those of a more purely theoretical nature. Of the latter, the 1859 Preface to A Critique of Political Economy has achieved canonical status. However The German Ideology, co-written with Engels in 1845, is a vital early source in which Marx first sets out the basics of the outlook of historical materialism. We shall briefly outline both texts, and then look at the reconstruction of Marx's theory of history in the hands of his philosophically most influential recent exponent, G.A. Cohen.

The German Ideology

In The German Ideology Marx and Engels contrast their new materialist method with the idealism which had characterised previous German thought. Accordingly they take pains to set out the 'premises of the materialist method'. They start, they say, from 'real human beings', emphasising that human beings are essentially productive, in that they must produce their means of subsistence in order to satisfy their material needs. The satisfaction of needs engenders new needs of both a material and social kind, and forms of society arise corresponding to the state of development of human productive forces. Material life determines, or at least 'conditions' social life, and so the primary direction of social explanation is from material production to social forms, and thence to forms of consciousness. As the material means of production develop, 'modes of co-operation' or economic structures rise and fall, and eventually communism will become a real possibility once the plight of the workers and their awareness of an alternative motivates them sufficiently to become revolutionaries.

1859 Preface

In the sketch of The German Ideology, all the key elements of historical materialism are present, even if the terminology is not yet that of Marx's more mature writings. Marx's statement in 1859 Preface renders much the same view in sharper form. Cohen's reconstruction of Marx's view in the Preface begins from what Cohen calls the Development Thesis, which is pre-supposed, rather than explicitly stated in the Preface. This is the thesis that the productive forces tend to develop, in the sense of becoming more powerful, over time.

This states not that they always do develop, but that there is a tendency for them to do this. The productive forces are the means of production, together with productively applicable knowledge: technology, in other words. The next thesis is the primacy thesis, which has two aspects. The first states that the nature of the economic structure is explained by the level of development of the productive forces, and the second that the nature of the superstructure-the political and legal institutions of society-is explained by the nature of the economic structure. The nature of a society's ideology is also explained in terms of its economic structure, although this receives less emphasis in Cohen's interpretation. Revolution and epoch change is understood as the consequence of an economic structure no longer being able to continue to develop the forces of production. At this point the development of the productive forces is said to be fettered, and, according to the theory once an economic structure fetters development it will be revolutionised-'burst asunder'-and eventually replaced with an economic structure better suited to preside over the continued development of the forces of production.

In outline, then, the theory has a pleasing simplicity and power. It seems plausible that human productive power develops over time, and plausible too that economic structures exist for as long as they develop the productive forces, but will be replaced when they are no longer capable of doing this. Yet severe problems emerge when we attempt to put more flesh on these bones.

Functional Explanation

Prior to Cohen's work, historical materialism had not been regarded as a coherent view within English-language political philosophy. The antipathy is well summed up with the closing words of H.B. Acton's The Illusion of the Epoch 'Marxism is a philosophical farrago'. One difficulty taken particularly seriously by Cohen is an alleged inconsistency between the explanatory primacy of the forces of production, and certain claims made elsewhere by Marx which appear to give the economic structure primacy in explaining the development of the productive forces. For example, in The Communist Manifesto Marx states that: 'The bourgeoisie cannot exist without constantly revolutionising the instruments of production.' This appears to give causal and explanatory primacy to the economic structure-capitalism-which brings about the development of the forces of production. Cohen accepts that, on the surface at least, this generates a contradiction. Both the economic structure and the development of the productive forces seem to have explanatory priority over each other.

Unsatisfied by such vague resolutions such as 'determination in the last instance', or the idea of 'dialectical' connections, Cohen self-consciously attempts to apply the standards of clarity and rigour of analytic philosophy to provide a reconstructed version of historical materialism. The key theoretical innovation is to appeal to the notion of functional explanation (also sometimes called 'consequence explanation'). The essential move is cheerfully to admit that the economic structure does indeed develop the productive forces, but to add that this, according to the theory, is precisely why we have capitalism (when we do). That is, if capitalism failed to develop the productive forces it would disappear. And, indeed, this fits beautifully with historical materialism. For Marx asserts that when an economic structure fails to develop the productive forces-when it 'fetters' the productive forces-it will be revolutionised and the epoch will change. So the idea of 'fettering' becomes the counterpart to the theory of functional explanation. Essentially fettering is what happens when the economic structure becomes dysfunctional.

Now it is apparent that this renders historical materialism consistent. Yet there is a question as to whether it is at too high a price. For we must ask whether functional explanation is a coherent methodological device.

The problem is that we can ask what it is that makes it the case that an economic structure will only persist for as long as it develops the productive forces. Jon Elster has pressed this criticism against Cohen very hard.

If we were to argue that there is an agent guiding history who has the purpose that the productive forces should be developed as much as possible then it would make sense that such an agent would intervene in history to carry out this purpose by selecting the economic structures which do the best job. However it is clear that Marx makes no such metaphysical assumptions. Elster is very critical-sometimes of Marx, sometimes of Cohen-of the idea of appealling to 'purposes' in history without those being the purpose of anyone.

Cohen is well aware of this difficulty, but defends the use of functional explanation by comparing its use in historical materialism with its use in evolutionary biology. In contemporary biology it is commonplace to explain the existence of the stripes of a tiger, or the hollow bones of a bird, by pointing to the function of these features. Here we have apparent purposes which are not the purposes of anyone. The obvious counter, however, is that in evolutionary biology we can provide a causal story to underpin these functional explanations; a story involving chance variation and survival of the fittest.

Therefore these functional explanations are sustained by a complex causal feedback loop in which dysfunctional elements tend to be filtered out in competition with better functioning elements. Cohen calls such background accounts 'elaborations' and he concedes that functional explanations are in need of elaborations. But he points out that standard causal explanations are equally in need of elaborations.

We might, for example, be satisfied with the explanation that the vase broke because it was dropped on the floor, but a great deal of further information is needed to explain why this explanation works. Consequently Cohen claims that we can be justified in offering a functional explanation even when we are in ignorance of its elaboration. Indeed even in biology we have had detailed causal elaborations of functional explanations only relatively recently.

Prior to Darwin, or arguably Lamark, the only candidate causal elaboration was to appeal to God's purposes. Darwin outlined a very plausible mechanism, but having no genetic theory was not able to elaborate it into a detailed account. Our knowledge remains incomplete to this day.

Nevertheless it seems perfectly reasonable to say that birds have hollow bones in order to facilitate flight. Cohen's point is that the weight of evidence that organisms are adapted to their environment would permit even a pre-Darwinian atheist to assert this functional explanation with justification. Hence one can be justified in offering a functional explanation even in absence of a candidate elaboration: if there is sufficient weight of inductive evidence.

At this point the issue, then, divides into a theoretical question and an empirical one. The empirical question is whether or not there is evidence that forms of society exist only for as long as they advance productive power, and are replaced by revolution when they fail. Here, one must admit, the empirical record is patchy at best, and there appear to have been long periods of stagnation, even regression, when dysfunctional economic structures were not revolutionised.

The theoretical issue is whether a plausible elaborating explanation is available to underpin Marxist functional explanations. Here there is something of a dilemma. In the first instance it is tempting to try to mimic the elaboration given in the Darwinian story, and appeal to chance variations and survival of the fittest. In this case 'fittest' would mean 'most able to preside over the development of the productive forces'. Chance variation would be a matter of people trying out new types of economic relations. On this account new economic structures begin through experiment, but thrive and persist through their success in developing the productive forces.

However the problem is that this would seem to introduce a larger element of contingency than Marx seeks, for it is essential to Marx's thought that one should be able to predict the eventual arrival of communism. Within Darwinian theory there is no warrant for long-term predictions, for everything depends on the contingencies of particular situations. A similar heavy element of contingency would be inherited by a form of historical materialism developed by analogy with evolutionary biology. The dilemma, then, is that the best model for developing the theory makes predictions based on the theory unsound, yet the whole point of the theory is predictive. Hence one must either look for an alternative means of producing elaborating explanation, or give up the predictive ambitions of the theory.

Rationality

The driving force of history, in Cohen's reconstruction of Marx, is the development of the productive forces, the most important of which is technology. But what is it that drives this? Ultimately, in Cohen's account, it is human rationality. Human beings have the ingenuity to apply themselves to develop means to address the scarcity they find.

This on the face of it seems very reasonable. Yet there are difficulties. As Cohen himself acknowledges, societies do not always do what would be rational for an individual to do. Co-ordination problems may stand in our way, and there may be structural barriers. Furthermore it is relatively rare for those who introduce new technologies to be motivated by the need to address scarcity. Rather, under capitalism, the profit motive is the key. Of course it might be argued that this is the social form that the material need to address scarcity takes under capitalism.

But still one may raise the question whether the need to address scarcity always has the influence that it appears to have taken on in modern times. For example, a ruling class's absolute determination to hold on to power may have led to economically stagnant societies. Alternatively it might be thought that a society may put religion or the protection of traditional ways of life ahead of economic needs.

This goes to the heart of Marx's theory that man is an essentially productive being and that the locus of interaction with the world is industry. As Cohen himself later argued in his essays such as 'Reconsidering Historical Materialism' this may appear one-sided, and ignore other powerful elements in human nature. This criticism chimes with a criticism from the previous section; that the historical record may not, in fact, display the tendency to growth in the productive forces assumed by the theory.

Morality

The issue of Marx and morality poses a conundrum. On reading Marx's works at all periods of his life, there appears to be the strongest possible distaste towards bourgeois capitalist society, and an undoubted endorsement of future communist society. Yet the terms of this antipathy and endorsement are far from clear. Despite expectations, Marx never says that capitalism is unjust to the workers.

Neither does he say that communism would be a just form of society. In fact he takes pains to distance himself from those who engage in a discourse of justice, and makes a conscious attempt to exclude direct moral commentary in his own works. The puzzle is why this should be, given the weight of indirect moral commentary one finds.

There are, initially, separate questions, concerning Marx's attitude to capitalism and to communism. There are also separate questions concerning his attitude to ideas of justice, and to ideas of morality more broadly concerned. This, then, generates four questions: (1) Did Marx think capitalism unjust?; (2) did he think that capitalism could be morally criticised on other grounds?; (3) did he think that communism would be just? (4) did he think it could be morally approved of on other grounds? These are the questions we shall consider in this section.

The initial argument that Marx must have thought that capitalism is unjust is based on the observation that Marx argued that all capitalist profit is ultimately derived from the exploitation of the worker. Capitalism's dirty secret is that it is not a realm of harmony and mutual benefit but a system in which one class systematically extracts profit from another. How could this fail to be unjust? Yet it is notable that Marx never concludes this, and in Capital he goes as far as to say that such exchange is 'by no means an injustice'.

Allen Wood has argued that Marx took this approach because his general theoretical standpoint excludes any trans-epochal standpoint from which one can comment on the justice of an economic system. Even though one can criticize particular behaviour from within an economic structure as unjust (and theft under capitalism would be an example of this) it is not possible to criticise capitalism as a whole. This is a consequence of Marx's analysis of the role of ideas of justice from within historical materialism.

That is to say, juridicial institutions are part of the superstructure, and ideas of justice are ideological, and the role of both the superstructure and ideology, in the functionalist reading of historical materialism adopted here, is to stabilise the economic structure. Consequently to state that something is just under capitalism is simply a judgement applied to those elements of the system that will tend to have the effect of advancing capitalism. This is further explained through Marx's dictum that in any society the ruling ideas are those of the ruling class; the core of the theory of ideology.

Ziyad Husami, however, argues that Wood is mistaken, ignoring the fact that for Marx ideas undergo a double determination in that the ideas of the non-ruling class may be very different from those of the ruling class.

Of course it is the ideas of the ruling class that receive attention and implementation, but this does not mean that other ideas do not exist. Husami goes as far as to argue that members of the proletariat under capitalism have an account of justice which matches communism. From this privileged standpoint of the proletariat, which is also Marx's standpoint, capitalism is unjust, and so it follows that Marx thought capitalism unjust.

Plausible though it may sound, Husami's argument fails to account for two related points. First, it cannot explain why Marx never described capitalism as unjust, and second it does not account for the distance Marx wanted to place between his own scientific socialism, and that of the utopian socialists who argued for the injustice of capitalism. Hence one cannot avoid the conclusion that the 'official' view of Marx is that capitalism is not unjust.

Nevertheless, this leaves us with a puzzle. Much of Marx's description of capitalism-his use of the words 'embezzlement', 'robbery' and 'exploitation' &mdash belie the official account. In my view the only satisfactory way of understanding this issue is, once more, from G.A. Cohen who proposes that Marx believed that capitalism was unjust, but did not believe that he believed it was unjust. In other words Marx, like so many of us, did not have perfect knowledge of his own mind. In his explicit reflections on the justice of capitalism he was able to maintain his official view. But in less guarded moments his real view slips out, even if never in explicit language. Such an interpretation is bound to be controversial, but it makes good sense of the texts.Whatever one concludes on the question of whether Marx thought capitalism unjust, it is, nevertheless, obvious that Marx thought that capitalism was not the best way for human beings to live. Here points made in his early writings remain present throughout his writings, if no longer connected to an explicit theory of alientation. The worker finds work a torment, suffers poverty, overwork and lack of fulfillment and freedom. People do not relate to each as humans should.

Does this amount to a moral criticism of capitalism or not? In the absence of any special reason to argue otherwise, it simply seems obvious that Marx's critique is a moral one. Capitalism impedes human flourishing. Marx, though, once more refrained from making this explicit; he seemed to show no interest in locating his criticism of capitalism in any of the traditions of moral philosophy, or explaining how he was generating a new tradition. There may have been two reasons for his caution. The first was that while there were bad things about capitalism there is, from a world historical point of view, much good about it too. For without capitalism communism would not be possible. Capitalism is to be transcended, not abolished, and this may be difficult to convey in the terms of moral philosophy.

Second, and perhaps more importantly, we need to return to the contrast between scientific and utopian socialism. The utopians appealled to universal ideas of truth and justice to defend their proposed schemes, and their theory of transition was based on the idea that appealing to moral sensibilities would be the best, perhaps only, way of bringing about the new chosen society.

Marx wanted to distance himself from this tradition of utopian thought, and the key point of distinction was to argue that the route to understanding the possibilities of human emancipation lay in the analysis of historical and social forces, not in morality. Hence, for Marx, any appeal to morality was theoretically a backward step.

This leads us now to Marx's assessment of communism. Would communism be a just society? In considering Marx's attitude to communism and justice there are really only two viable possibilities: either he thought that communism would be a just society or he thought that the concept of justice would not apply: that communism would transcend justice.

Communism is described by Marx, in the Critique of the Gotha Programme, as a society in which each person should contribute according to their ability and receive according to their need. This certainly sounds like a theory of justice, and could be adopted as such. However it is possibly truer to Marx's thought to say that this is part of an account in which communism transcends justice, as Lukes has argued.

If we start with the idea that the point of ideas of justice is to resolve disputes, then a society without disputes would have no need or place for justice. We can see this by reflecting upon Hume's idea of the circumstances of justice. Hume argued that if there was enormous material abundance-if everyone could have whatever they wanted without invading another's share-we would never have devised rules of justice. And, of course, Marx often suggested that communism would be a society of such abundance.

But Hume also suggested that justice would not be needed in other circumstances; if there were complete fellow-feeling between all human beings. Again there would be no conflict and no need for justice. Of course one can argue whether either material abundance or human fellow-feeling to this degree would be possible, but the point is that both arguments give a clear sense in which communism transcends justice.

Nevertheless we remain with the question of whether Marx thought that communism could be commended on other moral grounds. One compelling argument is that Marx's career simply makes no sense unless we can attribute this belief to him. But beyond this we can be brief in that the considerations adduced in section 2 above apply again. Communism clearly advances human flourishing, in Marx's view.

The only reason for denying that, in Marx's vision, it would amount to a good society is a theoretical antipathy to the word 'good'. And here the main point is that, in Marx's view, communism would not be brought about by high-minded benefactors of humanity. Quite possibly his determination to retain this point of difference between himself and the Utopian socialists led him to disparage the importance of morality to a degree that goes beyond the call of theoretical necessity.

Karl Marx and Friedrich Engels strove to put into practical effect the humanitarian concept of Feuerbach. In so doing, they founded a new economic movement called Socialism. According to Marx, the supreme end of man is an immanent and material one, and consists in happiness. This material happiness must be obtained through organized collectivism. In fact, according to Marx, reality is governed by economic needs (historical materialism). Economic reality develops according to Hegel's dialectical principles; that is, reality must deny itself in order to reach a higher degree of being.

In application, this principle means that the present organization of society must be destroyed (even through violent revolution, if necessary, because only through such destruction can a better political, economic, and social organization be achieved. To establish this new format of society, working men (the proletariat) must be organized and take up the struggle against the capitalists who defraud them. Thus the actors in this drama are the social classes--the proletariat is arrayed against capitalism. This struggle, according to Marx and Engels, will end in victory for the proletariat, that is, in the triumph of universal Socialism.

Life and Works

Karl Marx (picture) was born on May 5, 1818 and died on March 14, 1883. He was a German economist, philosopher, and revolutionist whose writings form the basis of the body of ideas known as Marxism.

With the aid of Friedrich Engels (picture) he produced much of the theory of modern socialism and communism. Marx's father, Heinrich, was a Jewish lawyer who had converted his family to Christianity partly in order to preserve his job in the Prussian state. Karl himself was baptized in the Evangelical church. As a student at the University of Berlin, young Marx was strongly influenced by the philosophy of Georg Hegel and by a radical group called Young Hegelians, who attempted to apply Hegelian ideas to the movement against organized religion and the Prussian autocracy. In 1841, Marx received a doctorate in philosophy.

In 1842, Marx became editor of the Rheinische Zeitung in Cologne, a liberal democratic newspaper for which he wrote increasingly radical editorials on social and economic issues. The newspaper was banned by the Prussian government in 1843, and Marx left for Paris with his bride, Jenny von Westphalen.

There he went further in his criticism of society, building on the Young Hegelian criticism of religion. Ludwig Feuerbach had written a book called The Essence of Christianity, arguing that God had been invented by humans as a projection of their own ideals.

Feuerbach wrote that man, however, in creating God in his own image, had "alienated himself from himself." He had created another being in contrast to himself, reducing himself to a lowly, evil creature who needed both church and government to guide and control him. If religion were abolished, Feuerbach claimed, human beings would overcome their alienation.

Marx applied this idea of alienation to private property, which he said caused humans to work only for themselves, not for the good of their species. In his papers of this period, published as Economic and Philosophic Manuscripts of 1844, he elaborated on the idea that alienation had an economic base. He called for a communist society to overcome the dehumanizing effect of private property. In 1845, Marx moved to Brussels, and in 1847 he went to London. He had previously made friends with Friedrich Engels, the son of a wealthy textile manufacturer who, like himself, had been a Young Hegelian. They collaborated on a book which was a criticism of some of their Young Hegelian friends for their stress on alienation.

In 1845, Marx jotted down some notes, Theses on Feuerbach, which he and Engels enlarged into a book, The German Ideology, in which they developed their materialistic conception of history. They argued that human thought was determined by social and economic forces, particularly those related to the means of production. They developed a method of analysis they called dialectical materialism, in which the clash of historical forces leads to changes in society. In 1847 a London organization of workers invited Marx and Engels to prepare a program for them. It appeared in 1848 as The Communist Manifesto. In it they declared that all history was the history of class struggles. Under capitalism, the struggle between the working class and the business class would end in a new society, a communist one.

The outbreak of the Revolutions of 1848 in Europe led Marx to return to Cologne, where he began publication of the Neue Rheinische Zeitung, but with the failure of the German liberal democratic movement he moved permanently, in 1849, to London. For many years he and his family lived in poverty, aided by small subventions from Engels and by bequests from the relatives of Marx's wife. From 1851 to 1862 he contributed articles and editorials to The New York Tribune, then edited by Horace Greeley. Most of his time, however, was spent in the British Museum, studying economic and social history and developing his theories. Marx's ideas began to influence a group of workers and German emigres in London, who established the International Workingmen's Association in 1864, later known as the First International. By the time of the brief Commune of Paris in 1871, Marx's name had begun to be well known in European political circles. A struggle developed within the International between Marx and the Russian anarchist Mikhail Bakunin, whom Marx eventually defeated and expelled, at the cost of destroying the International.

In 1867, Marx published the first volume of Das Kapital. The next two volumes, edited by Engels, were published after Marx's death. The fourth volume was edited by Karl Kautsky. Marx's last years were marked by illness and depression. Marx continued to write treatises on socialism, urging that his followers disdain softhearted bourgeois tendencies. At Marx's funeral in Highgate Cemetery in London, Engels spoke of him as "the best-hated and most-calumniated man of his time." The importance of Marx's thought, however, extends far beyond the revolutionary movements whose prophet he became. His writings on economics and sociology are still influential in academic circles and among many who do not share his political views. The main philosophical works of Karl Marx that are of interest to most students are the Communist Manifesto and Das Kapital.

9

Political Traditions in the West

Since September 11, 2001, the fog of war has enveloped political thought. Bright hopes of perpetual peace and prosperity collapsed in the debris of the World Trade Centre.

The fog grew thicker with the invasion of Iraq in 2003, as the nations of the Atlantic alliance collided over policy and principle, law and interests. By the time the postwar in Iraq became a civil war and produced more casualties than the war, the dominoes that neoconservatives dreamed would democratize the Middle East were falling helter-skelter into new uncertainties. On the other side of the debate, the most dire antiwar prophecies seemed exaggerated if not hollow, when Iraqis managed to hold elections for the first time in decades.

Neither the advocates nor the opponents of the war in Iraq had any sure insights into the uses of war on behalf of democracy. When, by the fall of 2006, the number of Iraqis being killed every month as a result of civil strife exceeded the number of Americans who had been killed in the September 11 attacks that had supposedly justified the invasion of Iraq, American policy was losing its political as well as moral bearings.

Combatants easily lose their sense of direction in the midst of battle, confuse comrade and foe, mistake progress for setback and setback for advantage, and retreat when on the verge of victory or hurl themselves into certain devastation convinced of their invincibility. Nor does war spare political thought from disorientation and uncertainty. Fundamental questions of war and democracy had scarcely begun to emerge into public awareness after September 11 when they were swept up in the whirlwind of preemptive war in Iraq. Among those fundamental questions are:

> What role do arms have in a democracy? How does military power alter, as well as protect, the polity that uses it? What is the possibility and even the meaning of the international rule of law? Can force effectively spread liberty and democracy abroad?

The spectacularly successful interventions that overthrew the Taliban and then Saddam Hussein were quickly compromised by the occupations of Afghanistan and Iraq. A pattern emerged. The United States overestimates the effectiveness of military might and underestimates the ordeal of democracy. Responsibility for the appalling shortcomings of the postwar rebuilding of Afghanistan and Iraq falls squarely on the presidency of George W. Bush-but not exclusively. The crisis runs deeper than any one administration when the world's oldest democracy and sole superpower does not comprehend the wellsprings of democracy or understand the nature of might. Opponents of Bush, neoconservatives, and the Republican Party delude themselves when they are satisfied merely with opposition to administration policy. The fundamental questions of war and democracy are even more difficult to answer today than on September 11, 2001. The threat of terrorism has likely grown rather than shrunk since 2001, and the Middle East has been turned into a laboratory of democracy where any failed experiment risks producing civil war, dictatorship, theocracy, or worse.

Diplomatic and military decisions are prepared and justified by a discourse authored by many hands: historians and ideologues, politicians and journalists, scholars and pundits. A range of discourses, from think-tank manifestos to "Great Power" historiography, from secret reports to presidential speeches, from strategic studies to op-ed pieces, produces the intellectual-but also the symbolic-webbing of the decisions and actions taken in foreign affairs. Since September 11, this symbolic-conceptual webbing has teemed with terms like "lone superpower," "hyperpower," "liberal imperialism," and "progressive interventionism," and slogans like war on terror or power-vs-weakness and Hobbesian-vs-Kantian. All these slogans imply some understanding of power; they all imply, to draw on a distinction made by Hannah Arendt, some understanding of political power and military might. Metaphors as well as ideas are at work in foreign policy discourse, for not only are there conceptions of power-and various methods of analyzing, say, the relative power of states or calculating their interests-but there is also an imagination of power. When it comes to military force no one can truly know how its use will enhance or diminish the power of the state that wields it. Might exists primarily in potential, and therefore it always exists in the imagination.

In liberal democracies all newly elected leaders, all new heads of state, find themselves suddenly in possession of power. And, inversely, they find themselves possessed by power. There is an inescapable ambivalence in the enjoyment of power. Max Weber turned to a bodily image when he identified the greatest of the "inner enjoyments" of the vocation of politics: "the feeling of holding in one's hand a nerve fiber of historically important events." To enjoy power-or to be empowered-is at the same time to be enjoyed by power. Having the means of coercion and violence in your grasp puts you in the grip of those very means of coercion and violence. That is why Weber, attentive to the insights of Nietzsche and riveted to the upheavals of war and revolution in his own time, insisted that the ethics of political life must include an awareness of politics' inherent potential for tragedy. Such an awareness alone tempers the intrinsic temptation to a kind of power beyond responsibility.

To become president of the United States in 2001, as happened to George W. Bush, was to find oneself suddenly in possession of power-beyond-responsibility, since the American body politic itself had been in the grip of power in excess of responsibility for a decade. The collapse of the Soviet Union left the United States with unmatched military might. It faced historic questions: For what ends does the nation possess such means of violence? Should this nation, or any nation, have unmatched military might? What responsibilities attend overweening power? The body politic never answered these questions or even seriously debated them. There were, of course, many discussions in the government, foreign policy think tanks, and opinion and policy journals, but the presidential campaigns of 1992, 1996, and 2000 avoided the controversy altogether. It became commonplace to refer to the Gulf War as the watershed of the United States's emergence as sole superpower, and politicians and theorists coined such grandiose names for the new era of American supremacy as the New World Order, the end of history, hyperpuissance, Empire. None of the labels took into account the stark fact that the American body politic remained silent and indecisive.

September 11 changed all that, though not because a great national debate finally occurred. Such a debate did not occur. Rather, after the Taliban and al Qaeda were routed in Afghanistan, the Bush administration was emboldened to advance an answer to the historic post-Cold War questions. In the 2002 document called The National Security Strategy of the United States, President Bush called upon the United States to embrace the role of supreme global power. With this appeal came the declaration of America's unique right over other nations, a threefold right to preemptive war, the overthrow of regimes considered hostile, and immunity from treaties and constraints imposed on other nations.

Hobbes versus Kant?

The doctrine of unilateralism and preemption contributed perhaps more than anything else to the showdown between the United States and major European allies, especially France and Germany, in the buildup to the war in Iraq. The U.S.-European divergence seemed neatly to confirm Robert Kagan's diagnosis that "Americans are from Mars and Europeans from Venus." Kagan is a particularly pertinent reference point, since the vision put forth in the Bush doctrine finds its intellectual backing in that strand of contemporary conservative thought represented by Kagan and preoccupied with the theory of "great powers." In his book Of Paradise and Power, which grew out of the essay "Power and Weakness" that stirred considerable discussion in the United States and Europe in the summer of 2002, Kagan ostensibly attempts to explain the markedly different views of Americans and Europeans in foreign affairs, in particular, the American inclination to unilateralism and force and the European preference for internationalism and negotiation in responding to crises: "On the all-important question of power-the efficacy of power, the morality of power, the desirability of power-American and European perspectives are diverging. Europe... is entering a post-historical paradise of peace and relative prosperity, the realization of Kant's "Perpetual Peace."

The United States, meanwhile, remains mired in history, exercising power in the anarchic Hobbesian world where international laws and rules are unreliable and where true peace and security and the defense and promotion of a liberal order still depend on the possession and use of military might."2 Kagan makes many interesting arguments and observations on U.S.-European relations, all more or less debatable, but it is the axioms that frame his whole discussion which throw a light on the mentality of the Bush administration and its understanding of power and military force. The fundamental axiom is simply a tautology: weak is weak, strong is strong: "When the United States was weak [in the eighteenth and nineteenth centuries], it practiced the strategies of indirection, the strategies of weakness; now that the United States is powerful, it behaves as powerful nations do.

When the European great powers were strong, they believed in strength and martial glory. Now, they see the world through the eyes of weaker powers. These very different points of view, weak versus strong, have naturally produced differing assessments of threats and of the proper means of addresing threats, and even differing calculations of interest."3 The tautology radiates out into the entire essay as the words nature, normal, perfectly normal, predictable, naturally alight on every aspect of current American policy just to say that a powerful nation does as powerful nations do. Policy flows from might. This axiom, presented by Kagan in the flat, frankly amoral tones of the historian of "great powers," undergirds the moral hyperbole by which the politicians Bush and Cheney justify the ambitious designs of the new National Security Strategy.

Is it really Kantians versus Hobbesians, Venus versus Mars? Both slogans are catchy, and Kant-versus-Hobbes has even caught on among serious political philosophers. But these oppositions do not hold up philosophically or politically. It is hard to imagine a thinker less venereal than Kant. And, just as strikingly, there is nothing at all martial about Hobbes. For starters, Hobbes fled England during the Civil War and wrote Leviathan in Paris in order to exorcise his horror at the image of civil order breaking down. Such a breakdown exposes a "state of nature" in which every man would have the right to do whatever he deems necessary "for the preservation of his own Nature; that is to say, of his own life." A commonwealth, Hobbes reasoned, arises from the fear of death that pervades the hypothetical state of nature, that is, the "condition of Warre of every one against every one." Contrary to Kagan's depiction, Hobbes's view of international relations little resembles that of the neoconservatives. "An anarchic Hobbesian world where international laws and rules are unreliable" is in fact not Hobbesian at all. Hobbes considered states to be less prone to violence than individuals, primarily because a ruler has responsibility for the peace and security of his subjects, and thus was inclined in Hobbes's view to be measured in assessing when their benefit and general welfare was best served by war or conquest.

Leviathan

Although Hobbes's ideas do not truly support the neoconservatives' vision of power, there is surely something that prompts Kagan and others aptly to consider the Bush doctrine Hobbesian. What stirs their imagination is the image of the body politic as leviathan. This image evokes something that is conveyed less in Hobbes's own words than in the famous engraving that graced the first edition of Leviathan. The monarch, his body composed of nothing but the multitude of his subjects, a scepter in one hand and a sword in the other, wearing a crown, rises above the land, whose gently rolling hills and little villages are at once the realm his outstretched arms protect and a kind of robe spread out around him. The undulations of the hills also suggest the waves that are the element in which the biblical leviathan lives. For the leviathan, as Melville well knew, is a sea monster, the whale as grasped in the ancient Hebrew imagination. There, in the more symbolic stew of Hobbes's thought, where body politic, sea monster, and monarch blend together, the Anglo-Saxon political imagination has found, precisely, an image of state power. The state is a monster, the One preventing the anarchy of the Many, that floats unperturbed in the sea or sails the oceans of the world to keep its multitude at peace, prosperous, and safe. That Britain-the island commonwealth, the commonwealth as island-would imagine the body politic a great sea monster makes nearly immediate sense. Hobbes has not, however, enjoyed extensive influence on American political thought. The American imagination of power has historically been more isolationist (the stay-at-home leviathan of the Monroe Doctrine) and territorial (the land-bound behemoth of Manifest Destiny). So how has the Hobbesian image come to fit America?

In a news conference in April 2004, as Iraq was being shaken by the simultaneous insurgencies of Sunnis in Falluja and militia loyal to Moktada al-Sadr in the Shiite South, and as the 9-11 Commission was probing how much warning the administration had prior to the al Qaeda attacks, President Bush uttered, as though revealing something for the first time, an astonishing anachronism. "We can no longer hope," he declared, "that oceans protect us from harm." Americans have, of course, been quite aware that oceans do not protect us from harm ever since 1957, when the Soviets sent the first Sputnik into space and raised the specter of intercontinental ballistic missles raining nuclear warheads on American cities. Bush's own chief preoccupation in defense matters before September 11 had been the renewal of Star Wars, the missile shield project that was predicated on just such vulnerability across oceans. Not only had Americans known for nearly fifty years that the Atlantic and Pacific afforded no guarantee against attack, but the September 11 attacks themselves, though they were an unprecedented assault by foreigners against American civilians at home, did not originate from abroad: the planes all took off on American soil.

Was Bush's anachronism then simply a historical lapsus? Not at all. For what it did, like so many other carefully crafted misstatements and innuendoes of that moment, was to associate the September 11 attacks carried out by al Qaeda with the presumed weapons of mass destruction in the hands of the United States's self-styled enemy Saddam Hussein. The anachronistic image of the protective oceans created a link between September 11 (attack on U.S. soil) and Saddam Hussein (weapons of mass destruction). According to polls, by the time the war in Iraq began 45 percent of Americans believed Saddam Hussein had planned September 11, just as many believed that his missiles with their range of a few hundred kilometers could reach the United States.

The war on terrorism and the war in Iraq had nothing to do with one another. We are engaged in the first because we have to be; we engaged in the second because the Bush administration wanted to, and could. They could because they took office in possession of unmatched military might. The attack on the Twin Towers and the Pentagon showed our vulnerability; the invasion of Iraq was meant to show our superior strength. The illusion of invulnerability that had shattered on September 11 was quickly transformed into an illusion of insuperability in preparation for war in Iraq. Put the two scenarios together and America becomes Hobbesian: the American body politic, no longer unperturbed floating in its oceans, gets transformed in the political imagination into the unvanquishable monster sailing the seas of the world. Shock and awe in Iraq answered, in symbol and fantasy, the shock and awe of September 11. Americans were called upon to see America the global power in leviathan imagery: "When he raiseth up himself, the mighty are afraid.... The sword of him that layeth at him cannot hold: the spear, the dart, nor the habergon....Upon earth there is not his like, who is made without fear."

The new national leviathan, however, hardly seems like one "who is made without fear." After September 11, political leaders and the media cultivated and relentlessly fertilized an all-pervasive fear within the American body politic. The sense of vulnerability and dread often seemed far more intense in the country at large than among the New Yorkers who had actually witnessed the destruction in their own city. Small towns in rural areas believed themselves to be targets in imminent danger when they learned that the federal government was furnishing local authorities with gas masks or special medical supplies. Unlike Roosevelt declaring that the only thing to fear was fear itself or Churchill exhorting Londoners to persevere in the face of the bombings that nightly ravaged their city, President Bush used September 11 to stoke citizens' fear for their lives. The most striking characteristic of the national mood between September 11 and the invasion of Iraq was how this excessive fear was strangely combined with inordinate confidence that military might could guarantee international and national security. Even as the administration purveyed fear and vulnerability, it promised that the army would topple dangerous tyrants armed with weapons of mass destruction and create new democracies. Therein is the mainspring of the administration's pseudo-Hobbesian vision and rhetoric. The national leviathan fuses an all-pervasive amorphous fear of death and an overweening faith in military power.

What are the origins of this combination of fear and hubris? Why was this combination so effective in cementing public opinion in support of the war? The answer undoubtedly has a lot to do with the post-Vietnam demise of a military of citizen-soldiers. Having first professionalized and now increasingly privatized the nation's armed forces, the Pentagon has so separated citizens from soldiers that citizens are free to indulge in debilitating fear while fully expecting their soldiers to bravely conquer all. Another factor is the tendency within contemporary culture to privilege the figure of the victim.

Symbolizing oneself as a victim lends an aura of moral rightness, a privileged viewpoint on what is just and unjust-and considerable entitlement and ultimately a certain license. The shock of September 11 was from the beginning nurtured into this dangerous mix of victimage, righteousness, and license. The leviathan motif expresses well the post-September 11 fear. This cultivated fear, this exaggerated yet real fear of death, has been integrated into the symbolic-discursive webbing of foreign policy. A wounded, half-blind leviathan thrashing about in geopolitical seas does not see the fragility of democracy at home and the difficulty of inaugurating it abroad.

The Neoconservative Illusion

The neoconservatives confuse power and might. Hannah Arendt makes the distinction in the sharpest of terms. Power "corresponds to the human ability not just to act but to act in concert." It is utterly distinct from might and violence. Might is the capacity for violence, and violence itself marks the breakdown of power, whether within the polity (where "violence functions as the last resort of power against criminals or rebels-that is, against single individuals who, as it were, refuse to be overpowered by the consensus of the majority") or externally in war, where in fact strength or might does not in itself secure power: "as for actual warfare, we have seen in Vietnam how an enormous superiority in the means of violence can become helpless if confronted with an ill-equipped but well-organized opponent who is much more powerful."

From the Arendtian standpoint, all the tautologies of the neoconservative hawks exemplified by Robert Kagan's writings are false. Policy does not flow naturally, normally, predictably, from might. The nature of the polity is not immune to the effects of wielding the available means of violence. The unilateral exercise of force does not necessarily defend and protect the polity. That the colossal failure of America's anticommunist foreign policy in Vietnam, which stimulated the creation of neoconservatism in the first place, might turn out to be the very model of their own deepest errors is more than an exquisite irony. It risks becoming a historic tragedy. The consequences of the neoconservatives' conflation of power and might are seen not simply in theory but in practice. The crisis-ridden occupation of Iraq exposed the fundamental flaws in neoconservative thought, especially its Great Power discourse.

The neoconservative hawks seem to have seriously believed that once American military might overthrew Iraqi tyranny, Iraqi democracy would spontaneously flower in its place; meanwhile, the more hard-nosed members of the administration assumed, just as naïvely though callously, that a strongman allied with the West could always step in to impose order if need be. The two attitudes resulted in gross negligence when it came to planning the occupation. Defense Department planning, directed by Donald Rumsfeld's undersecretary Douglas Feith, thoroughly ignored the need for civil order. The American occupation created the conditions for Hobbesian anarchy inside Iraq. Iraq turned into a breeding ground for Islamic terrorism because it lacked civil order and was awash in weapons and rife with contending factions. The

Coalition Provisional Authority headed by L. Paul Bremer III replaced Sad-dam Hussein's rogue state with an insecure failed state.

Iraqis owe their tyrant's overthrow to the Americans, but those Iraqis who heroically risked life and limb in an effort to salvage a democratic path owe Americans little else. For months on end after the invasion, Iraqis were driven to arm themselves and ally, often unwillingly, with militias or mullahs in the face of absolute uncertainty over their own safety. They felt the naked insecurity of the state of nature. The millions who exercised their right to vote under threat of death added a new and poignant symbol to democratic imagery-and, indeed, to the Hobbesian image-bank too: their ink-stained fingers are forever an emblem of individuals mastering the fear of death in order to create a civil order that might protect them all. What these Iraqis have Rumsfeld and Bush, Feith and Bremer, to thank for is leaving them unprotected. Fear and death swirled around their first election and continued to plague their civil covenant.

The neoconservative understanding of power also fails to comprehend that the might which a democracy possesses and uses can flow back-or blow back-to alter the very nature of its own democratic institutions. The neoconservatives conceive of the nation's liberal order and rule of law as an unalterable internal feature of American democracy, while armed force is simply the means of protecting the nation against external threats. The illusion that American democracy itself cannot be harmed by the might it wields abroad has proved costly. Consenting to war is the most serious decision that citizens have to make. When the reasons by which citizens are persuaded to give their consent are, as with Iraq, erroneous (weapons of mass destruction) and deceptive (Iraqi ties to al Qaeda), the very fabric of democratic deliberation is damaged.

The insistence that the errors and deceptions did not ultimately matter, since the result was good, even further undermined the very principle of accountability; a re-elected George Bush retained or promoted all the officials most responsible for the errors and deceptions. The posture that right-or-wrong we are right weakened the value put on truth in public affairs; the administration successfully fostered, with the help of the Fox-led media, a hatred of dissent, all the more intensely when the dissenters accurately exposed administration falsehoods. The willful distortion of international and domestic law through enemy combatants, detainees, homeland security, coercive interrogations, extraordinary rendition eroded civil liberties and the rule of law at home just as it severely damaged the United States's moral standing abroad. And the transformation of the border into a digital fortress that indiscriminately makes every visitor and immigrant a suspect has estranged the very foreigners most likely to value the United States as a symbol and example of a democratic way of life. So many essential features of American democracy-open deliberative politics, a public sphere valuing debate and truthfulness, due process, the furnishing of a symbolic and real haven of freedom for people around the globe-have been strained and damaged by the use of force in Iraq.

The reassuring view that arms are merely the instrument of a secure democracy in an insecure world is the fateful illusion at the heart of American policy. This illusion has its pseudo-Hobbesian variation in Kagan's equation of political power and military might in the amoral language of Great Power discourse, and it has its romantic-messianic variation in Bush's rhetoric of the axis of evil, the forward strategyof freedom, the end of evil, and so on. In calling this vision of foreign affairs an illusion, I have in mind the sense that Freud gave to the term in The Future of an Illusion, namely, an account of reality that coincides with what one wishes reality to be. An illusion in this sense is not necessarily demonstrably false, but wherever reality seems to coincide with one's wishes, doubt and skepticism ought to precede action, especially when the action is making war.

Crises of the Republic

Mindful of the extraordinary legacy of Arendt's political thought, we hope to preserve something of her spirit of inquiry and interpretation in the following chapters. Trying to reflect on the crises of the republic in the midst of those crises is an abrupt reminder that political thought never enjoys a firm grounding. Such intellectual ideals as the unity of theory and practice, the proceduralist commitment to philosophically justified norms, or the pragmatist belief in shared values and tested methods all prove rather feeble when it comes to understanding a democracy at war. The difficulties are all the more acute because the crises of the American republic since September 11 have disguised themselves by masquerading as the self-assured, democracy-protecting, faith-soaked assertion of national strength. The temptations to deception and self-deception are always great in the midst of war, and in some fundamental way they are intrinsic to political life. The public realm, in Arendt's account, is where individuals "disclose themselves as subjects, as distinct and unique persons" through "their deeds and words." It is a space of appearance but not transparence, of self-revealing but not necessarily self-understanding: "Although nobody knows whom he reveals when he discloses himself in deed or word, he must be willing to risk disclosure....It is more than likely that the 'who,' which appears so clearly and unmistakably to others, remains hidden from the person, like the daimon in Greek religion which accompanies each man throughout his life, always looking over his shoulder from behind and thus visible only to those he encounters."

While Arendt renewed the import of ancient democracy for modern politics, no one revealed the ethical paradoxes of modern politics more penetratingly than Max Weber. Looking at the professional politician's psychological and ethical existence, Weber identifies the enjoyments of this vocation in the "feeling of power" and "knowledge of influencing men." The aptitude for such a career amalgamates "passion" for a cause, "a feeling of responsibility" for the consequences of decisions and actions, and "a sense of proportion." Passion, responsibility, and proportion are, however, perpetually vulnerable to two essential instruments of political power: pretending and violence. Since every politician "works with the striving for power as an unavoidable means," he "is constantly in danger of becoming an actor as well as taking lightly the responsibility for the outcome of his actions and of being concerned merely with the 'impression' he makes." The politician is, moreover, drawn into a realm of recurrent ethical paradox, since at bottom "politics operates with very special means, namely, power backed up by violence." Whoever holds or vies for political power "lets himself in for the diabolical forces lurking in all violence."

Max Weber and Hannah Arendt are largely irreconcilable thinkers. The sociologist of modernity and the political philosopher of the ancient polis diverge sharply in their understanding of power and violence, and their respective projects are more dissonant than consonant. And yet Weber's thoughts on the vocation and ethics of modern politics and Arendt's on the ancient resources of the modern polis create a productive strife, a meaningful dissonance, for an understanding of democracy at war today. Drawing on the contradictory traditions of democratic thought is in fact vital to political thinking.

The plurality and debate so essential to democracy render disputes over the meaning of democracy a feature of democracy itself. Just as I draw on the contradictory ideas of politics and power developed by Weber and Arendt, so too we will adhere to the contradictory ideas of freedom found in Arendt and Isaiah Berlin.

Arendt's supreme value is self-rule through participation in a body politic, that is, in government; Berlin's supreme value is the individual's freedom from the constraints of others and especially government, that is, the body politic. Therein lies the permanent clash between the civic and the liberal dimensions of modern democracy. As American democracy plunged into war, it fused its justifications for self-defense with the ambition to overthrow tyrannies and spread democracy. Its understanding of self-rule, liberty, and power is at stake in these acts and justifications, just as the acts and justifications are at stake in the understanding of self-rule, liberty, and power.

In taking democracy at war as my theme, we try our best to understand how political thought faces the difficult questions prompted by September 11 and the war in Iraq. These two unprecedented events have forced new avenues of inquiry and interpretation. Al Qaeda's September 11 attacks were an act of war by a nonstate actor, whereas political thought and foreign policy have long understood war as armed conflict between states or, in civil war, within a state. Unsettled questions abound concerning sovereignty, the meaning of the "war against terrorism," and its sources of legitimacy. The invasion and occupation of Iraq were no less unprecedented than September 11. The United States under George W. Bush not only justified the invasion of another country on the grounds of overthrowing tyranny and spreading democracy, but did so under the banner of unilateralism and preemption and in effect as a display of its own global supremacy.

This step onto uncertain terrain was taken without public deliberation and decision, for even though the invasion itself had overwhelming public support, the reasons for going to war in Iraq were to overcome the impending if not imminent danger of its weapons of mass destruction and to sever its ties with Islamic terrorism.

There were no weapons of mass destruction and no link existed between Iraq and Islamic terrorism until the American invasion and occupation created one. Whether the overthrow of tyranny and inauguration of democracy were the real motive of the invasion all along or the rationale retrofitted to an intervention that lost its original justification or, as is most likely, some mix of the two, the United States has been firmly set on a course in which the spreading of democracy is now the principal justification of its foreign policy, and the precedent of unilateral preemptive intervention remains for the moment unchallenged.

Democracy at war stirs turmoil in political thought because the very aim of the internal workings of a democracy is to eliminate or transcend the use of force. Its institutions sustain that "unreliable and only temporary agreement of many wills and intentions" in which the democratic mentality delights. Neither military action abroad nor national-security measures at home foster such delight. On the contrary, military action stirs profound uncertainty, and security measures introduce the risk that the steps taken to protect democracy will dessicate its very values and institutions.

By the same token, any realistic assessment of the threats and dangers posed by terrorism, rogue states, and weapons of mass destruction confirms that the security of democratic nations requires concerted action on the international scene backed by the capacity and willingness to use force. It all depends on judgment, and one role that political thought ought to play in the political life of a democracy is to broaden and enrich the capacity for judgment.

The Argument

"September 11 and Fables of the Left": Beyond the ill-tempered response of some leftists immediately after the terrorist attacks against the World Trade Centre and the Pentagon, the unprecedented confrontation between Western democracy and Islamic radicalism has brought out how thoroughly the political judgment and imagination of the so-called Left is limited by its underlying sensibility now that the world is no longer defined by the polarities of the Cold War. The faultlines of this sensibility become discernible in Noam Chomsky's moral absolutism and Michael Hardt and Antonio Negri's prophetic lyricism.

"Iraq: Delirium of War, Delusions of Peace": The claims of American unilateralism and the invasion of Iraq unleashed intellectual and diplomatic disputes that suggest that no simple dichotomy of Left and Right explains international politics. Leftists are split on questions of values as well as strategy. Paul Berman's defense of the war in Iraq evoked an idealism of ends (and the supreme value of freedom from tyranny), while Jürgen Habermas's opposition to the war drew on an idealism of means (and the supreme value of the international rule of law). The very idea of an international rule of law in the framework of the United Nations was, by the same token, belittled from the neoconservative perspective of Michael J. Glennon and the neo-Marxist perspective of Perry Anderson. On the diplomatic scene, the Atlantic alliance was shaken by the dispute that pitted Germany and France against the United States and Britain. In scrutinizing this dispute, it becomes apparent that it derived from a complex weave of principles and interests, not a clearcut division between Kantian peacemakers and Hobbesian warriors. Moreover, even as the justifications for the war were soon exposed as unfounded and erroneous, many of the premises of peace-including the effectiveness of sanctions-turned out to have strengthened rather than challenged Saddam Hussein's tyranny.

"The Ordeal of Universalism": While the neoconservatives' freedom-versus-tyranny theme and Habermas's postnational cosmpolititanism have the look of a sharp Right-Left dichotomy, neither adequately grasps the international conflicts it is supposed to address. Islam, which is often said to be engaged in a civil war, is embroiled rather in a geopolitical civil war. American policy ran aground in Iraq because it misunderstood this geo-civil war and then exacerbated it by neglecting to secure the country after the invasion. The grand project of overthrowing a tyrant in order to initiate democracies throughout the Muslim world yielded, instead, a civil war within Iraq itself that drew terrorists from all over the world, strengthened the radical regime in Iran, and trained suicide bombers to be sent back to London. As alternatives to the Bush doctrine are sought by Western thinkers and politicians, the interpretation of Europe's postwar project has become crucial. Is it the delusional Kantian paradise caricatured by Kagan or the beginnings of the "global domestic policy" idealized by Habermas? Or is it, as I argue, an innovative political body-an Empire of Rights-that is still reluctant to embrace its own transformative ambitions? In light of Islam's geo-civil war and Europe's halting project of extending democracy and capitalism, I challenge Walter Russell Mead's vision of a global neoliberal religious conservatism that would unite the capitalist West and conservative Islam. "Prelude to the Unknown": Admittedly, this is an equivocal title for a conclusion, but it is true I think to the fact that as American ambitions in Iraq have faltered, the global situation of terrorism, geo-civil war, and tyranny is more desperately than ever in need of vigorous responses. Have the failings in Iraq and elsewhere squandered the very idea that freedom and democracy be the guideposts of American foreign policy? Or, conversely, might the rich tradition of ideas of self-rule (Arendt's positive liberty) and individual freedom (Berlin's negative liberty), both of which affirm human plurality, serve as a language of political criticism for assessing the failures and dilemmas of American policy itself?

Threaded throughout the book is a reflection on two political thinkers, Hobbes and Kant, whose ideas are as irreconcilable as those of Arendt, Weber, and Berlin. The evocation of Hobbes and Kant in debates over American foreign policy has simplified and warped the relation between their respective ideas; irreconcilable though they are, Hobbes and Kant do not conform to the current caricatures, and their relevance for the dilemmas and problems of the present can be startlingly unexpected, when it is recognized that Hobbes's thought hinges just as much on the body politic's founding covenant as on the war of all against all, and that Kant puts the darkness of human nature at the very heart of his reflection on perpetual peace.

The idealistic fervor and self-confident messianism that have infused American declarations of an armed crusade for democracy betray a dangerous disregard for the prospect of tragedy that Weber said inevitably accompanies politics when it turns to violence as a means for achieving its ends. The denial of tragedy amounts to a denial of responsibility. Not just moral responsibility, but ultimately political responsibility. Consider the silence regarding civilian casualties in Iraq. The United States made no effort to estimate civilian deaths, or even to assist Iraqis in accounting for their dead. Neither the press nor the Democrats insisted that an invading force and occupying power had such an obligation and duty. The gross negligence should arouse the intensest moral outrage, but also patriotic outrage. Our country has gone to war not wanting to know what it does. From the day of the invasion right through the destruction and depopulating of Falluja and beyond, America's leaders, its press, its representatives, its public-in short, ourselves-have indulged in this cowardly wanting-not-to-know. The silence is a form of lying. But the deception may be nearer self-deception than deceit. For it is well-known in much of the world that America does not have the courage to take a real look at the destructiveness of its own acts. The country's prevaricating silence on the tens of thousands of Iraqis killed is all the starker when juxtaposed to the exaggerated and vociferous fear of death in the United States since September 11. There is no reliable calculus for measuring what damage this kind of irresponsibility does to American interests abroad and the spirit of American democracy at home.

Political decisions and military actions are often thoroughly justified even though they violate valid moral standards. This is why, as Weber argued, politicians and statesmen must take responsibility for the foreseeable consequences of their decisions. A body politic incapable of accepting responsibility for politically justified but morally wrong acts cannot long operate effectively on the stage of world affairs. A body politic that wants not to know the harm it does loses its capacity to judge how its use of force accords with its political goals. How long before such refusal of responsibility and loss of judgment destroy the legitimacy of the foreign policy itself? I do not pose this question in order to launch into a jeremiad. Nor can the question be answered empirically. A body politic seldom has the benefit of reliable warning lights. A different metaphor is perhaps more apt. The body politic's institutions and, in Montesquieu's phrase, the spirit of its laws are its skeleton. Silence, lying, Orwellian misnaming, hypocrisy and hubris, negligence and bravado, wanting-not-to-know: these are all processes that resorb a democracy, ravaging the bones at a rate that is unfelt and unseen.

Main Contemporary Trends

The present chapter focuses on the most recent period in the development of Russian thought (1960s-1990s). Proceeding from the cyclical patterns of Russian intellectual history, we propose to name it 'the third philosophical awakening.' The main tendency of this period as 'the struggle of thought against ideocracy.' A classification of main trends in Russian thought of this period: (1) Dialectical materialism in its evolution from late Stalinism to neo-communist mysticism; (2) Neorationalism and Structuralism; (3) Neo-Slavophilism, or the Philosophy of National Spirit; (4) Personalism and Liberalism; (5) Religious Philosophy and Mysticism, both Christian Orthodox and Non-Traditional; (6) Culturology or the Philosophy of Culture; (7) Conceptualism or the Philosophy of Postmodernity.

> "The Karamazovs are not scoundrels but philosophers, because all real Russian people are philosophers..." — Dmitry Karamazov, in Fyodor Dostoevsky. The Brothers Karamazov

> It is a property of the Russian people to indulge in philosophy....The fate of the philosopher in Russia is painful and tragic. —Nikolai Berdyaev, The Russian Idea

> The fact that one can annihilate a philosophy.... or that one can prove that a philosophy annihilates itself is of little consequence. If it's really philosophy, then, like the phoenix, it will always rise again from its own ashes. —Friedrich Schlegel. Athenaeum Fragments, trans. Peter Firchow, 103.

The last period of the Soviet ideocracy, approximately from the early 1970s through the late 1980s, can be characterized as a period of "philosophical awakening," to use the felicitous expression of the theologian Georgy Florovsky (1893-1979). "Such awakening is usually preceded by a more or less complicated historical fate, the abundant and long historical experience and ordeal, which now becomes the object of interpretation and discussion. Philosophical life begins as a new mode or a new stage of national existence... One can feel in the generation of that epoch some irresistible attraction to philosophy, a philosophical passion and thirst, a kind of magical gravitation toward philosophical themes and issues."

Florovsky refers here to the first "philosophical awakening" of Russia in the span of years from 1830s to 1840s: roughly, the generation of Chaadaev, early Westernizers and Slavophiles, such as Belinsky, Herzen, Bakunin, Khomiakov, the brothers Aksakov, and the brothers Kireevsky.

Russia's second philosophical awakening occurred in the first two decades of the 20th century, following in the wake of the unsuccessful revolution of 1905 and disenchantment of the most refined part of intelligentsia with the low intellectual level of populism, Marxism and other socialist theories. This intellectual renaissance is associated with the philosophical collection Signposts (1909) and the work of Merezhkovsky, Rozanov, Berdyaev, Bulgakov, Frank, Florensky, Shestov, and other outstanding representatives of the so-called Silver Age.

Finally, after the soporific years of Soviet materialist scholasticism, a third philosophical awakening occurred in the 1970s-80s. In this period, philosophical works were circulated in various forms of "samizdat" ("self-publishing"), "tamizdat" ("there-publishing," i.e., in the West) and "togdaizdat " ("then-publishing," i.e., in prerevolutionary Russia).

Such works conveyed a mysterious charm that could not be explained in terms of "truth or falsity," "persuasiveness or dubiousness." The very touch of these books, by such authors as Berdyaev, Shestov, and Bakhtin, made one feel involved in the joy and mystery of self-reflective existence. Over the past forty years, several "philosophical" schools have emerged to challenge the ideocratic principles of Soviet Marxism which itself has undergone remarkable changes. Below, I will briefly outline seven principal trends of Russian thought of the 1950s-1980s.

Marxism

One principal vector of its transformation in the post-war period was the infusion of nationalism into Marxism, undertaken first by Stalin in his work on linguistics, where the class categories of traditional Marxism were abolished in favour of a notion of national unity, as exemplified in the integrity of national language. This tendency resurfaced in the 1980s, with the increasing rapprochement of official Marxism and grass-roots, nativist ideology, which later grew into a political alliance of communists and neo-fascists.

Another revisionist tendency, toward the humanization of Marxism, emerged in the mid-1950s with the publication of Marx's early Philosophical-Economical Manuscripts, and found expression in the writings of Evald Ilyenkov, Genrikh Batishchev, and Yakov Mil'ner-Irinin. This tendency suffered a severe political blow with the 1968 failure to build "socialism with a human face" in Czechoslovakia, which revealed the incompatibility of humanism and Soviet Marxism.

Later, in the 1980s, three new approaches to Marxism emerge. The first is an attempt to revitalize and modify Marxism in the wake of the failure of the Soviet communist project. This version of post-communist Marxism, exemplified in the work of Sergei Platonov, proposes the purification of Marxism from its Leninist and especially Stalinist contaminations and the incorporation of new realities, such as the persistent success of market economics.

The second approach argues that Leninism and Stalinism are consistent with the premises of Marxism, which must therefore be held responsible for all of communism's crimes against humanity. This version, developed in the writings of Aleksandr Yakovlev, the chief official ideologist of perestroika, involves the radical criticism of Marxism as a non-scientific and anti-humanist theory which, with its all-inclusive determinism, underestimates the sovereignty of consciousness, reducing personality to a function of social circumstances.

The third approach, which can be called post-Marxist communism (as distinct from post-communist Marxism), glorifies the religious aspects of communism, which were abandoned by classical Marxism in favour of a quasi-scientific materialism.

This position, articulated in the works of Sergei Kurginian and, to a lesser extent, Aleksandr Zinoviev, promotes a renewal of communism as a religious doctrine encompassing the deepest insights of many Eastern and Western faiths and opposed to the soulless hedonism and consumerism of capitalist civilization. Thus Marxism is presented as the latest form of "humanist religion" that might save humanity from the pitfalls of bourgeois individualism through high spiritual ideals and collectivist aspirations.

Methodological Approaches

A number of new methodological approaches starting from the late 1950s may be united under the title of neo-rationalism. Yury Lotman (1922-1993), the founder of the Tartu school of Russian structuralism, undertook comprehensive research on what he calls the "semiosphere"-the universe of signs. He offers many penetrating methodological insights on the role of sign systems throughout history and culture.

This project of rapprochement between the sciences and humanities was also developed in the Moscow school of structuralism (Vladimir Toporov, Vyacheslav Ivanov and others).

Merab Mamardashvili (1930-90) and Aleksandr Piatigorsky (some of their works were written in collaboration) undertook a phenomenological analysis of consciousness, with a special interest in non-classical, post-rationalist and Oriental types of logic.

The theory of systems and general methodology, as related to the philosophical problems of artificial intelligence and cybernetics, have been elaborated in the works of Georgy Shchedrovitsky, Vasily Nalimov, Yuly Shreider, and Georgy Mel'nikov.

Neo-rationalism, and especially structuralism, achieved its greatest impact in the 1960s and 1970s when it boldly challenged the social mysticism of orthodox Soviet Marxism; but later, in the 1980s, the role of the primary philosophical alternative passed from structuralism to religious thought, which increasingly opposed itself to old-fashioned Marxist rationalism.

Religious Orthodox Thought

Among the most influential intellectual trends in the 1970s-1980s are varieties of religious Orthodox thought. Christian visions of history and contemporary society were powerfully expressed by such major writers as Boris Pasternak and Aleksandr Solzhenitsyn, who inspired many other thinkers. Father Aleksandr Men. (1935-1990) was by far the most influential Russian theologian and Orthodox spiritual leader of the 1970s-80s. In his seven-volume treatise, In the Search of the Way, Truth, and Life, as well as in his other books, he elaborates a philosophy of spiritual ascension that leads humanity from paganism to the Christian revelation of Godmanhood. The next generation of Orthodox thinkers is represented by Tatiana Goricheva (who writes on the topics connecting and contrasting Orthodox spirituality with postmodernism and feminism), Sergei Khoruzhii, Evgeny Barabanov, and Vladislav Zelinsky.

A remarkable feature of this new religious thought is its sharp critique of the Platonic traditions of Russian religious philosophy (including Vladimir Solovyov's "total-unity" and its numerous repercussions). According to Khoruzhii, genuinely Christian philosophy would abandon such Platonic and Neo-Platonic conceptions as the total unity and would focus instead on existential intercourse between man and God, meditating on such spiritual processes as prayer, repentance, grace, introspection, silence, the unification of mind and heart-those acts of free will that truly mediate between the human and divine as distinct entities.

Marxist philosophers used to criticize Russian religious thought ('idealism') as the manifestation of a reactionary, bourgeois or feudalist worldview, incompatible with scientific and social progress. New critics, including Barabanov, Khoruzhii, and Boris Paramonov, on the contrary, blame Russian idealism for its secret or unconscious complicity with the communist Revolution, by supposedly preparing the ground for this social cataclysm through the dissemination of apocalyptic forebodings and totalitarian metaphysics ("total unity"). In this view, Russian society proved so receptive to the messianic revelations of Marxism and the mystique of the last bloody battle and coming golden age, precisely because Solovyov, Fyodorov, Berdyaev, and Merezhkovsky had already tuned the soul of the nation to the key of eschatological expectations that would be fulfilled, or at least precipitated, by their contemporaries and compatriots-by Russia as the vanguard of post-history.

Effects of Spiritual Teachings

Synthetic and spiritualist teachings proliferated in Russia since 1970s. Some of them, occult and para-scientific, are close to what in the USA is called "New Age." The most unified and solid among them is Cosmism (sometimes called "Anthropo-Cosmism") originating in Nikolai Fyodorov's (1829-1903) "the philosophy of the common cause" and his ideas about the universal resurrection of the dead, physical immortality, and the technological transformation of the cosmos. Such outstanding scientists as the father of Soviet cosmonautics Konstantin Tsiolkovsky and the pioneer of biogeochemistry Vladimir Vernadsky are considered the major authorities in Cosmism. Cosmism is a philosophy of active evolutionism, presupposing the possibility and necessity for the human mind to regulate and transform the laws of nature.

Cosmism explains historical, social and psychological processes by the influences of cosmic energies and asserts a reciprocal dependency of the fates of the universe on the activity of human mind. A leading exponent of this movement, Svetlana Semyonova, is one among very few women engaged in contemporary philosophical debates in Russia.

Paradoxically, Fyodorov's system which she advocates is based on extremely patriarchal views and denigrates the role of women as "seducers" of men preventing them from fulfilling their duties of resurrection toward the "fathers." Contemporary Cosmism is also related to the metaphysics of environment and ecological and neopaganist mysticism in the works of Fyodor Giryonok.

A different, more explicitly ecumenical and synthetic trend was expressed by Daniil Andreev (1906-1959) in his treatise The Rose of the World (1950-1958). Andreev develops an original "meta-historic" and "trans-physical" vision that attempts to absorb the religious wisdom of both West and East and to pave a way for a future "inter-religion" and harmonious world order based on a universal theocracy.

Nikolai Roerikh's (1874-1947) and his wife Elena Roerikh's (1879-1955) version of Oriental-Occidental esoteric synthesis-Agni-Yoga-is also being intensely promoted and publicized by hundreds of intellectual groups famous as "Roerikh centers" in Russia.

Concept of Freedom

Many thinkers and intellectual writers represent various trends of personalist philosophy whose supreme values are freedom and the individual. Owing to Dostoevsky's overwhelming domestic influence and further contributions by Rozanov, Berdyaev and Shestov, Russian philosophy started on the existentialist path sooner than its Western counterparts. No comprehensive systematic treatises have been produced in this field, but there are numerous essays, articles and philosophical diaries by Mikhail Prishvin (1873-1954), Iakov Druskin (1902-1980), Lidiia Ginzburg (1902-90), Andrei Siniavsky, Grigory Pomerants, Boris Khazanov, Mikhailo Mikhailov, and Boris Paramonov. The formation and self-awareness of personality, its attitudes towards nature and society, love and death, and time and fate are the central motifs of personalist thought. This tradition of philosophical liberalism and pluralism has attracted influential supporters in the field of politics, such as academician Andrei Sakharov and historian Natan Eidel'man (1930-89), as well as outstanding proponents in poetry and fiction, including Joseph Brodsky (1940-1996) and Andrei Bitov, both of whom express personalist views in their essayistic writings and philosophical prose.

Nationalist Ideology

Nationalist ideology, which emerged in the early 1970s and escalated rapidly in post-communist Russia, has produced its own intellectual elite: writers, critics, historians, and scientists who attempt to create a philosophy of national spirit (which is routinely, though not necessarily, linked to rightist views). Its major intellectual predecessors include the Russian Slavophiles of the 19th century and the Eurasianists of the 1920s. 20th-century German, French and Italian sources, such as Rene Guenon (1886-1951) and Julius Evola (1898-1974), the founders of contemporary traditionalism as a metaphysical system, are also abundantly cited.

The influential publicistic writings of Aleksandr Solzhenitsyn and the historio-ethnographic treatises of Lev Gumilev (1912-90) can be placed in this category insofar as they concern general philosophical issues, such as the relation between culture and nation, collective responsibility and guilt, biological energy and the moral patterns of ethnic groups. For example, Gumilev advances an original theory (which sometimes echoes Oswald Spengler's "morphology of culture") that explains the rise and decline of ethnic formations by biological rather than social factors, namely by disproportionate infusions of cosmic energies into the biological mass of humankind.

Gumilev's key concept is "drive," or "passionality," which accumulates in the "heroic personalities" of certain nations and epochs, accounting for their historical accomplishments. Even more extreme representatives of the same conservative nationalism are critic Vadim Kozhinov and mathematician Igor Shafarevich, who have developed a pessimistic view on Russian and Soviet history as permanently threatened and undermined from within by non-Russians, particularly Jews.

Finally, two modifications of nationalism surfaced in the 1980s-90s. One presented by Viktor Aksiuchits is moderate conservatism, claiming the timeless values of Orthodox Christianity as a specifically Russian legacy destined to introduce the spirit of national reconciliation into a society torn apart by militant pluralism and partisanship. The other promoted by Aleksandr Dugin is radical traditionalism, proclaiming the restoration of a paganist, esoteric legacy and the unification of Eurasia into one Empire under Russian guidance with the aim of waging spiritual war on the secularized and materialist West.

Unlike other conservatives, with their exclusively Russian or Slavic nationalism, traditionalists attempt to unite the extreme Rightist movements of the entire world, which reveals that they are more indebted to German, French, and Italian fascist or para-fascist ideologists than to the nineteenth-century Russian Slavophiles. Radical traditionalists believe that after the fundamentally leftist and democratic revolutions in France, America and Russia, the world abandoned Tradition and sold its soul to the devil of material prosperity. That is why a new, metaphysical revolution is needed, this time a rightist one, antithetical to the conventional revolutionary formula insofar as it pursues the restoration of the spiritual foundations of the world that were buried by decadent civilization in its pursuit] of "progress."

Culturology

Another important trend of the 1970s-1980s is culturology, the philosophy of cultural dialogue and self-determination through "otherness." Culturology approaches culture as the integral system of various cultures-national, professional, racial, sexual. Thus culturology can be defined as a metadiscipline investigating the interconnections among the various phenomena of culture-in the realms of politics, science, art, literature, and religion. One reason for the ascendancy of culturology is the traditional tendency of Russian culture to overcome the extreme specialization of various disciplines and professions so characteristic of Western modes of cultural production. In communist Russia this unification was achieved on ideological grounds that submitted the entire range of cultural activities to the domination of politics. Culturology became a field of interdisciplinary interaction, posing an alternative both to excesses of scholarly specialization and to the pressures of ideological totalization. In culturology, "culture" is treated as a descriptive rather than a normative concept, the term itself being used both in the singular and in the plural. Culture as the ultimate unity of disciplinary spheres presupposes the diversity of cultures as multiple national and historical types, each having its own formative principle irreducible to others. Culturology attempts to approach culture on its own specific terms and to develop a holistic language that avoids lapsing into politicism, scientism, aestheticism, moralism, or the absolutization of any single aspect of culture.

Culturology received powerful impetus from Mikhail Bakhtin (1895-1975), who asserted in his later works that "a culture exists only on the border of other cultures." Another strong influence came from Aleksei Losev (1893-1988), who developed his philosophy of "dialectical idealism" and "absolute mythology" primarily on the material of classical antiquity (History of Classical

Aesthetics, in 8 volumes, 1963-1988). Representatives of culturology include Vladimir Bibler who managed to create his own methodological school of "dialogical logic" in the history of sciences and humanities; and Sergei Averintsev, a brilliant scholar in the field of antiquity and Byzantine civilization who has elaborated the philosophical aspects of cultural heritage and innovation, giving special emphasis to the problems of symbol and the interaction between religious and secular types of culture.

Poststructuralism

The latest trend worthy of mention corresponds to the post-structuralist paradigm in the West. One of its most original versions may be identified as conceptualism. This name usually refers to a well-known movement in Russian arts and literature of the 1970s and 1980s, but it can also be aptly applied to a broad spectrum of critical and philosophical ideas that complement and highlight this movement. Conceptualism assumes that certain conceptual schemes underlie the ideological construction of reality and determine its artificial, conventionalized character. Conceptual thinking is imbued with irony, parody, and a sense of relativity, since "truth" and "reality" are considered to be empty categories. The relationship between conceptualism and Marxism is somewhat reminiscent of the dispute between nominalists and realists in the epoch of the medieval scholastics: whereas Marxists assert the historical reality of such concepts as collectivism, equality, and freedom, conceptualists demonstrate that these notions are either contingent on mental structures or derived from linguistic structures. Every cultural form is conceived in terms of combinations of pre-established codes, such as Soviet ideological language or the code of the Russian psychological novel. The general approaches of conceptualism can be found in theoretical and artistic works by Andrei Siniavsky, Ilya Kabakov, Vitaly Komar and Aleksandr Melamid, and Boris Groys.

Another version of philosophical poststructuralism is presented by the Laboratory of Non-Classical Philosophy at the Institute of Philosophy in Moscow, in particular, by such authors as Valery Podoroga, Mikhail Ryklin, and Mikhail Yampolsky. They publish a philosophical collection Ad Marginem (book series and an annual) which is methodologically inspired by contemporary French thinkers (Jacques Derrida, Gilles Deleuze and Felix Guattari and others). Podoroga's works represent an original combination of phenomenological, hermeneutical and deconstructionist readings of German philosophers and Russian writers, with a special emphasis on the "communicational strategy" of writing and reading and corporeal and spatial quality of texts as "landscapes."

Of course, the above-mentioned eight movements do not exhaust the entire complexity of intellectual life in Russia, nor do they even account for the "hybrid" work of some individual thinkers. For example, Georgy Gachev has created an original holistic genre of writing that includes such components as "living-thinking" (zhiznemyslie), "national images of the world," and a "humanitarian approach to natural sciences." His thinking combines peculiar qualities of such disparate trends as culturology, personalism, and the philosophy of national spirit. Contemporary Russian thought is polyphonic, not just pluralistic, in the sense that different positions and voices interact in the consciousnesses of the most creative individual thinkers. Rarely in the history of thought has philosophy represented such a liberating force as it did in Russia from the 1960s through the 1980s. The Soviet State had generated a rigid system of "once and forever proven" ideas that aimed to perpetuate its mastery over the individual mind. For this reason, philosophical thinking, which by its nature transcends the limits of the existing order and questions sanctioned practices, was under permanent suspicion as an anti-State activity: to philosophize was an act of self-liberation via an awareness of the relativity of the dominant ideological discourse. Philosophical ideas in the Soviet Union rarely matured into well-balanced, self-sufficient systems, because the State arrogated to itself the privilege of consummating and elaborating ideas in a systematic way.

The fate of non-Marxist thinkers was to dissolve these ideocratic systems in a stream of critical, spontaneous thinking that attempted to go beyond all possible systems, in order to undermine rather than consolidate them. Since official philosophy functioned as a tool of power, it was the task and merit of non-official philosophy to advance anti-totalitarian modes of thinking, thus de-centralizing the structure of discourse and deconstructing any possible principle of systematization. Thought tried to free itself from ideocracy by putting down roots in authentic, concrete entities beyond ideological generalizations, such as faith in a living God, the existential uniqueness of personality, the organic soul of the nation, the empirical credibility of science, the symbolic meanings of culture, or, finally, by challenging the master-discourse of Soviet ideology through its parodic imitation and exaggeration.

All of these trends in philosophy-neo-rationalist, religious, personalistic, national, culturological, post-structuralist-were initially and intentionally forms of intellectual self-liberation. The internal logic of development, however, has led some of these schools of thought, especially the philosophies of national spirit and religious syncretism, to renovated and "improved" projects of postcommunist ideocracy. Indeed, if we attempt to summarize the most recent developments in Russian thought (the 1990s), we discover a general tendency for the radicalization of its metaphysical ambitions. This tendency may be identified in such diverse movements as Marxism, with the eschatological communism of Sergei Kurginyan; nationalism, with the radical traditionalism of Aleksandr Dugin; religious philosophy, with the increasing popularity of Nikolai Fyodorov's Cosmism and Daniil Andreev's "interreligious" teaching of The Rose of the World. Even the movements that would seem to be the most resistant to metaphysical assumptions, such as Structuralism, culturology and conceptualism, reveal a growing propensity for universalist claims. For example, the later works of Yury Lotman and Vasily Nalimov are rife with a metaphysics of chance, contiguity, indeterminism. Georgy Gachev builds much more ambitious cosmosophical constructions than did his predecessors in culturology, Bakhtin, Losev and Likhachev. Is it a coincidence that this proliferation of new, radical metaphysical discourses has arisen with the degradation and collapse of the ideocratic system of Soviet power?

The Soviet system was not merely a political and legislative entity but was founded on a metaphysical, even eschatological, vision, officially called Marxism but stemming also from the prophetic philosophizing of the late 19th and early 20th centuries. Hence the collapse of the Soviet regime left something more than just a need for governmental reform: it left a metaphysical vacuum, eager to be filled. If the prevailing mood among intellectuals in the late Soviet period was to challenge and demystify ideocracy, then the collapse of that ideocracy generated numerous emulations and simulations among various intellectual groups, which attempted, at least in theory, to build a new ideocratic regime on a more firm, nationalistic, technological and/or religious foundation. Traditionally in Russia, political platforms have been constructed on a framework of the most general, "filosofical" ideas; in the early 1990s, competing metaphysical theories were rushing in to fill the demolished and excavated site with a foundation for a new political architecture. The death of one "big" totalitarianism gave birth to a number of smaller ones. Many politicians, of both leftist and rightist orientation, such as Vladimir Zhirinovsky, Aleksandr Rutskoi, and even the new communist leader Gennady Zyuganov more or less consistently wielded metaphysical ideas to justify their ambitions for intellectual leadership. This overall tendency, characteristic of the Russian mentality in general but aggravated in the early 1990s by increasing political instability, can be called "metaphysical radicalism." Political radicalism flows from the very core of this type of metaphysics, which, following Marxist paradigm, does not limit itself to explaining the world but attempts to change it. At the same time, any politics with pretensions to radically transforming the world cannot limit itself to the social, economic, and legislative dimensions, but must entail metaphysical assumptions. In the contemporary West, politics usually pursues less expansive goals of partially improving existing systems, and therefore, it is divorced from metaphysical considerations, or at least pretends to be.

Since Russia's historical dynamics are not evolutionary but disruptive and catastrophic, each break in political continuity necessitates renewed metaphysical speculation and indoctrination designed to justify the entirely new social order. It is the privilege of metaphysics to address the world as a whole, as it is the objective of political radicalism to transform this whole completely. Thus metaphysical and political radicalism are mutually dependent, as the totalitarian experiments of the 20th century have shown: both communist and fascist radicalism advanced strong metaphysical claims. Russian philosophy, which during the 1950s-80s had resisted the stranglehold of Soviet ideocracy, may now be preparing the foundation for a new type of ideocracy, potentially based on the ideas of Cosmism, universal theocracy, radical traditionalism, Eurasianism or eschatological communism. The options are varied. Metaphysical radicalism is a specific type of philosophical discourse that ignores the Kantian critique of metaphysics and claims to "transcend" the epistemological limits imposed on human cognitive capacities. It relies on 'revealed', 'self-evident' or 'generally accepted' truth or values that are directly accessible for human mind.

However, this philosophical mode cannot be identified with the naive metaphysics that Kant criticized; it aspires not to adequate knowledge but to the practical transformation of the world, not to truth but to power. For metaphysical radicalism, epistemological limits remain effective, but irrelevant, since they can be transcended politically, volitionally, as the projection of a different world is implemented by the forces of social, national and technological revolution. This is not a pre-critical, descriptive but a post-critical, prescriptive metaphysics, one that draws on suppressed desires and taps the collective unconscious. Western intellectuals are familiar with this type of fiery speculation through the works of New Left thinkers such as Herbert Marcuse, but the principal distinction of the majority of contemporary Russian "New Right" thinkers is their appeal to the absolute past, to the resurrection of ancestors or the restoration of Tradition.

It is known that sentences in the imperative mood cannot be subjected to the criteria of verification. As Roman Jakobson puts it, "The imperative sentences cardinally differ from declarative sentences: the latter are and the former are not liable to a truth test." "Do this!" as distinct from "S/he has done this" or "This is done," cannot be challenged by the question "Is it true or not?" The same may be said of "metaphysics in the imperative mood," which, unlike the "indicative mood" of pre-Kantian metaphysics, evades critical challenges to its truthfulness. Kant's critique of philosophical dogmatism was crucially conclusive in respect to metaphysical "declarations," but to what extent can it help to demystify the metaphysical "imperatives" that began proliferate in the 19th and 20th centuries precisely as a result of Kantian limitations on theoretical reason?

The alliance between metaphysics and politics has benefits for both of them: as practice, it concentrates on one goal, on one direction of change; as philosophy, it posits itself beyond truth and falsehood. A diversity of positions is possible in philosophy only insofar as it interprets the world, but the task of changing the world leaves one position-the one that is sanctioned as correct and mandatory. One of the most famous Karl Marx's statements on the tasks of philosophy is his 11th thesis on Feuerbach: "The philosophers have only interpreted the world, in various ways; the point, however, is to change it." There is a curious asymmetry in this proposition: the transition from "interpreting" to "changing" is achieved at the price of "variability" which is dropped in the second part of the thesis. It is possible to interpret the world in various ways, but presumably there is only one way or direction of its practical transformation. This is how totalitarian implications are inherent in the very project of the philosophy as the practical/ political action. There are strong tensions, originating from diverse ideological sources, among the representative trends of metaphysical radicalism. For example, radical traditionalists inspired by such extreme rightist thinkers as Rene Guenon and Julius Evola, condemn Fyodorovian Cosmism as a leftist, technocratic heresy obsessed with the idea of progress and active, self-governed human evolution. Neo-fascist ideologists of Zhirinovsky's camp condemn radical traditionalists for their romantic alienation from the contemporary scene and their obsession with the past. Nonetheless, these antagonisms serve to underscore the substantial unity of metaphysical radicalism, not in the specific contents of the individual projects that fall within its scope, but in the very mode of projective thinking that establishes a set of ideas about what the world should be, while utterly rejecting the world as it is. Fyodorov, the founder of Russian Cosmism, wrote: "...philosophy must become the knowledge not only of what is but of what ought to be, that is, from the passive, speculative explanation of existence it must become an active project of what must be, the project of universal action."

Not only Fyodorovians but radical traditionalists and Neomarxist utopians could subscribe to this statement of what philosophy should do in the face of the world problems and what the world should become in the name of philosophical ideas. The formula for the political implications of this metaphysical radicalism can be found in Nietzsche's prophecy: "The time of the struggle for domination of the globe is upon us; it will be undertaken in the name of basic philosophical teachings." Russian metaphysical radicals invoke as model the fate of Nietzsche's own teachings: German recruits going into the trenches of the first World War with volumes of Zarathustra in their rucksacks.

The ideological incompatibility among Marxist, nationalist and religious discourses, which sharply divided them in the late Soviet period, now becomes more and more irrelevant as these positions merge in the overarching type of radical discourse. Consider the words of Sergei Kurginyan, one of the chief ideologist of post-Marxist revival of communism who was the principal political advisor of the conservative, pro-communist forces in the Soviet leadership that organized the failed putsch of August, 1991, and attempted to preserve the Soviet Union as a communist superpower: "We regard communism not only as a theory but as a new metaphysics which leads to the creation of a new, global religious teaching... It contains many fundamental features vitally important for civilization, features of a new world religion with its own saints and martyrs, apostles and creed....Among the indisputable predecessors of communism we identify Isaiah and Jesus, Buddha and Lao Tse, Confucius and Socrates... [...] Today there is no alternative to the communist meta-religion..." Further, Kurginyan insists that Russia, since its ancient history "has experienced a need for an idea with global-messianic potential capable of unifying Eurasia. She found this in communism. [...] The red field, Communist eschatology and Communist mysticism existed, exist and will exist in Russia and, most probably, these ideas... will find their place within Eurasian expanses, merging with Orthodox, Sufi, Buddhist, and possibly, Catholic mysticism."

This example of the discourse of "metaphysical radicalism" reduces or even erases any difference among communist, nationalist and religious rhetoric. Another example comes from the head of the renovated Communist party, Gennady Zyuganov, the strongest contender for Russian political and ideological leadership in Russia today: "From the standpoint of ideology and world view, Russia is the keeper of the ancient spiritual tradition: its fundamental values are sobornost' (collectivism), the supreme power of the State [derzhavnost'], sovereignty [literally: self-sufficiency of statehood], and the goal of implementing the highest 'heavenly' ideals of justice and brotherhood in earthly reality." Within a single sentence, phrases imbued with religious meaning-"spiritual tradition," "sobornost'" and "heavenly ideals," merge together with "derzhavnost'" and "statehood," taken from the vocabulary of nationalists, and with "collectivism" and "brotherhood," the key words of communist jargon.

Thus we can single out metaphysical radicalism as one of the most powerful tendencies in contemporary Russian thought, as a kind of metadiscursive strategy transcending the ideological differences among previously oppositional movements. Russian intellectual history is a history of thought that fights desperately to escape the prison of an ideocratic system created by the strenuous and sacrificial efforts of thought itself. What makes Russian thought so unique is its internal tension, its struggle against itself, against its own ideational constructions and social extensions.

In the West, the field of philosophy is more or less clearly divided into ontology, the theory of being, and epistemology, the theory of knowledge. In Russia, such a division is almost irrelevant since philosophy addresses a conception of being that is itself constructed by thinking.

Beginning with Chaadaev, and the Westernizers and Slavophiles, Russian philosophy focused on the secondary reality, one created by ideas. In Russia, thought tried to confront the triumph of thought. One speculative capacity, "intelligentsia," opposed itself to another speculative capacity, "ideocracy, "-but the former also created the latter. This self-contradictory movement of thought, shattering its own foundations, gives an unprecedented, sometimes "suicidal" quality to Russian philosophy. It may have been "derivative" and "secondary," but not so much in respect to Western thought, as in relation to properly Russian, utterly artificial, fabricated, and "ideational" reality.

Till now, Russia never played an important role in world philosophy, but philosophy did play an enormous role in Russia, especially in the 20th century. Now that the system of ideocracy is not only theoretically deconstructed but, hopefully, historically transcended, one can envision the reversal of these tendencies. As philosophy will play a lesser role in a Russian society increasingly motivated by materialistic, economic goals, Russian philosophy, rethinking its unique experience of self-denial and self-liberation, will assume a more prominent role on the international scene.

Neo Classical Social Democratic Marxism

Neo classical Marxism refers to a style of thinking about Marxism that was prominent amongst English-speaking philosophers and social scientists during the 1980s. It was mainly associated with the September Group of academics, so called because of their biennial September meetings to discuss common interests. The group also dubbed itself "Non-Bullshit Marxism", and was characterized, in the words of David Miller, by "clear and rigorous thinking about questions that are usually blanketed by ideological fog." The most prominent members of the group were G. A. Cohen, John Roemer, Jon Elster, Adam Przeworski, Erik Olin Wright, Philippe van Parijs, and Robert-Jan van der Veen.

Origin

Analytical Marxism is usually understood to have taken off with the publication of G. A. Cohen's Karl Marx's Theory of History: A Defence (1978). More broadly conceived, it might be seen as having originated in the post-war period in the work of political philosophers such as Karl Popper, H. B. Acton, and John Plamenatz, who employed the techniques of analytical philosophy in order to test the coherence and scientificity of Marxism as a theory of history and society.

Those thinkers were all hostile to Marxism. Cohen's book was, from the outset, intended as a defence of historical materialism. Cohen painstakingly reconstructed historical materialism through a close reading of Marx's texts, with the aim of providing the most logically coherent and parsimonious account. For Cohen, Marx's historical materialism is a technologically deterministic theory, in which the economic relations of production are functionally explained by the material forces of production, and in which the political and legal institutions (the "superstructure") are functionally explained by the relations of production (the "base").

The transition from one mode of production to another is driven by the tendency of the productive forces to develop. Cohen accounts for this tendency by reference to the rational character of the human species: where there is the opportunity to adopt a more productive technology and thus reduce the burden of labour, human beings will tend to take it. Thus, human history can be understood as the gradual development of human productive power.

Theory

Exploitation

At the same time as Cohen was working on Karl Marx's Theory of History, American economist John Roemer was employing neoclassical economics in order to try to defend the Marxist concepts of exploitation and class. In his General Theory of Exploitation and Class (1982), Roemer employed rational choice and game theory in order to demonstrate how exploitation and class relations may arise in the development of a market for labour. Roemer would go on to reject the idea that the labour theory of value was necessary for explaining exploitation and class. Value was in principle capable of being explained in terms of any class of commodity inputs, such as oil, wheat, etc., rather than being exclusively explained by embodied labour power. Roemer was led to the conclusion that exploitation and class were thus generated not in the sphere of production but of market exchange. Significantly, as a purely technical category, exploitation did not always imply a moral wrong.

Rational Choice Marxism

By the mid-1980s, "analytical Marxism" was being recognised as a "paradigm". The September group had been meeting for several years, and a succession of texts by its members were published. Several of these appeared under the imprint of Cambridge University Press's series "Studies in Marxism and Social Theory", including Jon Elster's Making Sense of Marx (1985) and Adam Przeworski's Capitalism and Social Democracy (1986). Elster's account was an exhaustive trawl through Marx's texts in order to ascertain what could be salvaged out of Marxism employing the tools of rational choice theory and methodological individualism. His conclusion was that-contra Cohen-no general theory of history as the development of the productive forces could be saved. Like Roemer, he also rejected the labour theory of value and, going further, virtually all of Marx's economics.

The "dialectical" method is savaged as a form of Hegelian obscurantism. The theory of ideology and revolution continued to be useful to a certain degree, but only once they had been purged of their tendencies to holism and functionalism and established on the basis of an individualist methodology and a causal or intentional explanation. Przeworski's book uses rational choice and game theory in order to demonstrate that the revolutionary strategies adopted by socialists in the twentieth century were likely to fail, since it was in the rational interests of workers to strive for the reform of capitalism through the achievement of union recognition, improved wages and living conditions, rather than adopting the risky strategy of revolution.

Justice

The analytical (and rational choice) Marxists held a variety of leftist political sympathies, ranging from communism to reformist social democracy. Through the 1980s, most of them began to recognise that Marxism as a theory capable of explaining revolution in terms of the economic dynamics of capitalism and the class interests of the proletariat had been seriously compromised. They were largely in agreement that the transformation of capitalism was an ethical project. During the 1980s, a debate had developed within Anglophone academic Marxism on whether Marxism could accommodate a theory of justice. This debate was clearly linked to the revival of normative political philosophy after the publication of John Rawls's A Theory of Justice (1971). While analytic moral philosophy holds that one is free in all situations to make a moral judgement that is in the interests of all equally, some commentators remained hostile to the idea of a Marxist theory of justice, arguing that Marx saw "justice" as little more than a bourgeois ideological construct designed to justify exploitation by reference to reciprocity in the wage contract. The analytical Marxists, however, largely rejected this point of view. Led by G. A. Cohen (a moral philosopher by training), they argued that a Marxist theory of justice had to focus on egalitarianism. For Cohen, this meant an engagement with moral and political philosophy in order to demonstrate the injustice of market exchange, and the construction of an appropriate egalitarian metric. This argument is pursued in Cohen's most recent books, Self-Ownership, Freedom and Equality (1995) and If You're an Egalitarian How Come You're So Rich? (2000b).

In contrast to traditional Marxism, Cohen rejects the argument that capitalism is unjust because under it workers experience alienation, or a lack of self-fulfilment as workers. For Cohen, this thesis is based on an untenable metaphysical account of human nature and historical development: the claim that all persons have one purpose and aim toward one end, productive labour. Because such a claim cannot be inferred from a priori truths of logic or from experience, it is not justifiable by the restricted means available to analytic philosophy.

Cohen further departs from previous Marxists by arguing that capitalism is a system characterised by unjust exploitation not because the labour of workers is "stolen" by employers, but because it is a system wherein "autonomy" is infringed and which results in a distribution of benefits and burdens that is "unfair". In the traditional account, exploitation and injustice occur because non-workers appropriate the value produced by the labour of workers, something that would be overcome in a socialist society wherein no class would own the means of production and be in a position to appropriate the value produced by labourers.

Cohen argues that underpinning this account is the assumption that workers have "rights of self-ownership" over themselves and thus, should "own" what is produced by their labour. Because the worker is paid a wage less than the value he or she creates through work, the capitalist is said to extract a surplus-value from the worker's labour, and thus to steal part of what the worker produces, the time of the worker and the worker's powers.

Cohen argues that the concept of self-ownership is favourable to Rawls's difference principle as it ensures "each person's rights over his being and powers"-i.e. that one is treated as an end always and never as a means-but also highlights that its centrality provides for an area of common ground between the Marxist account of justice and the right-wing libertarianism of Robert Nozick.

However, much as Cohen criticises Rawls for treating people's personal powers as just another external resource for which no individual can claim merit, so does he charge Nozick with moving beyond the concept of self-ownership to his own right-wing "thesis" of self-ownership. In Cohen's view, Nozick's mistake is to endow people's claims to legitimately acquire external resources with the same moral quality that belongs to people's ownership of themselves. In other words, libertarianism allows inequalities to arise from differences in talent and differences in external resources, but it does so because it assumes that the world is "up for grabs", i.e. to be appropriated as private property.

Criticisms

Analytical Marxism came under fire from a number of different quarters, both Marxist and non-Marxist.

Method

A number of critics argued that analytical Marxism proceeded from the wrong methodological and epistemological premises. While the analytical Marxists dismissed dialectically oriented Marxism as "bullshit", many Marxists would maintain that the distinctive character of Marxist philosophy is lost if it is understood non-dialectically. The crucial feature of Marxist philosophy is that it is not a reflection in thought of the world, a crude materialism, but rather an intervention in the world concerned with human praxis.

According to this view, analytical Marxism wrongly characterises intellectual activity as occurring in isolation from the struggles constitutive of its social and political conjuncture, and at the same time does little to intervene in that conjuncture. For dialectical Marxists, analytical Marxism eviscerated Marxism, turning it from a systematic doctrine of revolutionary transformation into a set of discrete theses that stand or fall on the basis of their logical consistency and empirical validity. Analytical Marxism's non-Marxist critics also objected to its methodological weaknesses. Against Elster and the rational choice Marxists, it was argued that methodological individualism was not the only form of valid explanation in the social sciences, that functionalism in the absence of micro-foundations could remain a convincing and fruitful mode of inquiry, and that rational choice and game theory were far from being universally accepted as sound or useful ways of modelling social institutions and processes.

History

Cohen's defence of a technological determinist interpretation of historical materialism was, in turn, quite widely criticised, even by analytical Marxists. Together with Andrew Levine, Wright argued that in attributing primacy to the productive forces (the development thesis), Cohen overlooked the role played by class actors in the transition between modes of production. For the authors, it was forms of class relations (the relations of production) that had primacy in terms of how the productive forces were employed and the extent to which they developed. It was not evident, they claimed, that the relations of production become "fetters" once the productive forces are capable of sustaining a different set of production relations.

Other non-Marxist critics argued that Cohen, in line with the Marxist tradition, underestimated the role played by the legal and political superstructure in shaping the character of the economic base. Finally, Cohen's anthropology was judged dubious: whether human beings adopt new and more productive technology is not a function of an ahistorical rationality, but depends on the extent to which these forms of technology are compatible with pre-existing beliefs and social practices. Cohen recognised and accepted some, though not all, of these criticisms in his History, Labour, and Freedom (1988).

Justice and Power

Many Marxists would argue that Marxism cannot be understood as a theory of justice in the rather narrow sense intended by the analytical Marxists. The question of justice cannot be seen in isolation from questions of power, or from the balance of class forces in any specific conjuncture. Non-Marxists may employ a similar criticism in their critique of liberal theories of justice in the Rawlsian tradition. Most of these theories fail to address problems about the configuration of power relations in the contemporary world, and by so doing appear as little more than exercises in logic. "Justice", on this view, is whatever is produced by the assumptions of the theory. It has little to do with the actual distribution of power and resources in the world.

Denouement

As a project, analytical Marxism had largely disappeared by the end of the 1990s. Most of its practitioners agreed that the Marxism that in the beginning they had set out to interrogate and, to an extent, defend, was not theoretically or politically defensible. They concluded that as a theory for the explanation of human action, Marxism was a failure on both theoretical and practical grounds. The leading lights of analytical marxism now focus their energies in other areas-such as moral and political philosophy (Cohen, van Parijs), and democratic theory employing economic models (Roemer, Elster).

Bibliography

Ackrill J. L. 2001. *Essays on Plato and Aristotle,* Oxford University Press, USA

Alex Callinicos, *The Revolutionary Ideas of Karl Marx* (Bookmarks, 1983)

Allen, R.E. (2006). *Studies in Plato's Metaphysics II.* Parmenides Publishing.

Ambuel, David (2006). *Image and Paradigm in Plato's Sophist.* Parmenides Publishing.

Anglo, Sydney, Machiavelli - the First Century: Studies in Enthusiasm, Hostility, and Irrelevance, Oxford University Press, 2005.

Bertram, Christopher (2003). *Rousseau and The Social Contract.* London: Routledge.

Bock, Gisela; Quentin Skinner and Maurizio Viroli, ed. (1990). *Machiavelli and Republicanism.* Cambridge University Press.

Bolotin, David (1998). An Approach to Aristotle's Physics: With Particular Attention to the Role of His Manner of Writing. Albany: SUNY Press.

Cassirer, Ernst (1945). *Rousseau, Kant, Goethe.* Princeton University Press.

Cottret, Monique and Bernard Cottret. Jean-Jacques Rousseau en son temps, Paris, Perrin, 2005.

Cranston, Maurice (1991). *The Noble Savage.* Chicago: University of Chicago Press.

Fine, Gail (2000). *Plato 1: Metaphysics and Epistemology* Oxford University Press, USA.

Frederick Rosen, Classical Utilitarianism from Hume to Mill (Routledge Studies in Ethics & Moral Theory), 2003.

Knight, Kelvin. 2007. Aristotelian Philosophy: Ethics and Politics from Aristotle to MacIntyre, Polity Press.

Kochin, Michael S. (2002). *Gender and Rhetoric in Plato's Political* Thought. Cambridge Univ. Press.

Krämer, Hans Joachim (1990). Plato and the Foundations of Metaphysics. SUNY Press.

Macpherson, C. B. (1962). The Political Theory of Possessive Individualism: Hobbes to Locke. Oxford: Oxford University Press.

McLellan, David. *Karl Marx: his Life and Thought* Harper & Row, 1973.

Michael St. John Packe, *The Life of John Stuart Mill,* Macmillan (1952).

Paul Blackledge, Reflections on the Marxist Theory of History (Manchester University Press, 2006)

Pocock, J.G. A.. The Machiavellian Moment: Florentine Political Thought and the Atlantic Republican Tradition. Princeton.

Rose, Lynn E. (1968). *Aristotle's Syllogistic*. Springfield: Charles C Thomas Publisher.

Sallis, John (1996). *Being and Logos: Reading the Platonic Dialogues.* Indiana University Press.

Samuel Hollander, *The Economics of John Stuart Mill* (University of Toronto Press, 1985)

Simpson, Matthew (2006). *Rousseau's Theory of Freedom*. London: Continuum Books.

Soll, Jacob (2005). Publishing The Prince: History, Reading and the Birth of Political Criticism. University of Michigan Press.

Starobinski, Jean (1988). Jean-Jacques Rousseau: Transparency and Obstruction. Chicago: University of Chicago Press.

Strauss, Leo (1936). The Political Philosophy of Hobbes; Its Basis and Its Genesis. Oxford: Clarendon Press.

Sullivan, Vickie B., ed. (2000). The Comedy and Tragedy of Machiavelli: Essays on the Literary Works. Yale U. Press.

Talmon, Jacob R. (1952). *The Origins of Totalitarian Democracy*. New York: W. W. Norton.

Index

M

N

P

R

S

T

□□□